SANCTIONED

1

I should have known better when William Callahan called. I mean, a chill ran right through me. But still, I should have known better.

Callahan is the top lawyer for RTG, Cleveland's biggest company by a mile. It's one of those companies traded on the New York Stock Exchange, and Callahan is always first on the list of Cleveland's highest paid lawyers. He makes over seven million a year, if you can believe it. Anyway, it's not every day that someone like Callahan calls me. Actually, it's not any day that someone like Callahan calls me.

I'm a lawyer, too, although it still sounds funny to say that. But if there's a pecking order of lawyers, Callahan is at the top of the totem pole. And I'm the guy who digs the ditch and pours the cement and holds the pole while the cement dries. I mean, sure, I went to law school and passed the bar last year, but in Ohio nearly everyone does. As one of my professors told my class, if you can spell your name, you've got a really good shot at being a lawyer in Ohio. And of course he was looking at me when he said that.

Anyway, I passed the bar and couldn't get a job. I tell myself it's because the economy for lawyers is in the toilet, but I guess I know better. Finishing at the bottom of my class may have had something to do with it. I like to think that I'm street smart, not book smart. That description, my buddy Rett from law school always tells me, is half right.

So with no other options, I hung up my own shingle. I worked out of my apartment in

Cleveland Heights, a suburb east of Cleveland, until an office opened up on the second floor in my building. The first floor is a dirty diner, which people only go to once. The second floor has ten offices, five on each side of a dark hallway, all with oak doors and frosted glass panels, kind of like the detective offices you see in the old movies. There's a staircase at the end of the floor leading outside. It's kind of weird, but there's nothing but psychologists in those offices. Second floor shrinks, I call them. The top three floors are apartments, and I live on the fourth floor. Anyway, one of the shrinks vacated his office. Turns out the guy committed suicide, which I find ironic, given his profession. So I asked, and the landlord let me have his office for 200 bucks a month. A great deal, and I like the space. Plus, you can't beat the commute.

My law practice is really sad. All I have is a few landlord – tenant matters. I started out helping one of my softball buddies who was having trouble with his scumbag landlord, and after awhile, my name got passed around. If you quit paying rent because you have no heat, and the landlord is spending his time trying to evict you instead of fixing the furnace, I'm the guy to call. I've tried drafting a few simple contracts for my buddies, and that's about it. As my professor said, if you can spell your name…

Anyway, people like William Callahan never call me. Why would they? Callahan's one of those movers and shakers who does deals all over the world and plays golf four times a week. I have a sorry little website, and I'm guessing that's how he found me.

But miraculously, he called. He told me that an employee at RTG, a Ms. Allen, had a legal issue. He said he was fond of her, but the company's lawyers couldn't help because it involved "an internal company matter." He said she was a "striking woman," one I would find "intriguing," and he would be happy to have RTG pay for my time. No one had ever paid for my time. He asked if I could squeeze her in that day. I asked him to hold on while I pulled up my calendar. I had only one hour booked the whole week, and that was for a dentist appointment. I told him I thought I could make time in the afternoon.

The afternoon was good because I like to play basketball at lunch. There's a gym down the street at Case Western Reserve University where I went to law school. I like to get on the floor with the college guys. I'm not winning any awards for my legal work, so I guess it makes me feel good to hold my own at something. Plus, I don't really have much else to do.

Anyway, Callahan said she'd be by at 3:00. I was back at my office at 2:30. It's just a big room, nothing fancy at all. There are a bunch of plants the prior tenant forgot to take with him, and great floor-to-ceiling windows facing the street at the end opposite the door. I've got a beat up couch in there that one of the shrinks down the hall gave me when I moved in. It's crazy how an ugly couch can change things.

After the landlord let me have the office, I started moving things down from my apartment. On about my fifth trip, I struggled off the elevator with my law books stuffed into shopping bags, and a couch was sticking out the door a few down from mine and blocking the hall. I put the sacks on the couch and sat down to take a break just as this gorgeous woman squeezed out of the office and into the hall.

"Hello," she said, looking down at me. "Our timing is off."

"That's a shame," I said. "Story of my life."

She looked at her watch. "When was your appointment?"

She looked straight at me, very calm and direct. She didn't look like a shrink. Probably 30-something, long, silky dark brown hair tucked behind her ears. No makeup. High cheekbones, a narrow face, voluptuous lips and big brown eyes full of life. Man, she was something! She was thin and fit and spry and wore running shoes and jeans and a white tank top that she filled out perfectly. I tried not to be too obvious staring at her.

"Did you come from the hospital?" she asked.

"No! Well, originally. Maybe I should make an appointment. I have lots of baggage," I said, pointing to my sacks on the couch. "I'm moving into the office down the hall."

She grinned. "Sorry, I'm expecting a patient, I thought you were him. Got a minute? Want to help me lug this monstrosity down to the dumpster?"

"Sure. Although I'd be happier to lug it to my office if you're parting with it. I'm a little thin on furniture at the moment."

"Ok," she said. "Let's go."

She exuded energy but somehow was steady and detached at the same time. We wiggled the couch into the hall. I offered to drag it down to my office. She couldn't have been more than five-five and 120 pounds, but she smirked at me. She grabbed one end of the couch and lifted it like it was nothing. She waited for me to get my end, and we carried it down the hall. I put my end down in front of my door and fished around one of the sacks for my keys. I don't know if she was trying to make a point, but she kept holding her end of the couch in the air until I got the door open. We carried the couch into the barren space and placed it against the wall.

"Looks like we carried it to the dumpster after all, huh?" I said.

She dusted her hands off on her butt. I would have liked to do that.

"Freudian?" she asked.

"Pardon me?"

"What kind of therapist are you?"

"Oh, ha! I'm not. I'm a lawyer."

"I guess that explains the dirt in here," she said, grinning. "Hey, we're both counselors, right?"

"Right," I said. "That should earn me some respect, no?"

She smiled at me. "No."

She put her hand on my shoulder and squeezed by me and out my door. A second later she poked her head back in.

"I'm Jocelyn Levy. Joss. Welcome to the neighborhood."

"Thanks, Joss. I'm Ben Billings."

"Really? A lawyer named Billings? That's too good to be true." She chuckled and left.

Yeah, a lawyer named Billings and no clients to bill. Story of my life.

Anyway, my office is pretty bare bones. It's big, maybe 20 feet wide, 30 feet deep. Joss's couch is on the left as you come in. I've screwed a plastic nerf ball hoop into the wall above the couch to help me pass the time. There's a beat-up old lounge chair to the right of the door. At the end of the office, I've got an old oak desk that was once my grandfather's. It's the only nice thing I have in the office. It's got lots of drawers and a green leather insert on top that's perfect for writing. I sit with my back to the window that overlooks the intersection that forms a Y where Fairmount Boulevard curves into Cedar Road. There are two ratty old chairs facing me on the other side of the desk, just in case anyone ever comes to see me.

I ran upstairs to my apartment to change into

my suit and tie and dress shoes before the woman Callahan was sending over showed up. When I came back, this incredible looker was standing outside my office door.

"Hello," I said. "I'm Ben Billings. Can I help you?"

She turned and looked me up and down but made no effort to shake my hand. She was wearing large, dark movie star sunglasses. She looked to be about 35. Callahan was right; she was striking. She was wearing an expensive business suit, dark blue with a knee-length skirt and a tight fitting white blouse underneath the jacket. She had long straight blonde hair and a wary expression.

"You're the lawyer?"

"Yes, ma'am." Her disappointment was palpable. "Come on in."

I walked in and stood behind my desk. How do these meetings work? "Can I get you some coffee?" I had one of those big old coffee makers on the windowsill, and a pot brewing.

"Yes," she said.

I poured us each a cup. She sat down across from me. She was still wearing her sunglasses. I was nervous but tried not to show it.

"So how can I help you, Ms. Allen?"

"How old are you? Are you really a lawyer?"

Ouch. "I get that all the time," I said. "I'm 26 and yes, I'm a lawyer. I went to law school and much to everyone's surprise, even passed the bar on my first try."

"First try, huh? You must be so proud." She didn't try to hide her sarcasm. "I'm just trying to figure out why William sent me to you. Have you worked for RTG before?"

"No, ma'am, I haven't." Man, she was a

stunner. And impenetrable. "Why don't you tell me what's going on, and then maybe we can figure it out. I'm kind of curious myself."

She leaned back and sipped her coffee. She finally took off those big sunglasses. They fit her. She had a movie star face, thin and angular. She reminded me of Gwyneth Paltrow.

"I got fired Friday. I've been an administrative assistant with RTG for 20 years, since the day I graduated high school, and they fired me."

She stopped and looked at me. "Before we go further," she said, "William told me that RTG would pay your bill. Is that your understanding?"

"Yup, he said they'd pay."

"Does that work?"

"Sure." Actually, I had no idea. "If it looks like there may be a problem at some point, we'll figure it out."

She stood and walked around the office. She touched the leaves on a few of the plants absent-mindedly. She looked at the nerf ball hoop above the couch and came back and sat down. She picked her purse up off the floor, put it in her lap, and pulled out a manila envelope and handed it to me.

"They fired me Friday. They offered me a separation agreement. William said I should get the advice of experienced counsel before I sign."

"He obviously doesn't know me," I said. I pulled the contract out of the envelope and flipped through it. It was seven pages long, single spaced, and filled with legalese. Reading it would be drudgery. And completely foreign to me.

"Do you mind if I get some info from you?" I asked. "I don't even know your first name."

"Liza. My name is Elizabeth Allen. "

I got her address and phone number and email

11

and all that. She seemed annoyed with the whole process. Finally, I asked what happened at work.

She stood and stared at me. She was smoldering. It made me uncomfortable and I stood as well. She watched me across me desk like a gunslinger about to draw in an old western.

Liza put her sunglasses back on. "Just review the contract, ok? Let me know if I can sign it."

"Sure."

She turned and walked out.

That was weird. And now I would have to figure out what's supposed to be in a separation agreement.

2

About 20 minutes later, I got another call from Callahan. He wanted to make sure I'd met with Liza, and asked if there would be any problem representing her. I told him that I didn't see any difficulty at all. He was pleased, and suggested that if this went well, he might send more work my way. This was fantastic!

It did seem strange that Callahan was taking such an active interest in this matter. I looked up RTG on the Internet. It was a behemoth, an aerospace, technology, and communications "systems provider," whatever that meant. RTG did 97 billion dollars in annual sales. It had 120,000 employees around the world, and 127 lawyers scattered in 14 different countries, although most were here in good old Cleveland at RTG's headquarters. Callahan was Chief Counsel, the top lawyer. It was weird that the head lawyer of such a massive operation was so interested in the firing of a secretary.

I read through the contract. It was clearly a form, probably the same one companies used everywhere. It didn't say why Liza was fired or anything about her. All it said was that she and the company had "agreed to part ways," and RTG would pay her one year's salary, which was 60 thousand bucks. Awfully good, I thought. More than I would make in the next five years, that's for sure. RTG promised to pay her health care for a year. All in all, it sounded like a good deal. A year's paid vacation.

The contract also had form language saying that the parties agreed that they wouldn't say anything disparaging about each other, and would keep the agreement and the facts leading to it confidential. It seemed fair. It was dull and harmless.

Since I was getting paid by the hour, I called Loretta Anderson. We were best friends since our first year of law school. I actually met her when I was playing intramural basketball. My team was losing as usual, since, to be honest, I was the only one who had any basketball skills. Just not many athletic types in law school. Anyway, we only had five on our team, and one of the guys turned an ankle. We were about to forfeit the game, but then Rett – that's what I call her - was walking by the court, on her way out after a yoga class. I recognized her from school. She was hard to miss, because she looks like a model. Just not an ounce of fat on her, firm and fit and rounded in all the right places. Anyway, I called out to her, and asked if she wanted to play, even though it was an all-guys league.

Without a word, she dropped her bag and walked on the court. "Are you any good?" she asked.

"No."

We started playing, and next thing I know, she's hitting jumpers, cutting to the hoop and making layups with both hands. She was lightning quick, stealing the ball from the guys, just a natural athlete. She loved trash talking, which was hilarious with a bunch of overweight, spastic law students. No one knew what to make of her, but we clicked, hitting each other with passes in rhythm. We whupped the other team. We were pretty much inseparable after that, which made us a really funny combination. She's black and I'm white. She was first in our class and I was last. She's really intense and I'm as laid back as they get. But there's just something I love about her. She's feisty and irreverent and the farthest thing from a snob you'll ever meet, quite the exception at law school.

Anyway, unlike me, Rett had her pick of jobs when we graduated, and she went with Warner Levitt, one of the big employment firms in town. So she'd been doing this kind of work for the last year and a half, and knew way more than I did. Rett was so damn competitive, and over-prepared for everything. In law school, whenever the class wasn't on top of the cases we read for the day, the profs would turn to Rett to explain what was going on. She was always two steps ahead of everyone else. And four steps ahead of me.

So I called Rett and asked if I could take her to lunch and pick her brain. We agreed to meet downtown near her office the next day.

I pulled out a yellow pad and wrote down my time on Liza's case for the day. I didn't have one of those time-keeping software programs that the real lawyers use. So far all of the work I'd done had been for an agreed fee. Usually for an agreed beer, to be honest. So finally, 18 months into my legal career, I was billing out my time. It was exciting and a little weird to know that no matter how bad a job I did, I was going to get paid. No wonder lawyers got a bad rap.

It was 5 o'clock, and I figured I could pick this up in the morning. I locked my door and heard a ruckus in the stairwell. I wandered over and there were two people standing with Joss laughing their heads off about something.

"Counselor!" Joss said. "Doctors, this is Ben Billings, who is, naturally, a lawyer." They got a good chuckle at my expense. "We're headed out for a drink. Want to join us?"

"Do you promise no lawyer jokes?"

"Nope. This is Dr. Katrina Wilkens, and this is

Dr. David Peterson."

I shook hands with them. They were both in their fifties, I'd guess. Katrina looked like a hippie from the 60s, now all gray, with pale blue eyes. Thick in the middle, but still pretty, with no makeup and something earthy about her. David looked like a nerd. Skinny with black glasses, a neatly trimmed gray beard and thinning hair. Joss seemed completely out of place, barely constrained energy and athletic and not the least bit bookish. She was wearing a blue cardigan over a tank top, which made her look professional and sexy at the same time.

"We're headed to Nighttown," Joss said. "We like to drink to get the crazy out of our heads."

We walked outside. David and Katrina led the way, and Joss and I followed.

"Do all of you caregivers hold your patients in such high regard?" I asked.

"Only those of us who are well-adjusted." She leaned into me and whispered, "That means I'm the only one. All the other shrinks are nuttier than their patients. That's why they got into this field. Don't tell them I said that."

"Ok," I said. "I promise."

"A lawyer calling it a day at 5 o'clock? You must not have much work, huh, Counselor?"

"You're right, Counselor," I said. "Or maybe the right amount of work. A lawyer can have a balanced life, right?"

"Shhhhh." She had this breathy way of talking, sexy and intimate. She made me feel like I was the only one there. And her eyes, my god, her eyes were intoxicating. They said so much more than her words. She leaned into me and said, "Don't repeat that. We'll lose our clients. Seriously. Did you know that half our patients are lawyers? And the rest are their families?"

"That's scary. Is that really true?"

"Well, it's not a scientific study."

The way she leaned into me when she talked, her whispering meant only for me, was surprisingly arousing.

We walked the short block and a half to Nighttown. Nighttown is one of Cleveland's great spots, a lively old bar with a big dining hall and fantastic food.

"Dr. Levy!" the bartender called out as we walked in. "What are the good doctors up to?"

"Screwing their patients, as usual," Joss said.

The bartender laughed. Joss walked into the restaurant and slid into a table in the back. I sat next to her. David and Katrina sat opposite us and Katrina immediately started talking about insurance issues. David just nodded every time she said something.

Joss leaned her shoulder against mine and asked, "What kind of law do you do?"

"I'm a generalist." I thought that sounded better than telling her I take whatever I can get. "Today I was working on an employment case."

Joss nodded and waved to the waiter. She leaned into me. "It's on me today, Benny. What'll you have?"

I liked that she called me "Benny." No one had done that since I was a kid. I ordered a Burning River, a hometown brew. Joss got one as well.

"So what was your day like, Joss?"

"Oh god, please don't make me re-live it. Eight hours of poor souls complaining about their parents. And one 60-year-old self-absorbed lawyer who can't get his life together because his girlfriend dumped him. Seriously. He's married and has kids and a fortune and he's cheating on his wife with a 25-year-old secretary who everyone knows is using him for his

17

money. But now she's dumped him and he can't function. Can you believe that? This is my contribution to society?"

"You don't like your job?"

"Oh sure, I love my job."

I couldn't tell if she was being sarcastic.

"Hey," she said, "it's better than the crap most people do everyday." She punched me in the shoulder and grinned. "Right?"

"You're not helping, Counselor."

She looked at me and flashed a sexy smile. Her eyes asked me to save her.

We talked and joked for a couple hours. Katrina was matronly, a wonderful combination of open and direct and earthy. David was content to listen all evening, nodding and stroking his beard. Joss was, well, a mystery. Observing everything and everyone, watching and joking. She was funny and quick and insightful and captivating. I was thrilled there was no mention of a spouse or boyfriend.

We ate and drank and called it a night around 9. We all walked to the parking garage under our building. Katrina gave us each a hug. David waved and walked out without a word. Joss looked at me ambiguously. I'm usually pretty good at reading people, but not Joss. Her eyes were so hungry. Somehow she was engaged and distant at the same time. I wanted to give her a hug or invite her up to my apartment, but worried about chasing after her and being rejected and looking pathetic. I figured I'd just play it cool, but before I could impress her with my coolness, she got in her car and drove off.

I went up to my apartment and quickly remembered that being cool is no fun at all.

3

I met Rett for lunch the next day at Pura Vida, a trendy place downtown near Rett's office. It was packed with nothing but lawyers, it seemed. Rett is like a magnet, and people kept coming by our table to talk. To Rett, not me. When our food came, I was finally able to get her attention.

I was used to seeing Rett at school in jeans and a t-shirt and loved how down-to-earth she was. But looking at her in a business suit, so conscious of the time and constantly checking her phone for messages, she seemed like a different person.

"So what's the legal issue you want to talk about, Ben?"

"Well, I saw a new client yesterday. She just got fired after 20 years on the job."

"Stop right there!"

"There's more to the story."

"No, you moron," she said. "Of course there is. Just don't tell me where she worked. If you do, then I'll have to check if we represent the company. If we do, I won't be able to talk to you. Got it?"

"Got it."

"Ok, keep going," she said, digging into her salad with gusto.

"Right. So she gets fired after 20 years. She was a secretary at her company. And they've offered her a one-year severance package. She's asked me to look over the contract. The company's paying for my time."

"Nice."

"Is that weird? I mean, I know I'm one of the shining lights in the legal community, but why would the company pay me to help her out?"

"Yeah, clearly they don't know you."

"Funny woman."

"It's common with executives. The company wants to make sure they get a deal done so that they'll never hear from her again. If she signs the agreement and waives all her rights, they've got their peace and quiet, except for one risk: the only thing that can screw it up is if she later says the deal is unconscionable because she didn't know what she was doing. By having a lawyer review it before she signs, the company is guaranteed she can't back out of the settlement later on. So it's in everyone's best interests that she has competent legal help before she signs."

"Or even help from me?"

Rett laughed. There was that beautiful smile I loved. Rett laughed from deep in her belly, like she was laughing with her whole body. Her whole face lit up. It made me laugh as well.

"Having you look at it is better than nothing, I guess," she said. "As long as you're a lawyer, it gives the company the protection it needs."

"So is it weird for them to do this for a secretary? And to give her a whole year's pay?"

Rett kept attacking her salad. As usual, she was going to finish before I started. "Yeah, it's a little weird. Normally a big company will pay one week of severance for every two years worked, up to a maximum of 26 weeks. So it sounds like she's getting a good deal, barring other issues."

"What do you mean, 'other issues'? Couldn't they just boot her out and give her nothing?"

Rett rolled her eyes. "You're lucky you're so damn loveable, Benjamin. Where were you all those years in law school? Generally, yes, it's true. She's an employee at will and they can fire her any time for any reason and not owe her a penny. But there's a big exception. They can't fire her because of her sex, her race, her age, or her religion. They can't retaliate against her if she complained of illegal behavior. If any of those are the reasons they fired her, then it's illegal, and she shouldn't settle unless she's getting compensated for waiving her right to sue them. That's a whole different ballgame. So before you let her sign that contract, you'd better know the reason she was fired. Make sense?"

"Sure," I said, nodding. I had asked Liza why she was fired, but she didn't talk about it. I should probably ask her again. At least now I could tell her why I needed to know.

I drove back to my building after lunch. I paused as I wandered by Joss's office. The hall was empty, and I leaned against her door and listened. I could hear the mumble of voices, a world separate from me. I knew it wouldn't be cool to be caught eavesdropping, so I hurried down to my office.

I had a landline in my office. At first I just used my cell phone, but somehow it seemed more professional to have a separate office phone. So I splurged for the monthly phone service. When I walked into my office, the yellow message light was blinking. I listened. Callahan had called, wanting to set a time to exchange the signed contract.

Callahan intimidated the hell out of me. He was 58 years old, according to RTG's "Leadership Team" webpage. He'd gone to Northwestern undergrad, and the University of Michigan Law School. Those were two of the top schools in the whole country, ones I would never have dreamed of applying to. He'd worked for a federal appellate judge after law school, about the most prestigious job a law grad can get. Then he spent five years at Stallon Moore, the world's largest law firm, which is headquartered right here in good old Cleveland. He moved over to RTG after that, and his career just skyrocketed. Counsel, Senior Counsel, Assistant Chief Counsel, Associate Chief Counsel, and then the last seven years, Chief Counsel, the top lawyer in the whole company. In addition to the 127 lawyers who reported to him, he was also in charge of the Mergers & Acquisitions, Securities, and Compliance functions. He'd been at RTG for a quarter century.

It wasn't just that he lived in a world that was foreign to me. He was around my dad's age, or at least the age my dad would have been. My dad died when I was 12. He owned a little automotive supply company, and basically worked every waking moment. I don't have many memories of him, just images of him being angry on the phone, barking directives, talking about things that were Greek to me. My mom fell apart after he died, and was never really there until she died a few years later. After that, I moved in with my cousin. My predominant feeling growing up was a rumbling panic, and I spent my time ducking and hiding, feeling lost, trying to stay safe and keep the world from crashing down on me. Thinking about working with Callahan gave me that same feeling of dread.

So I wasn't anxious to get back to him. I took a nap instead.

It was evening when I woke up. I needed to follow-up with Liza, and called her cell.

"Hi, Liza, it's Ben. How are you?"

I could hear music in the background. It sounded like she was at a party.

"Who is this?" she asked.

"Uh, it's Ben."

There was no response. "You know," I said, "your lawyer?"

She didn't respond, so I kept going. "So I've been over the contract, and there's a few things I hoped we could talk about. I wondered if you had time to get together?"

She didn't respond. I could hear laughter.

"Liza? Are you there?"

She didn't respond. I heard her say, "Danny! Not now! Put that away, you pervert." Then I heard shuffling and muffled voices. She sounded like she'd been drinking.

After a minute, I said, "Hello? Liza? Hello?"

There was no response. I waited another minute, but couldn't make anything out. Finally I hung up. I sat there in my office feeling like a complete putz. I called her back. It went to voicemail.

"Um, hi, Liza. It's Ben. You know, I'm the guy who's your lawyer. Anyway, I can't sign off on the contract until we talk, so if you wouldn't mind giving me a quick call, that would be great. Thanks."

I hung up and immediately felt guilty for being pushy with her. I spent the next hour typing a letter for my one other open matter – a friend couldn't get his landlord to fix the lock on his door – and then decided to call it a day. I hadn't called Callahan back. I'd deal with him tomorrow.

It was Thursday, and I figured I'd spend the night watching the Indians on TV. Boring, but I wasn't really in the mood for much else.

I walked down the hall and most of the shrinks' offices were dark behind the frosted glass doors. I slowed as I approached Joss's office. The door was half open and a cone of light split the dark hallway.

I stopped and looked in. Her office was the same as mine, but about a thousand times more tastefully decorated. Just inside the door was a round marble table surrounded by three dark brown leather chairs. She had dozens of framed pictures on the walls, all close-ups of people with searching expressions on their faces. She had a desk in front of the window like I did, and a leather couch along the wall, obviously the new purchase that replaced the ratty one I inherited. There was a chair at the end of the couch to the side of her desk. Joss was lying on the couch with her eyes closed, rubbing her temples. I tapped lightly on her door. She opened her eyes and smiled at me.

"Hey there, Counselor," she said.

"Aren't you supposed to be in the chair, Counselor?"

"Oh, man, I need someone in that chair for me today."

"Well, here," I said, "allow me." I stepped around the couch and sat down. With her head on the couch, she couldn't see me behind her.

"How do you stay awake in this thing?" I asked.

"I rarely do."

I looked down on her. She was seriously gorgeous. She was wearing a light blue tank top, and from where I sat I had a lovely view of her cleavage. Her arms were lean and muscular. She had broad shoulders and a tiny waist. She was wearing a long red skirt that had slid up above her knees.

I turned off the lamp on her desk. The sun had set, and we were ensconced in darkness. "So, Dr. Levy, tell me how I can help."

She chuckled. "It's a long story."

"Yes," I said. "But that's why we're here."

"What made you decide to be a psychologist, Dr. Billings?" she asked. Her voice was soft and near.

"I guess it's the gratification of helping people. Feeling admired and appreciated and being a part of their lives. Being needed, you know?"

"That's lovely. So you have no patients?"

"It's growing thin," I said.

"What is?"

"My patience."

"Ha!" Joss said. "I hope you have other career

options."

"I could always be a lawyer. But everyone hates lawyers."

"True."

"Ok, Dr. Levy, tell me about yourself."

"What do you want to know?"

"Where'd you grow up?"

"I haven't."

"That's apparent."

"What makes you think I'm a parent?"

"Funny woman. So no kids?"

"I'm not suited for it."

"Few are. But the world is littered with them."

"No litter for me," Joss said.

"No husband? No boyfriend?" I couldn't help myself.

"Dr. Billings!" Joss feigned surprise. "Do you have an inappropriate interest in me?"

"That's what we're here to find out."

"Doctor! You could lose your license."

"No loss there."

Joss giggled. I sat in the chair, my elbows on my knees. Joss's head was on the pillow just a few inches away. I heard her sit up on the couch. Her face was just inches from mine. I could feel her breath on my cheek. I leaned my forehead against hers, and she flinched and started to pull away. Gradually, she leaned back into me. We sat there in the dark, breathing slowly. I loved her smell, earthy and arousing. Joss leaned her cheek against mine, and I felt her breath on my ear. She reached and turned on the lamp on her desk.

I blinked to get used to the light. Joss was standing before me.

"Ok, Dr. Billings. I think our time is up."

"It's ok," I said. "Really, I don't have any more

patients today."

"Yes, I know. You have no patience."

"I don't bill by the hour. Really. It's ok."

She walked around and sat at her desk and pulled some paperwork out of a drawer. She looked up at me. I had no idea what to say. What just happened?

"Well, ok," I said. "I guess we'll have to continue where we left off at our next session."

"We'll see about that," she said, smiling while she flipped through papers. She looked at me again and cocked her head. I guess she couldn't make things more clear. She dipped her toe in the water and had no interest.

"Ok, Joss. See you later."

I turned and left. It was another dull night drinking beer and watching the Indians on TV. For the first time, I was starting to dislike baseball.

4

I stopped by my office at 8:30 the next morning before leaving for my dentist appointment. Another week at the forefront of the pressing legal issues of our times.

As I was about to leave, the phone rang. I shouldn't have answered it. It was Callahan.

"Hi Mr. Callahan. How are you today?"

"You didn't return my call yesterday."

"Yeah, sorry about that. I need a little more time."

"Jesus Christ, Ben. What could possibly be the delay? This is a simple form contract. The same one we use for everyone. It's very generous for Liza. I would like this wrapped up today. Are you capable of doing that?"

"I'm sorry, Mr. Callahan, I'll do my best. I 'm just on my way to a proceeding." No need to tell him it was to get a cavity filled. "But I need to make sure Liza's getting good legal advice, just like you asked."

"Let me remind you who's paying your bill, son. I did you a favor by sending you work and offering to pay for your time. I expect you to show me the courtesy of calling me back when I call you. And I expect you to be honest about your time and not take advantage of the fact that you've got a Fortune 50 company funding you. Don't you dare pad your bill."

"I've really got to go, Mr. Callahan, I can't be late. Don't worry about me padding my bill. I would never do that." This was humiliating. "I'll be back in touch just as soon as I have a chance to go over the contract with Ms. Allen. Hopefully today."

I hustled down to my car. What was with that guy?

I got back to my office before lunch and my message light was flashing. I hit the play button.

"It's Liza Allen. We need to talk. Call me."

Now that kind of pissed me off. First, she didn't even acknowledge that she'd blown me off yesterday. And I couldn't help but think that Callahan called her to push her to get this done. If he had, he committed a major ethical violation. She was my client, and he's not allowed to talk to her if she has a lawyer. I can't believe he would be so stupid. He could lose his law license for that, and the seven million a year he's getting from RTG.

I called Liza.

"We need to get this contract done," she said. "Are you free today?"

"I think so. Let me check my calendar." I pulled up my calendar on my computer. It was the end of May. I had nothing scheduled for the rest of the year.

"I can move some things around and meet you for lunch today if you're free," I said.

"That works."

"Ok. Where should we meet?" I asked. She lived just a few blocks away from me in Cleveland Heights. "We could go to The Fairmount. Do you know it? It's right across the street from my office."

"I'll see you there at noon." She hung up.

Charming.

5

I got to the Fairmount Wine Bar at noon. It was a classic Cleveland restaurant. Good food for lunch and dinner, and morphing into a sports bar at night for the college crowd. I walked around the restaurant looking for Liza. She wasn't there, so I got a table near the door so she would see me.

She finally showed up at 12:20, wearing expensive jeans, a red blouse, and those movie star sunglasses. Her blouse was form fitting, inviting looks but still classy somehow. She was thin and well built. She walked up and stood across from me.

"I want the back."

"Pardon me?"

"The back. Of the restaurant. Not the front. Get it?" She looked back and forth, like she was hoping to find someone. "It's so fucking crowded in here."

Holy cow.

We moved to a booth in the back. The guys watched Liza as she walked through the restaurant. She sat with her back to the wall, and I sat across from her.

"How are you doing?" I asked.

She took off her sunglasses. Finally. She had tired blue eyes. "How do you think? I've worked at RTG my whole life. I don't know what to do with all this free time."

"Do you want to tell me what happened?"

"Is there any point?"

"Well, yes, there is. I mean, first of all, it might do you good to talk about it. Do you have anyone to talk to about something like this?"

"This isn't middle school, Ben."

Ouch.

"I don't need to talk about it," she said. "And Callahan told me not to talk to anyone if I want the severance package. He said there's a non-disclosure requirement, and if I 'run my mouth,'" she said, making air quotes, "the offer would be off the table."

"Ok. But you can talk to me. I'm your lawyer."

She didn't respond.

"By the way," I said, "did Callahan call you?"

"Yeah. He wanted to know how I was doing." She shook her head. "Like he's so concerned about me. What a dick. I worked there for two decades and he never showed the slightest interest in me. And now suddenly he's so concerned. Does he think I'm an idiot? I know exactly what's going on."

"What's going on, Liza?"

She didn't respond.

"Did he ask you about our conversation?" I asked.

"He wanted to know if I was comfortable with you and when I thought we would have a signed contract for him."

Man, that made me mad. "Ok, so listen. He's not allowed to talk to you. There are rules, and he knows that since I'm your lawyer, he can only talk to me about this. If he calls you again, please tell him he's not allowed to speak with you and he'll have to talk to me. Ok?"

Liza smirked at me.

"So here's the deal, Liza. I need to know why they fired you. If I'm going to advise you on this contract, I need to know what happened."

"Why does it matter? They don't want me there. I can't be there anymore. They'll pay me some money and forget about me. And that's the end of it. They've done it a thousand times and now it's my turn. I can't believe I have to put a resume together and start applying for jobs. Do you know how long it's been since I've done that?"

The waitress came by and asked if we were ready. "Give us a minute," I said. "C'mon, let's figure out what we want and then we'll talk."

She stared above my head but didn't respond. I turned to see if someone was there.

Liza ordered a small Caesar salad and a glass of Pinot Grigio. I got a cheeseburger and fries and a beer. When the waitress left, I said, "So listen, Liza. It does matter what happened. I mean, if they just decided after all these years that they don't like you, or that you're not doing a good job, then they can fire you..."

"I've never had anything but the highest performance reviews. They gave me a bonus at the end of January of 30 percent of my base pay. It's not my performance."

"Ok, well here's the thing. If they fired you for an illegal reason, then this is an entirely different discussion. What I mean is, if they fired you because of your sex, you know, they decided they wanted a man in your job instead of a woman, then they've got a real problem on their hands. If they fired you because of your religion, or your race, they've got a problem."

"Jesus Christ, Ben. I'm a white girl. Have you seen the management team? All white men. It's got nothing to do with my race. Every secretary in the whole building is a woman. I don't know who's going to replace me, but you can bet it'll be another white woman. It's not because of my sex. And it's not because of my religion. They're going to hire a good looking white girl with big tits."

"Well, my point is, if they fired you illegally,

then they face a whole different risk of damages."

"Like what?"

Shit. I had no idea. I should have asked Rett what Liza should get if they fired her illegally.

The waitress brought our drinks. Liza sipped her wine. "I'll take the year," she said without looking at me. "I'll take their money and be done with those bastards."

We sat. Liza was angry and didn't want to talk. I thought maybe it would be best to change gears.

"So you live near here? Are you from Cleveland?"

She nodded. She kept looking to see who was around.

"So how'd you wind up at RTG?"

"I grew up here in Cleveland Heights. I always dreamed of owning a business, somewhere exotic, you know, Paris, London, Rome, somewhere like that. I wanted to go to college, but I come from a fucked up family and there were money issues. I got into Cornell and was planning to study economics. But my father is a prick. He and my mom divorced when I was a kid. My mom had cancer and he said he'd pay for half the cost of a two-year community college and not a penny more. Five hundred bucks a year. I don't think he wanted me going to a school that was better than where he'd gone. He didn't care about my mom's situation or what I wanted.

"I decided I was done with my dad. He was always trying to control me like he did my mom and I wouldn't have it. And I needed to be here to help my mom. I graduated high school and took a job with RTG. I can't believe I'm almost 40. And I'm still here in Cleveland, living three blocks from where I grew up."

"I'm sorry. What happened with your mom?"

"She died a few months later."

"I'm sorry."

Liza polished off her wine. She lifted her glass to let the waitress know she wanted another.

"In a way, RTG saved me back then, with all that was going on. It's hard not to like working at the Crystal Palace."

"Where?"

She shot me a look. "Obviously, you haven't been to RTG. They call the headquarters here the Crystal Palace. It's almost obscene. I mean, at a company that routinely lays off workers to cut costs and moves operations overseas to avoid taxes, it's insane how they spare no expense for the management team. All glass and opulence. Anyway, I'd go to work there everyday, go to all these glamorous dinners and parties and meetings around the world. They took care of me."

Liza was talking but we had no connection. She reminded me of a porcelain doll, like the ones I saw in the windows of Saks Fifth Avenue when my grandfather took me to New York at Christmas when I was a kid. Her features were sharp. Her skin was flawless. She was a strikingly beautiful woman. And yet she was impervious. She was an alabaster ice queen.

It seemed strange to me that a secretary got to travel so much. "It's nice that you got to travel for work." I said.

"I was part of the executive team the last eight years I was there. They have meetings all over the world. I got to travel with them when they wanted me. First-class flights. Five-star restaurants and hotels. As long as I was accommodating, I got to participate in everything."

The waitress brought our food and I started

eating. I was hungry and the burgers were great. Liza didn't touch her salad. She polished off her wine and signaled for another.

We sat in silence. I needed to keep her talking if I was going to learn anything.

"I'm from here, too," I said. "I grew up in Shaker Heights. I went to Ohio State for college, and came back here for law school. I never really thought about where I'd wind up. But I like it here. Of course, I'm young, as you pointed out the other day."

She looked at me and nodded. "Very."

I decided to take it as a compliment. "I get that all the time. Anyway, I have plenty of time to figure out where I want to be."

"No wife? No kids?"

"Oh god, no," I laughed.

"It's not a preposterous question."

"No, not unless you know me."

"Not the marrying type?"

"Oh, I don't know. I've never had a serious relationship, you know? They scare me. I mean, sure, I've dated. But nothing serious."

She looked me in the eye. "Just fun and games?"

"Well, yeah, fun and games. What's wrong with fun and games?"

She watched me.

"What about you?" I asked. She didn't wear a wedding ring.

"That's an impolite question to ask a 38 year-old woman. But no, I'm not married. No kids."

I finished my meal and she polished off her wine. The waitress brought the check. Liza didn't offer to contribute, so I paid it.

Liza got up to leave. I'd still learned nothing about why she was fired.

34

We walked outside. It was a beautiful spring day, nearly 65 and sunny. Liza put on her sunglasses and folded her arms across her chest. She scowled. "I don't know why I walked here." She started looking around, like she was trying to find something.

"I could drive you home. My car's in the garage across the street."

She looked at me quickly. "I don't like cars."

"I could walk you home."

"If you want."

We wound our way through the side streets of Cleveland Heights. Parts of this suburb are stunning, with 150-year-old houses set back a hundred yards from the street. Rockefeller built some of the houses near here. Wandering through the neighborhood, it felt like we'd gone back in time. A car drove by and some guy leaned out the window and honked at us.

"He must think I'm hot," I said.

Liza laughed. It was the first time I'd seen her smile.

I figured now was the time to try again. "So Liza, why'd you lose your job?"

She sighed. "Let me tell you about RTG. I started as a secretary in the finance department. And eventually they put a rising star in finance. A guy named Nicholas Stanton."

"Nick Stanton? The CEO?"

"Yeah, same guy. He apparently took a liking to me. Because after a while, he became the CEO, and when he did, he asked me to be his secretary. I hadn't ever worked for him, and it pissed off some of the other secretaries. It was a big promotion for me, and of course I took it. It put me in the Executive Circle."

"What's that?"

She looked at me impatiently. "The Chiefs run the company. There's the CEO, the Chief of Finance, the Chief of HR, the Chief of Environmental, the Chief of Operations, and Callahan, the Chief Counsel. The six of them are the Executive Circle. Their offices are in the top of the building, in this big circular area. All windows, so you have a 360-degree view of the grounds. Anyway, there's a pool of six secretaries working for them in the center of the circle. They call us the 'Pool Girls.' Our job is to take care of them. Whatever they need. Even though we worked for all of the Chiefs, I was Nick's private secretary in certain ways. I guess you could say that I was Nick's personal assistant for the last eight years or so."

We turned up a small street made of bricks. It wasn't hard to imagine horse-drawn carriages coming down the road. Massive oak trees, three deep in perfect rows, lined the yards.

"So what went wrong?"

Liza stopped and turned towards me. She folded her arms across her chest.

"Ok, Ben. Here's the deal. I think Nick had a thing for me. There was a constant flirtation. Our relationship was always professional, but he thought there was the prospect of something more. Always."

"Just fun and games?"

"No, not fun and games at all. We worked together. That's it."

I stood and waited. She was looking to see if I was judging her, and I knew if I did she'd stop talking.

"Look," she said, "every secretary in the Pool got there because of her looks and relationship with the Chiefs. It's not really how it sounds. You don't get to that level unless you're good. Every one of us in the Pool earned those jobs."

I nodded. She started walking again.

"Nick's married, anyways. He shouldn't be. There's always talk of Nick's women and his affairs."

I walked alongside her and didn't say anything.

"So I kept my distance," Liza said. "We had fun at work and there's no doubt there was sexual tension there. He's a very good-looking man. And then, about a year ago, I met a guy in the international finance group. A really good, solid guy. We started spending time together. He was the first guy at RTG who didn't treat me like entertainment. And then suddenly Nick gets hostile with me. He must have heard about Robby and didn't like it. I don't think Nick wanted to be with me; he just didn't want anyone else with me. Like I was his property. Ridiculous. So next thing I know, about nine months ago, Robby gets transferred to our joint venture in Sao Paulo. Can you believe what an asshole Nick is? I mean, it's a great career move for Robby. A big promotion, and he goes from a staff position to the head of finance for an international business. And then two days after Robby leaves, Nick comes up to me at the end of the day and is so sympathetic. He knows what a difficult time this must be. He wondered if I might like to go out for dinner.

"Well, I knew what he was doing. I told Nick that he's a prick for transferring Robby. He denied it, of course. Robby was in finance, and that's Marty's team. Marty Bishop is the Chief of Finance. Nick claims he had nothing to do with it, and if I wanted proof, I should go ask Marty. But it's bullshit. Marty would never do something like that unless Nick told him to."

"So what happened?"

"At first it was awkward. In front of others he was always polite. I kept doing my job in the Pool and things were ok. But I stopped working for Nick exclusively. All the chiefs started using me."

We crossed Coventry Boulevard and turned

onto Corydon.   After a few minutes Liza tilted her head and said.   "This is my house.   Let's go in the back."

Her house was a small, beautiful Tudor.   It was on a corner, and had a perfectly tailored wrap-around lawn.   The back yard was fenced in, a slotted five-foot high wooden fence that must have cost a ton.   She had a patio with a wrought iron table surrounded by four wrought iron chairs.   We sat at the table.

"In any event, Nick stopped flirting with me.   There was a chill between us and it was unpleasant."

"Then what happened?"

She got up and walked over to the fence and leaned against it.   I waited.   Eventually she turned and looked at me, her arms folded across her chest.   I couldn't see through the movie star sunglasses.

"Then last week they fired me."

"Did they say why?"

She looked away.   I waited.

"Liza?"

"They said they needed to make a change.   That's it."

"But why then?   I don't understand.   Why was Nick ok with you for months after you turned him down, but then he wanted you out?"

"How the hell would I know, goddamn it?"   Liza walked back to the table and sat down.   "Maybe he wanted a new conquest in the Pool.   Maybe I no longer have what it takes to titillate him."

"I doubt that.   Who told you that you were fired?"

Liza stared at me and then looked away.   She put her feet up on the chair next to her.   She sat there facing away from me.

"Liza?"

"Callahan.   Callahan told me I was fired, ok?

He called me into his office and told me they needed to make a change. That I needed to leave immediately and they would pack up my office. He had two people from HR waiting for me. They took my phone and my badge and escorted me out. They escorted me out like I was some kind of criminal."

"He didn't say why?"

"I told you!" She shot me an angry look. "He said they needed to make a change."

It still didn't sound right.

Liza stared off into the yard. "So that's it. I'll take their money and be done with the bastards."

"Can I ask? The $60,000 that they're offering. Is that what they paid you last year? You mentioned a bonus."

"Sixty thousand is my base pay. But there were bonuses for 'special contributions,'" she said, making air quotes. "Plus my annual bonus at the end of January. I got a 30 percent bonus this year."

"Wow, is that normal?"

"There's no normal for the Pool girls. They took care of us, you know? If they wanted to reward us for something we did, or encourage us, there was lots of money handed out."

"What'd you make last year?"

"Probably $120,000."

Holy shit. I wondered what she'd done for all that money. "So the $60,000 they're offering isn't really a year's pay?"

"Dammit, Ben. I'm telling you this isn't worth it. I've seen every severance package they've paid for the last decade. For a secretary to get this much is unusual. I'll take their money."

"You don't have the stomach for a fight?"

"Fuck you."

Wow. We sat in silence for a few minutes.

"Listen, Liza. The easy route is to take their money and be done with it. But we could fight to try to get more out of them. Maybe the $120,000 they paid you last year. That's a true year's pay."

Liza stood and wandered around her yard. She walked like a model. She stopped and stood by the fence. I walked over next to her and leaned against the fence. "Who are you so mad at, Liza?"

She turned and looked at me. She folded her arms across her chest. "Those fuckers. I had a goddamned career. They ended it! I'm furious. What, I'm going to go get hired somewhere and be the lowest ranked person in the company? Start over like I'm just out of high school again? You don't know what I did to get here. Every day I'm angrier and angrier. I don't know where to go with this."

"How much do you need the money?"

"Why?"

"Well, if we fight for more, you risk getting nothing. Or maybe something more, but not getting it for a few months. Do you have enough to live on for awhile?"

"I can get by for three months, that's it. Then I have no idea how I'm going to pay my bills. They said they wouldn't contest unemployment. I have to sign up for that and look for a job. Can you believe it? I have to go on goddamn government handouts."

I wanted to buy some time so I could talk with Rett and figure out where to go with this.

"So listen, Liza. Callahan is pushing for me to get back to him today. But if I tell him we're going to take a few days, I can't believe he's going to withdraw the offer. So why don't we take a little time? Let me do some research. If you're getting madder every day, I'd hate to make a rush decision. What might feel right today might not be what you want in a couple weeks.

Let me do some research, and then we'll talk again. What do you think?"

"Let's talk tomorrow," she said. "I can't bear this. I want this done. Call me in the morning."

I hadn't had much luck on the phone with her. "Wanna meet at the Fairmount for lunch again?"

"Fine. Let's meet at 11:00. I don't like crowds." She shook her head. "I can't believe I'm going through this. Do you know how many people they fired over the years? You should hear how they talk about them. It was always 'the fuckhead,' or 'the dickhead.' You know, 'let's get that dickhead out of here.' Now I'm the dickhead."

"I'm sorry, Liza. But they're the dickheads, not you. You didn't do anything wrong. Let's take a little time and we'll figure this out."

I reached out and put my hand on her shoulder. She jerked away violently and hurried into the house. She shoved the door shut behind her and I could hear her turn the bolt.

Yikes.

I walked back to my building at a complete loss, as usual.

6

My first instinct was to call Rett and share what I learned. But I had an inferiority complex with Rett. Well, with everyone, I guess. She was my best friend at school, and as great as she was to me, I couldn't help but be aware of her success, compared with my hapless floundering. Some of our friends called us "Rocky and Bullwinkle." Even though Rett is thin and firm, and I'm big and lanky by comparison, I have no doubt the reference was to her being smart and a leader, and me being content to follow her around. But she never made me feel bad about turning to her, and I knew I could count on what she told me.

I avoided calling Callahan. He'd be angry with me and I didn't want to deal with that. I wish he played sports so I could show him I was good at something. I had no clue about this lawyering game. He'd want to know what the holdup was, and the truth is, I couldn't even really answer the question. Something didn't feel right, but what did that mean? I'd spent two and a half hours with Liza, but decided I'd only bill Callahan for an hour of my time. I didn't want anyone thinking I'd done something wrong.

I sat with my feet on my desk. It occurred to me that instead of getting Rett to explain more about the law, I could go to the law library and try to learn something on my own. It sounded dull as, well, sitting in a library, but I figured I should try. Joss's light was on when I walked by her office, but the door was shut. I wondered if I would ever be able to walk this hall again without trying to find an excuse to see her.

I drove to the law library and spent two hours reading about wrongful termination. I think I dozed off the last hour, to be honest. It was Friday evening, and I couldn't believe I was in a library. I needed to get out of there.

I drove back to my building. I thought about calling some of my buddies to go out to a sports bar, but couldn't stop thinking about Joss. And how incredibly arousing it was to be near her. I decided to wander by her office just in case she was there.

The shrinks were all in Joss's office when I stopped by. The door was open and they were crammed around the couch. They were uncharacteristically somber.

"What's going on?" I asked.

"Katrina lost a patient," David said.

They seemed to be overreacting. "Is that unusual? There's got to be a million patients out there."

Joss shook her head. I looked at David.

"Her patient killed herself."

"Oh, geez, I'm sorry."

Joss was sitting on the couch, stroking Katrina's hair and whispering to her. She walked to her desk and got a box of Kleenex.

"Did you know him?" I whispered to Joss.

"No. I just feel so bad for Trina." Joss sat back down next to Katrina.

David walked behind Joss's desk and stood looking out the window. Katrina blew her nose.

"I'm sorry," Katrina said. "I know I should be more professional."

Joss put her hand on Katrina's knee. "You know it's not your fault."

"I should have had her hospitalized."

"You had no way of knowing, and you know

it."

"She seemed to be doing so well the last two months. She didn't show any signs."

"It's so sad," Joss said, "but it's not your fault, Trina."

I couldn't believe how compassionate Joss was. Katrina leaned against Joss like Joss was her mother. Joss put her arm around Katrina and stroked her hair.

"Beer," David said to the window.

"What?" I asked.

"Beer. We should drink beer."

Katrina looked at David and wiped her eyes. "You're right. Come on, let's get a drink."

Joss looked at me. "What are you doing tonight?"

Was that an invitation or was she telling me to go do something else? I would love to hang with Joss.

"I was thinking of going for a run," I said, hoping she'd ask me directly.

They got up to leave. Still no invitation.

"I'll be up in my apartment later if anyone feels like talking. Number 402. Just knock."

I hoped that wasn't too obvious.

We said our goodbyes and I wandered up to my apartment to change. My job might be dull, but at least I didn't need to worry about gut-wrenching stuff.

I went for a slow run through the streets of Cleveland Heights, plodding really, looking at the toney mansions, envious of the contented families I imagined inside their limestone walls, laughing and sharing intimacies and oblivious to me so nearby and so alone. I got back to my building around 9. I showered and straightened up the place. I lay down on the couch, hoping for a knock on the door. It never came.

7

I woke up at 11, stiff from sleeping on the couch. Shit. 11 o'clock. I was supposed to meet Liza.

I brushed my teeth and rushed over to The Fairmount. Liza was sitting at our table with her back against the wall, sipping a Bloody Mary. I sat down. She was wearing white, neatly pressed pants and a powder blue, sleeveless blouse that matched her eyes perfectly. The movie star sunglasses were on top of her head. She was dressed casually, but still looked like she could be on the cover of Vogue. She was a classically beautiful woman. I, on the other hand, looked like I just woke up after sleeping on the couch all night.

Liza shook her head condescendingly. "Nice outfit," she said. "Looks like you had a long night."

I groaned.

"Fun and games?" she asked.

"Not much. None, actually."

She looked past me.

We sipped our drinks. "So listen, Liza. I did some research. If they fired you for an illegal reason, we could be looking at more money. Basically, they have to pay you for what you're out of pocket. But not just up until today. Going forward, too. So if you can't find a job for like five years, then a jury could give you five years' pay. And we can try to force them to pay you for the emotional suffering they've caused you. We can even try to get punitive damages, you know, to punish them for really bad behavior. So I'm thinking that maybe one year's base pay doesn't really cut it."

"Why do you think they did something illegal?"

I looked at Liza. She still wasn't interested enough to look at me. She sat there fiddling with her drink. She was insolent and I was sure she had no faith in me to do anything for her. She was smart beyond her years.

"I don't know. Have you told me everything?"

She smirked at her drink. "Sure."

"See, there are some cases out there that say that if they fired you because you refused to go out with your boss, then yeah, that's illegal. I guess if he fired you because you went out with Robby and not him, then it's a form of sexual harassment. They can't condition your job on you being willing to date your boss."

"You don't seem very confident about it."

"Well, I guess what's weird is the time that passed before they fired you. I mean, if you told Nick you wouldn't go out with him, and then he fired you the next day, that would be easy. But he waited months. And you said he was professional during that time. That makes it really hard to show that they fired you because you refused to date Nick."

"How do you know how long it will take me to find a job? I could find one tomorrow. I might never get hired. Do we have to wait and see?"

Shit. I didn't know the answer to that. I hesitated, and she smirked at me again. Damn, I felt like a fool. I decided not to fake it. "You know, I'll have to research that. But I think maybe the thing is, we can ask for more, because there's the chance that you could be entitled to more. And if they're worried about that, then maybe they'll pay you more."

Liza sipped her drink and didn't say anything. We sat for a minute.

"Have you ever gone up against RTG on

anything?" she asked.

"No."

"Have you ever had a trial for an employment case?"

"No."

"Have you ever even had an employment case?"

"This is my first."

"Have you ever had a trial on any matter?"

"No."

Liza polished off her drink and stood up. She slid her glassed on.

"I'll take what they're offering," she said. "Get it done."

She walked out. Lovely.

8

I went to my office at 9 on Monday after a boring weekend watching ballgames and drinking beer with my softball buddies. I just couldn't enjoy myself with that gnawing fear of my looming call to Callahan. I kept telling myself that there was nothing to be nervous about, but I was a wreck. How ridiculous was that? But I didn't know what I was doing, and didn't want to look like a fool and screw things up.

I took a deep breath and called.

"William Callahan's office. Bonnie speaking."

"Hi, Bonnie. Is Mr. Callahan in?"

"May I ask who is calling?"

"This is Benjamin Billings."

"May I ask what this is regarding, Mr. Billings? Mr. Callahan is in a meeting at the moment."

"Sure. Of course. Well, I'm the guy who's working with Liza Allen."

"One second, I'll put you through."

Wow, that wasn't what I expected. I was on hold for nearly two minutes. I paced nervously, walking circles around my desk, listening to elevator music.

"Ben, how are you?"

Well, this was an entirely different tone. "I'm fine, Mr. Callahan, how are you today?"

"I'm quite well, thank you. Ben, I know that you're a busy young man, and I don't want to take too much of your time. I'm not happy about our last conversation, and was thinking that it would be nice for the two of us to meet, to sit and break bread together."

"Well…. Um, yes, that would be nice. But I'm really sorry, Mr. Callahan, I don't have a signed contract for you quite yet."

"That's fine. It's important for me to get to know the attorneys in town, and I think it's always wise to spend time before doing business. I was neglectful in not doing that with you. I wondered if you might join me for lunch today if you're not otherwise occupied."

"Hang on just a second, let me check my schedule."

I put the phone down on my desk. I wish I had one of those hold buttons. I thought of playing elevator music on my cell phone, but worried it wouldn't fool him. Anyway, I had nothing scheduled for forever. I held the phone next to my keyboard and hit a bunch of keys to make it sound like I was checking.

"Sure, I can move some things around and come there today if that works for you."

"It does. One second, let me see if I can get a room." Suddenly, he was bellowing. "Bonnie! Bonnie! Bonnie! Bonnie!" It reminded me of Stewie on Family Guy, hollering for his mom. He waited a few seconds and then started again. "Bonnie! Bonnie! Bonnie! Oh, you're here. Can you get me the Rogers Room at noon today?"

I could hear muffled conversation. Finally, he came back on the phone. "I'm sorry, Ben. I thought I could make this work at noon, but I'm not free until 1:30. Would that work for you?"

"Sure, that works."

"Let's meet at my office. I'll have Bonnie give you instructions."

Suddenly the elevator music was back. Bonnie

picked up and gave me directions. She was very precise about what to do when "confronted by the security guard at the gate." She asked me to confirm that I understood, and instructed me to ask for her when I arrived, not Mr. Callahan. What a rigmarole for grabbing a sandwich!

I was wearing shorts and a t-shirt. I chuckled at the idea of going like that. I had a few hours, and needed to go over the contract before our meeting. I started to read it, but a minute in I was dozing off. I figured I had a better chance of focusing if I walked down to Starbucks. I grabbed a yellow pad and pen.

As I left my office, Joss came bounding up the steps and around the corner. She nearly bowled me over. I wish she had.

"Counselor!" she said.

She was wearing black yoga pants that left nothing to the imagination, and a sleeveless white top. Damn.

"Uh, hi, Joss, I'm just going to grab a coffee before a corporate meeting this afternoon. How are you?"

"I'm fine. Got my run in. Seven miles today. Got in a rhythm and just went and went and went. Feels great. Don't you love Cleveland with a hint of summer in the air?"

"Yeah, I do." Smooth.

She bent and touched her toes, laid her palms flat on the ground. Damn. She stood up and tucked her hair behind her ears. "Ok. Gotta go," she said. "Can't let the patients lose patience."

And with that she was on her way down the hall to her office. Damnit! Why was I so inept? I would love to talk with her, go for a run with her. Why hadn't I suggested that? I should have invited her for coffee. Maybe I could do it now. I walked to her office, but her door was closed. I thought about knocking, but it seemed pathetic.

I sat in Starbucks sipping my coffee. I blew another chance with Joss. Not that I ever really had a chance. She was just way above my league, and since our intimate little moment, she'd had no interest in me. She was so damn self-sufficient, unlike me. And yet I was so drawn to her. How was that? As usual, I was hopelessly off the mark.

I sat at Starbucks, trying to go over the contract. I should come up with something that might make it a better deal for Liza, but I really had no ideas. And it was so incredibly boring, I couldn't really get myself to read it. I looked around the coffee shop, which was filled with college students. Always fun to watch, even though most wore earplugs and shut themselves off from me. A remarkably well-dressed woman stood in the aisle a few tables up, looking for someone. My pen rolled off the table and into the aisle. I got up to get it, and the woman walked up to me.

"Are you leaving?" she asked.

I stood and looked at her, and she wiped a tear off her cheek.

"I'm sorry, are you ok?" I asked.

She was attractive. Probably 45 years-old, blonde, green eyes. Her hair was parted carefully on the side and curled at the bottom just above her shoulders, just exactly the same length on both sides and with the same curls. It must take forever to get it perfect like that. Her skin was flawless and I could smell her perfume. She was wearing a tight white skirt and a soft green scoop-neck blouse that matched her eyes. She was definitely out of place with the college kids. She reeked of money.

"I wondered if you were leaving," she said.

"Sorry, I wasn't," I said. "Just trying to find my

pen."

I looked around and it was on the floor, resting under the arch between her toes and the 2-inch heel to her shoe.

"Um," I said, "there it is." She just watched me. I couldn't tell if she knew she was standing on it. Now what? I got down on one knee and reached under her shoe and grabbed it, careful not to touch her foot. I stood up and she watched me.

"Get what you were looking for?"

"Not really," I said, "but I found my pen."

She laughed out loud. "Thanks," she said, "I needed that." She sighed and looked around. "There aren't any open tables."

"They usually open up pretty fast," I said. "Just a lot of college kids here waiting for classes to start."

She looked at me and down at my table. There were two chairs, one on each side. Oh.

"Sorry," I said. "I've got to work on my table manners. You're welcome to join me."

"Why, thank you!" she said, pretending to be surprised.

She sat down in the chair opposite mine and crossed her legs. She looked like she went to great lengths to make herself attractive. Hours in the gym, no doubt. It was working though. She was clearly fit. She had an intelligent but weary look about her. I offered to get her a coffee.

"Wow, a gentleman. How refreshing." She pulled her Louis Vuitton wallet out of her Louis Vuitton handbag.

I told her not to worry, I'd get it.

I came back and handed her the coffee. "So what are you working on? Are you in school?" she asked.

I had my yellow-pad out with lots of notes on it.

Ok, just doodles. Not a single cogent thought.

"Me? No. I'm a lawyer. "

She glanced at my running shoes. Then my shorts. Then my t-shirt. As usual, I was an embarrassment.

"What firm?"

"I am happily self-employed," I said.

She nodded. I'm sure she was judging me.

"So what brings you to this legal mecca?" I asked.

"What brings you here?"

"My office is just up the block. I came here for a change of scenery to jumpstart my thoughts."

"How's that working for you?"

"Very well at the moment," I said.

She laughed and put her hand on my forearm for a moment. "God, you're refreshing."

Her hands were perfect. Long, slender fingers and flawless tan painted nails with white tips. She had rings on each finger on each hand.

"I'm Lynn Lawson," she said.

"I'm Ben Billings. We're both alliterative."

She raised her eyebrows.

"Yeah, yeah," I said. "I know. A lawyer named Billings. Pathetic."

"Oh, I don't know. Marketing would be easy with that name."

"True, if you're a fan of fiction."

She looked me up and down. "Give yourself credit, Ben. You're good-looking. With the right clothes and a little confidence, you could knock a client right off her feet."

"Maybe with football clothes."

"How old are you?"

"Twenty-six."

"And how's your law practice going?"

"It's not. People aren't banging on the door to hire this guy."

Lynn looked me in the eye. "You need coaching, that's all. It's all in the presentation. Put the right clothes on that frame of yours, learn to present yourself in the right way, and the clients will flock to you."

"Do you know any coaches? Or maybe a magician? Because I'm pretty sure you're talking about someone else."

She sat back and folded her arms. "I could be your coach."

"Yeah?"

"Yeah." She had this weird way of frowning when she grinned. "Why not?" she asked. "I was a star in marketing before my sentence."

"Your sentence?"

"Marriage. We were going to take over the world. And when I became successful, somehow that was threatening. So I retired. A jail sentence for peace at home."

"Well, at least you've got a good marriage."

She snorted. "Yeah, right."

I wasn't sure what to do with this. Here was a clearly accomplished woman offering to help me out. I couldn't imagine why.

"Well, I definitely could use coaching. But is there really any point? I'm a lawyer in the middle of the workweek hanging out by myself in shorts with a bunch of unemployed college kids. I don't think a different outfit will change much of anything for this sorry guy."

"Would you like to place a wager on that?"

I raised my eyebrows. "So what do you do instead of marketing?"

She sighed. "Nothing. Nothing at all. I'm on

some boards. I go to meetings and nod my head when I'm supposed to. I work out. But I was a successful business woman before my husband got his claws into me."

I didn't know anyone on a board, or what that really meant. It sounded important.

"And you think you can turn me into something productive?" I asked. "I applied for jobs at a bunch of law firms, and no one was interested. A nice wardrobe won't change my GPA."

"Are you willing to give it a shot?"

"How would we do that?"

"Spend some time with me. I'll get you some nice clothes and work on your presentation."

This was weird. "Uh, do you think your husband would like you buying clothes for some stranger?"

She snorted. "He'll never know. He's got so many suits he could compete with Nordstrom. I could get you 20 if you'd like."

She was intense. And this was a little uncomfortable.

"So, um, I'd definitely be interested in your advice. But believe it or not, I've got a meeting this afternoon with my one and only client. Maybe we could talk more some other time?"

She looked me in the eye. Then she nodded and looked away.

"I'm sorry," I said. "I do appreciate your offer. But I think if you knew me better, you'd be disappointed."

"Why?"

"I don't know. You seem so .... polished. I can't imagine you'd want spend your time with a clown like me."

She frown-grinned. "Ok," she said. She looked

at her watch and stood up. "Well, you've got to go, right?"

"Yeah, I'm sorry. I need to get ready for my meeting. I probably shouldn't show up dressed like this. Even I know that."

We walked out of Starbucks together and stood on the sidewalk.

"I'm headed this way," I said, pointing up the hill.

"I'm headed that way, too," she said.

We walked side by side.

"Marketing tip number one, Ben. When someone successful offers to work with you, say 'thank you' and accept. You never know where that will lead."

"Ok, got it."

We got to my building. "So," I said, "next time I'll get it right. Promise. Sorry, but I need to go in here."

She watched me. "I'm going here as well," she said.

"Oh, ok." I opened the door slowly. She walked in.

She stood in front of me in the vestibule. "I think getting together would be a good idea."

"Um, I'm headed up the steps to my office," I said.

She looked at me. "I'm headed upstairs as well."

She made a point of walking up the steps in front of me. That skirt was form fitting. She really was quite attractive. She waited for me at the top. I wondered what she had in mind. She was probably 20 years older than me.

"I'm down the hall this way," I said.

"Me too."

I started to walk down the hall, slowly. What would happen if Joss saw us? What would Lynn think of that ratty old couch in my office?

Lynn stopped and faced me. She put her hand on my forearm and nestled up to me. She kissed me on the cheek. I started to think that my couch really wasn't so bad.

"This is marketing lesson one. Lesson two is at the same time on Wednesday in your office."

"Uh, sure."

She turned and walked into a shrink's office.

9

I still had a couple hours before meeting Callahan. I went up to my apartment and lay on my bed and thought about what I needed to do. I had to go through the agreement and come up with a list of comments for Callahan. I needed to figure out how to get him to tell me why Liza was fired.

I must have dozed off, because the next thing I knew it was one o'clock. Shit! Damn. I couldn't be late. I threw on my suit and scurried down to my car and raced over to RTG, which was about 20 minutes away. When I was almost there, I realized I forgot the contract. And my pen. And my yellow pad. Damn.

RTG was nestled in a ridiculously affluent suburb called Gates Mills. I mean ridiculously, like you probably have to be a millionaire to live there. Anyway, I followed a drive through a forest for about a half-mile. Finally I came to a skinny little metallic rectangular sign about six inches off the ground and a foot wide that said "RTG Inc." That was it. For the headquarters of one of the world's biggest companies, it sure wasn't much.

I kept following the road, and eventually came to a small guardhouse. Just a hut in the middle of the woods with a mechanical arm blocking the path. Some guy in a dark suit came out and walked up to my car.

"How can I help you, sir?"

"I'm here to see William Callahan."

He raised an eyebrow and looked at me but didn't respond.

"Oh, shit!" I said. "No, I'm here to see Bonnie

Flannery."

He looked at my beat-up, dirty old Honda Civic and chuckled. "What's your name?"

I told him and he walked back to the guardhouse and came back with a clipboard. My name was printed on one side. He asked me to sign next to my name. After I did, he said, "Ok, pull through and follow the road until it ends. Follow the sign for 'Visitors' and park your car in the garage. Then go to the Visitors' Entrance and press the intercom. Got it?"

"Yes, sir, I do."

He walked back inside the hut and pressed a button. The gate went up. As I drove through, he stepped behind my car and wrote down my license plate.

I got buzzed into the Visitor's Entrance, and walked up a gleaming spiral wooden staircase. The railings were solid brass, polished so bright that I smudged them when I touched them. When I got to the top, I was stunned. I expected the usual office building, but I was in the middle of a green jungle, a huge atrium that went up five stories to a glass ceiling at the top of the building, with a forest of plants and trees all around and a cascading waterfall 30 yards wide pouring down from somewhere near the ceiling. If there were people and offices in this building, they were nowhere to be seen. And somehow, despite the avalanche of water pouring down, it was quiet as a library, like someone had pressed a mute button.

"Mr. Billings?" a voice asked.

I turned and saw a beautiful, smiling blonde woman sitting at a desk in front of a barrage of plants.

"Yes?"

"Ms. Flannery will be down to see you momentarily. Would you like to take a seat?"

There were four leather chairs next to her desk. I just stood and kept looking around. "This place is incredible," I said. "I've never seen anything like it."

She smiled at me politely.

"How is it so quiet?" I asked.

"White noise. The building has white noise pumped in to silence all sound."

Holy shit.

Just then another blonde appeared out of nowhere. "Mr. Billings?"

"Yes?"

"I'm Bonnie Flannery, Mr. Callahan's assistant."

She paused, and I looked up. She caught me admiring her chest. She shook her head at me.

"Follow me," she said, and turned and walked towards the waterfall.

"I can't believe this place," I said. "Seriously. If I worked here, I'd come in on weekends just to hang out."

She didn't respond. We walked down a brick path and behind the waterfall. I reached out and touched the water pouring down, as if maybe it weren't real. The water sprayed all over the back of Bonnie's dress, and she turned and glared at me.

"Oh shit! I'm so sorry!" I said.

She smoothed out her dress and resumed walking, following the brick path to a broad, curved wall made of solid oak. There was an elevator with a glass door cut into the wood. We stepped in and Bonnie pushed the button for the top floor.

"You must love working here." I said.

"It's a lovely place to work."

"This place is crazy."

She didn't respond. She had that same robotic quality that Liza had.

We reached the fifth floor and she strode

purposefully off the elevator. I stopped and leaned over the railing, smudging it while I looked at the luxuriant atrium below. She said, "This way, Mr. Billings."

I followed her down the corridor. The walls were lined with fancy artwork. I'm not an art buff, but this stuff was something. All sorts of sculpted, welded pieces made of brass and gold. It looked like some sort of combination of ancient Japanese and modern art. The sculptures just glistened. We walked into a large foyer. It had a dozen plush chairs tastefully scattered about, and a wet bar in front of floor-to-ceiling windows. Outside, there was a wrap-around balcony with another wet bar, and more lounge chairs overlooking the woods. I could see runners on jogging trails weaving through the trees. Crazy.

"Please sit here," Bonnie said.

I sat in a cushy chair and waited. There was a stack of magazines on the table next to me. The Economist, Foreign Affairs, The Weekly Standard, The National Review. Who read this crap?

Callahan came out of an office, looking like the puffy roboton he seemed from his picture on the web. He wore a dark gray suit, a perfectly ironed white, monogrammed shirt with his initials on the pocket: "WAC." His tie was dark red, and he had black, perfectly polished wing-tip shoes. I could see his gold cufflinks sticking out just below his coat sleeves. He wore Clark Kent glasses with dark gray frames that matched his suit and hair.

"Ben, how kind of you to come. I hope I didn't keep you waiting too long."

He shook my hand. "Come, let's get lunch."

I followed him. As we passed Bonnie, he barked, "Forty-five minutes."

I leaned over to Bonnie and whispered, "Sorry

again about your dress." She looked at me impassively.

Callahan and I went back to the glass elevator and headed down.

"This is an amazing place," I said. "I've never seen anything like it."

Callahan gave me a surprised look. "Oh. Yes. Well it is. You work here every day and after awhile you cease to notice it. But it is a lovely facility."

Sheesh. "I guess you can get used to anything."

"Do you mind if we eat in the cafeteria here? I had hoped to take you out but I'm pressed for time. It's quite nice, actually."

"Sure, that's fine."

We walked to another corridor branching off from the atrium and came upon a massive cafeteria. It was ringed by serving counters. Salad bars, sandwiches, soup, grilled food, vegetarian dishes, you name it.

"Wow," I said. "What a place."

"Yes, it's quite nice. I've reserved a private room for us."

We walked across the cafeteria to a hallway of rooms with glass windows and doors. Each room was filled with small groups in meetings. We walked into an empty room. There were two women servers about my age waiting for us. Callahan and I sat on opposite sides of a rectangular table, and one of the servers took our drink orders. Callahan asked for unsweetened ice tea. I got a Sprite. The other waitress placed menus in front of us. "If there is something you'd like that's not on the menu, our chef can prepare it for you," she said.

Callahan opened his menu but did not respond. "Thanks," I said. She looked at me and gave me a quick smile.

Callahan ordered a Maurice Salad, whatever

that was. I asked the waitress if I could just get a cheeseburger and fries. She smiled at me and nodded.

We made small talk for a minute, and then Callahan said, "Listen, Ben, I'm sorry we had cross words the other day. I wanted to sit and smooth things out. You know that RTG is a significant participant in the Cleveland community. We're the largest employer, and have been for over 100 years. We're the city's largest charitable donor. As the head of the law department, I make my own contribution in the ways available to me. I make sure that as many of the firms as possible in town get work. It's my own way of spreading the wealth in the legal community. I get a fair amount of grief for that, because if I sent it all to one firm, I'd be sure to get reduced rates for the company. So I'm cautious to make sure RTG is not being taken advantage of. You understand that, don't you?"

"Yes, of course." Rett had told me that Callahan had a different motive in spreading the work around like he did. By giving work to every large firm in town, those firms were unable to represent anyone who might want to sue RTG. They would have a conflict, and could not represent anyone adverse to RTG unless the company agreed to it. If Rett was right, it was Callahan's underhanded way of making it more difficult for anyone to sue the company.

"It's just my job, Ben, when the company agreed to pay for your time, to make sure you're not taking advantage of that generosity. You understand, don't you?"

"Yes, of course, that makes sense. But Mr. Callahan, I want you to know that I'm not trying to run up a bill or take advantage in any way. I'm just trying to do what you asked me to."

"Good. You know Ben, I may be old fashioned,

but I believe we lawyers hold a noble vocation. It's vital that we behave with class and professionalism at all times. If we treat each other with the dignity that our field calls for, all of society benefits. I hope you feel the same way.

"I certainly do."

"Good. Then the air is cleared?"

"It is!"

Our food came and Callahan began digging at his salad. He was hunched over, and the salad seemed to occupy him completely. I didn't want to disturb him. I turned to my burger, and the smallest Heinz ketchup and mustard bottles I had ever seen, no more than an inch high. I would have liked to take them to show Rett, but it would probably make the wrong impression if I slipped them into my pocket. Callahan was still plowing into his salad, and we ate in silence.

Finally, we finished and the servers cleared our plates. As they left, Callahan cleared his throat, and the server closed the door behind her. Callahan looked at me and said, "Tell me, Ben, where do you stand on the contract? It's a very straightforward form. As I've said, the same form we use any time an employee leaves us and we provide severance. Elizabeth Allen was a wonderful employee for quite some time, and we'd like to do what we can under the circumstances. Are there any concerns you have that I can address so we can move this forward?

"Well, Liza, I mean Ms. Allen, told me that you had promised not to contest unemployment benefits. But I didn't see anything about that in the contract."

"You're right, Ben. I did tell her that we would not get in the way of unemployment benefits, should she need them. I also told her that we'd be happy to give her a fine letter of reference. You're right. Those items are not in our standard form and I neglected to add them. I'll amend the contract right now to include those things. Do you have any other concerns?"

"Well, it doesn't say why she was fired, but other than that, no."

"Those forms never do. No reason to badmouth Ms. Allen unnecessarily, right? Do you have the agreement with you?"

"No. I'm sorry, I didn't bring it."

Callahan walked to a phone on the credenza at the back of the room. He punched four buttons and then said, "Bring the Allen agreement," and hung up.

Two minutes later, Bonnie hurried in and handed Callahan a manila folder. He took it and said, "Wait outside."

Bonnie turned and left the room and shut the door. Sheesh.

Callahan flipped to the last page and pulled out a fancy fountain pen. It was black with a white star on the cap and gold rings around the middle of the oversized shaft. He put an asterisk above the signature line and flipped the page over. He wrote quickly and slid the contract over to me. It said, "RTG agrees not to contest any application that Ms. Allen may make for unemployment benefits. If RTG is asked by any benefits agency the reason for Ms. Allen's departure, it will indicate that her position was eliminated through no fault of her own. At Ms. Allen's request, RTG will provide any potential employer with a reference letter indicating that her performance for RTG was outstanding in every regard and she is recommended without qualification for any position for which she might apply." It was to the point and everything I could have asked for. I told Callahan that it looked good.

He called Bonnie back in and handed her the contract. "We'll be upstairs in ten minutes. Have it ready."

She took the agreement and left.

"I still can't get over this place," I said. "Are those RTG's jogging trails I saw in the woods?"

"Yes. We have 7.4 miles of jogging paths on the grounds. Do you enjoy physical exercise?"

Callahan was shaped like a pear and looked like he hadn't worked out in his life. "Sure, I like to work out when I can."

He looked at his watch. "Come with me. You'll appreciate this."

We wound our way through a maze of oak-lined corridors. We walked up to two wooden doors carved into the wood. Callahan pulled one open and we walked into the largest, most glistening fitness room I had ever seen. It was filled with people working out, even though it was two in the afternoon.

"This is unbelievable," I said. "Why are all these people working out in the middle of the day?" It was what I did, but only because I had nothing else to do. I assumed these people had actual jobs.

"They're employees. We encourage them to work out during the day. Studies show that it improves morale and makes them more productive. Our health insurer gives us discounts the greater our usage. So we track when anyone uses the facility - - anonymously, of course - - and share the aggregate numbers with the insurance providers. We actually pay the employees to use the facility. Not a lot, but enough to make them motivated to use it. We also wash their workout clothes at the end of the day and put them back in their lockers so they have fresh exercise clothes waiting for them every day."

"That's unbelievable. Any chance you need any more lawyers here?"

Callahan smiled. "Well, Ben, the nice thing

about this project is that it allows me to get to know you and assess your abilities. I think the business folks would enjoy working with you. You have a natural way with people, a likeable quality. I'm always looking for lawyers who might thrive here."

I smiled. "Do you mind if I take a quick walk around?"

"No, go right ahead. But we have to be upstairs in a few minutes, so be quick."

I wandered through the room. It was insane. Rows of treadmills and ellipticals with TVs mounted on them. People would swipe a card as they got on the machines, I assume to track their workouts electronically. There were free weights and all sorts of weight machines. There were side rooms for aerobics and yoga. Like the rest of the building, the outside walls were all glass, giving a view of the woods. Amazing. I wandered back to Callahan. "I don't know how anyone gets work done here."

"They have no choice. But it's a fine place to make a career." He opened the door for me and we walked back to the glass elevator and rode up to his office. The contract was on his desk.

"Do you want to look it over?" he asked.

"No, I'm sure Bonnie got it right."

"Ok. Take it with you and make sure it's what we discussed. Let's try to get this signed today, or tomorrow at the latest, ok? Then maybe we can talk about you and RTG's law department."

"Sure," I said. "I'll talk to Liza and get right back to you."

He shook my hand and barked for Bonnie. Silently, she walked me out.

10

I intended to go back to my office and call Liza and get the contract signed. But I was exhausted. As polite as Callahan was, meeting him stressed the hell out of me. I stopped by my apartment, and lay down on my couch in my suit. I must have crashed, because next thing I knew it was 6 o'clock. Shit. I'm such a screw up. I needed to head down to my office, make copies of the settlement agreement, and get it to Liza.

As I walked down the hall, I could see the light on in Joss's office behind her closed door. I tiptoed up to the door and put my ear against it. I could hear music playing. It was Pink's song, "Beam Me Up." Nice. Clearly no patients in there. Should I knock? It was Monday night and it would be nice to hang out. Was there a tactful way to ask her without making a fool of myself? Why would she want to be with an idiot like me? Was I willing to keep getting pummeled by her lack of interest? For now she seemed to think I was cute and funny, but she drew the line at pleasantries. And she was a shrink, so she undoubtedly saw me for the hollow shell that I was.

Suddenly Joss's door swung open. Shit. Busted. Joss looked at me, as I jumped back.

"Ben! Are you eavesdropping on me?"

"What? No. No, of course not. I was just about to knock. I was trying to figure out if you were with a patient."

She grinned. Damn. She saw right through me.

"Nope," she said. "No patients after 5 o'clock. Just doing the endless insurance paperwork. It's the only way I get paid, you know. I spend as much time filling out forms as counseling patients."

She wore jeans and sandals, and a button down, untucked yellow shirt. Perfection. How could someone so calm and even-keeled be bursting with so much energy? I felt a rising desire, and then, quickly, panic.

"So, Ben, what do you have planned tonight?"

"Planned?"

"Yeah, what are you doing?"

Another almost invitation. "Oh. Well I never really plan, you know. Just play it by ear. Probably just go meet some of my softball buddies at a bar at Coventry and watch the Indians." Coventry was a popular street about a mile away. It was filled with bars and restaurants, and was a frequent hangout for the college and young professional crowd. The strip had blossomed during the Viet Nam era, a gathering spot for protests, pot, and music, and still had a tinge of the 60s to it.

"Bar hopping?"

"We don't hop much. Basically just plant ourselves and hang out, meeting people who wander in and join us. It's fun."

I thought about inviting Joss along, but what would she think of me? Beers and nachos, lots of bad jokes. My friends were crude and loud, and I was sure she would scorn us. Scorn me.

"So what are you doing tonight?" I asked. "Paperwork all night is no fun."

"No, not all night. I've got about half an hour more and then I'm out of here. I need a break. I'll head home, do my yoga, and then make some dinner and lose myself in my book so this endless sea of neuroses doesn't consume me."

She looked at me.

"Uh, well," I said, "that sounds like a nice

break, Counselor. Not too exciting, but a nice break."

"With the right mindset, you can find excitement in anything, Ben."

She stood there looking at me. Now was my chance. I might not get it again. Shit. I couldn't do it.

"Well," I said. "I guess I should let you get back to it. I've got to get upstairs and put on some presentable beer and nachos clothes."

"I'll tell you what, Mr. Excitement. How about you go and get yourself ready, and then come and get me. I'll hang with you and your buddies at the bar for a bit. My book won't be going anywhere."

She looked at me unblinkingly with those big brown eyes. No pretense about her. Her eyes challenged me, asked me to lose myself in her, and I fought being drawn in. "Sure, that would be fun. Hopefully you won't judge me by the guys I hang out with."

"No worries, Ben. It wouldn't occur to me to judge you by your friends or your clothes or your activities, really."

"Phew. Ok, so what, I'll come by in a half hour or so?"

"Sure, see you then."

She went back in her office and closed the door. Damn. I'll have to be a lot more subtle. It was humiliating to be caught hovering outside her door.

I called Liza and made arrangements to meet her at The Fairmount the next day at 11 to sign the contract. Then I ran up the steps to my apartment. I was going out with Joss!

11

I came down half an hour later wearing jeans and a t-shirt and flip-flops. I knocked on Joss's door. Her light flicked off and the door opened. She looked me up and down. "You do clean up nicely. "

I shrugged. "It's a bar. "

"Come on, you drive," she said, grinning.

We got to the bar before my buddies were there. We picked a booth in the back and I asked Joss what she wanted.

"A Corona, sir. With a lime."

I got two Coronas and came back to the table and sat across from her. She got up and slid in next to me. "Let's watch the world together. It's more fun."

I lifted my bottle. She clinked with me and took a swig. She put her bottle down and pulled her hair back and tied it in a ponytail. She took my breath away. She had a strong jaw line, not an ounce of fat on her angular face. Just strong and beautiful. And full, soft lips. Man I wanted to kiss her.

"What's occupying you these days, Ben?"

"Other than you? I'm working on this employment case."

"Are you enjoying it?"

"To be honest, it scares the shit out of me. I'm learning as I go. But it's interesting."

"Do you like your client?"

"Hmmmmm. I want to like her. I don't know what to make of her. She's made of ice, you know? I don't think she thinks much of me."

"Why did she hire you?"

"Well, she didn't really. Her company hired me

to represent her, and said they'd pay my bill. Kind of a sweet deal. Except of course they fired her, and she's stuck with me as her lawyer."

"Why'd they fire her?"

"I don't know. Nobody wants to talk about it."

Joss watched me. She raised her bottle and said, "Well, here's to money in the bank."

"Yes, that would be a new experience." We clinked bottles. "How's your work?"

She sighed. "Oh, same old, same old. We have the same conversations over and over, and if I'm lucky, after going over the same routine 50 times, I can say, 'See, you've just done this again. Do you see the pattern?' And my client shrugs and says, 'I guess so.' And then we repeat the conversation. But real changes in their lives? It's pretty much unheard of."

"Joss?"

"Yeah?"

"Maybe you're just not very good at what you do."

She laughed. "Did you ever see a psychologist?"

"Me? No! So you're saying it's not like you see in the movies? Ever see Good Will Hunting?"

She rolled her eyes. "Sure. Who hasn't?"

"Well don't you have those breakthrough moments? That's what all the good shrinks do in the movies. You know, there's a confrontation between patient and doctor, the patient cries, the walls come tumbling down, and the patient is healed. Maybe you're just not cut out for this."

"Yeah, maybe you're right. You know that's all crap, don't you? It makes for a nice story, that breakthrough moment, and then everyone goes off to live a happy, fulfilling life. But it's all crap. In real life, if they start to recognize a pattern, that's about as good as it gets. No one is ever healed."

"So once you're wounded, it's all over? There's nothing to be done?"

"Two tools, if you're lucky. Recognition and coping. That's it."

"Wow. That's depressing."

She watched me. I could not read her.

"I'm sorry," I said. "Was that rude?"

She watched me unblinkingly and I swear she was going to bore a hole through me with that look. I had no clue what she was thinking, and it made me feel vulnerable. It thrilled me and scared the hell out of me.

Finally, she looked away. "It's fine. It's the reality of psychotherapy. Hey, at least in your cases, you know when you've won, right? When you've made a difference? The jury rules in your favor. Your client gets - - I don't know, whatever it is you're fighting for. At least you have tangible signs of results, one way or another."

"I guess so. The respect of my peers? Not so much."

"Is that why you do it?" she asked.

"I don't know." I took a swig of my beer. "It's a living, I guess."

"Why'd you go to law school, Benny?"

"The truth?"

"No," she said. "Lie to me."

"Funny. I went to law school because of the dry cleaning."

"The dry cleaning?"

"So I always figured I'd go to college and then find a good job somewhere. I never really knew what."

Joss leaned back against the side of the booth, facing me. She pulled her knees up and wrested her chin on them, watching me. She kicked off her sandals. She had red toe nail polish and had the most perfect feet I had ever seen. Miss America feet.

"So anyway, I had this buddy in college. Collin Schwartz. We played sports together for years. He was a senior and I was a junior. And man he was smart. Dean's List every semester, academic scholarship, all that. So he graduated and I didn't see him. But the beginning of my last semester, senior year, I'm walking by the dry cleaner's, and I look in the window and there's Collin. So I go in and give him a hug and say, 'Collin! My buddy! What are you doing here?' And he says, 'I'm at the dry cleaners.' And I say, 'Yeah, I know, but I mean, why are you here? I haven't seen you since you graduated.' And he says, 'No, I work at the dry cleaners. It's the only job I could find.'

"And I figured, shit. If a guy like Collin couldn't find work other than that, who the hell is going to hire me? So I panic, and at the last minute decide maybe law school. There's a million lawyers out there, so there must be a good job market, right? And if not, it can only help to have a law degree, right?"

"How'd that work out for you?"

I looked at her and grinned. "Hey, it's Monday night and I'm drinking beer with a beautiful woman. So really well, right?"

She smiled and nudged my thigh with her foot. "I know why you went to law school."

"Why's that?"

"You want to help people. You're kind. A kind soul in a world of sharks."

"Truth is," I said, "when I finished law school, no one would hire me. So I haven't been slaying dragons or helping anyone, really, other than a few softball buddies. No one knows I exist, other than the bankers I'm indebted to for my student loans."

"Well, it's nice to be noticed," Joss said.

There was music piped in over the bar's speaker system. They were playing an old Beatles' song called "In My Life."

"Great song," Joss said.

"Want to dance?" I blurted out.

She looked around. There was a small area at the end of the bar that could be mistaken for a dance floor.

"Sure," she said.

She slid out, and I followed her. She turned and faced me and started moving to the song. Man, she moved like an athlete. Graceful, smooth, coiled strength. And incredibly sexy. "Did you play sports, Joss?"

"I played soccer at Dartmouth. For a year."

"Why'd you stop?"

She didn't respond. She put her hands on my shoulders, guiding me to move with her. I'm 6 feet tall, and she's seven inches shorter than me. She stepped in close and put her arms around my waist. We moved to the song, and I have to admit I got hard. It was embarrassing. She didn't do anything to acknowledge it, but there was no doubt she could feel me against her. She kept moving in perfect rhythm, deftly sliding her feet, somehow swaying to the beat while fitting snuggly against me. She was taking the lead. Moving slowly, and I could feel her pressing against me. Damn.

The song ended, way too soon. We stood there leaning against each other. I was hoping another slow song would start right up.

"Ben Billings! Where are your ballet tights?"

Shit. Here we go. The guys from the ball team.

All downhill from here. I stepped back from Joss. They were standing at the bar, laughing their asses off. Two of the guys started dancing, mocking us. I looked at them and blushed.

"Who'd you pay to dance with you, Ben? She must be having a tough time, scraping the bottom of the barrel!"

Shit. These guys had become my sports buddies in the last few years. I didn't feel like I had a best friend other than Rett, but I guess Bobby Buchanan was as close to it as I had. We played softball and basketball together, and had that camaraderie that only comes from sports

Bobby gave me a high five. "All-star! How you doing? Who's this we have here?" he said, turning to Joss.

Joss sat on a bar stool and spun her back to me and faced Bobby. "I'm Joss," she said, and shook Bobby's hand.

"Well, glad to meet you," Bobby said. "What brings you to our fine establishment?"

"This guy," she said, nodding towards me.

Bobby raised his eyebrows and shook his head. He looked at me. "You couldn't take her to a decent place? You brought your date here?"

I sighed. "Nice to see you, Bobby. I can tell this was a mistake already. How's it going?"

"Never better. The Tribe is winning. I'm drinking beer. Life is good." He started talking with Joss and had her laughing just like that. The guys from the team surrounded her and joined in. I tried to get in the conversation, but with Joss's back to me, and the music in my ear, I couldn't really participate. I must have offended her during our dance, getting aroused like a kid in middle school, because she paid no attention to me whatsoever.

They spent the night drinking and joking. Three college girls sat at a nearby table and Bobby found his way over to them, talking as if he'd known them all his life. He had that way with people. Joss was still at the bar, in the middle of the guys. No place for me.

"Hey Dopey!" Bobby called. I ignored him. "Yoooo hoooo! Benjamin Billings! Hellloooooooo!"

I turned. Bobby had pulled another chair over to the girls' table. Joss had forgotten me, so I went and sat with them. Bad move, I guess, dancing with Joss. A moment of intimacy, and another swift rejection. Lovely.

But the college girls were foolishly impressed with us, which was a welcome change. Bobby worked for one of the local TV stations in its marketing department. He sold advertising time, so he had all sorts of inside information about TV shows and whether they were being renewed for the next season. Between that and hearing that I was a lawyer, the girls were giving us way more respect than we deserved.

I wondered how Joss would react to the attention they were giving us. She couldn't think much based on my work, that was for sure. Anyway, it was fun being admired for a change. One of the girls told us that they were roommates and were heading back to their apartment and asked if we wanted to join them.

"Of course we do," Bobby said.

I looked around. "I don't think I should. I came here with someone."

Bobby punched me in the thigh under the table.

I got up, rubbing my leg. "Well, listen," I said. "I told my friend I'd give her ride home." I wasn't sure she still wanted it.

The blonde girl, Trisha, stood and stepped close

to me. "Here," she said. She took my hand and pulled a pen out of her jeans pocket. "Here's where we live." She wrote her name and address on the back of my hand. "Why don't you drop your friend off and come over? It'll be fun. Really." She gave my hand a squeeze. Damn.

I looked at Bobby. He raised his eyebrows at me and grinned. I looked at Joss. She was still at the bar laughing with the gaggle of guys.

Trisha gave me a hug. "We'll see you in a bit, right?"

"Uh, sure," I said. "I guess so."

I walked up to Joss. When she saw me she stood up. "Ready to call it a night, Ben?"

"Yeah, I think so."

"Still free to give me that ride back to the office?"

Damn. Ok, she noticed and wasn't impressed with the college girls.

We walked out of the bar in silence. I was embarrassed. I would blow off the girls in a second if Joss wanted to spend time with me, but she didn't seem interested.

We drove the short drive to the office and didn't say much. I pulled into the parking garage behind our building.

"My car's over there," Joss said, pointing towards the back. I pulled into the spot next to her car, a bright red Mini Cooper.

I looked at Joss. She turned in her seat and looked back.

"Well, Mr. Billings, I think you've got other plans for tonight."

"What? No."

She reached over and patted my hand. "I think you do."

"Really, I don't."

"Trisha and the writing on your hand say otherwise."

Shit. I forgot.

"Hey, I'd much rather be with you."

She smiled and opened her door. "That's ok, Benny. You go have fun with the girls. I'll see you around."

She shut the door and got in her car. Before I could react she pulled out and drove away.

Dammit! Was she mad or just uninterested? I had no clue.

It was 10:30 and the night was young. I wanted to somehow get Joss to spend time with me. But that was a lost cause. Still, she knew where I lived. Maybe she'd come find me. I sent a text to Bobby:

Ben: headed home bro.

Bobby: walking to car w/ babes. dont leave me hanging. blondie's apt in 10. dont let me down.

Shit. I didn't want Bobby to be disappointed in me. I turned my car back on and drove to the girls' apartment. Joss was long gone anyway.

The college girls were acting like they'd won the lottery. Bobby had bought a bottle of bourbon at the bar, and we were all drinking more than we should. I wanted to forget about yet another rejection by Joss. It was a joke that the girls thought we were such a catch. If they only knew. Anyway, I let the illusion that I was a successful litigator flourish. It felt good to pretend.

After a time, Bobby wandered into a bedroom with two of the girls. Trisha turned to me with a lascivious smile. She was nicely built, a thin waist and tight stomach. She was determined to impress me. It wasn't often that I was treated like something special, and I was happy to lean back and relish the attention.

She looked up at me and said, "I have a thing for powerful men and lawyers."

"I think you're confellating two things," I said.

"Do you mean 'conflating'?"

"No."

I don't remember much after that, other than waking up in the morning and looking at my phone and panicking. Fuck! It was 11:15, and I was late for my meeting with Liza. I sent her a quick text apologizing, and told her I'd be there by 11:30. I jumped in the girls' shower and did a 30-second wash. When I stepped out to dry off, Trisha came into the bathroom without any clothes on. She looked good, even with a hangover.

"Hi there," she said.

Man, no self-consciousness at all.

"We didn't get to finish our fun last night," she said.

"Hey, I'm really sorry, but I gotta run. I was supposed to meet an important client 20 minutes ago."

She frowned at me but didn't really seem to care. I thought about combing my hair, but decided the safest thing was just to get out of there.

"I've got to go, Trisha. I hope I don't seem like a jerk running out like this, but I have a huge case going on and an important client waiting. I'm really sorry."

I thought I should hug her, but she was naked, and that seemed weird, so I just patted her on the shoulder and hurried out. I ran down the steps and out onto the street. I found my car down the block, with a ticket on the windshield, of course. I raced to The Fairmount.

Not my proudest moment. Damn.

12

It was 11:40 when I got to the restaurant. Shit, 40 minutes late. I hate being late. What would Liza think of me? I looked around but she wasn't there. Damn. I checked my phone, but she hadn't called. Damn, she'd probably gotten fed up waiting for me and left. I tried calling her, but it went to voice mail.

I sat at the booth in the back that Liza seemed to like. I'm such a fuck up. I screwed up with Joss last night and missed a meeting with my client. And Trisha must think I'm a selfish jerk. Damn. Callahan was going to be pissed if I didn't get him the contract.

I ordered a beer and a burger. While I waited for my food, Liza walked up to my booth. She looked angry. She was wearing designer jeans and a sleeveless dark blue button down shirt. She carried a sweater over her arm. She glanced at me, tossed her sweater on the bench across from me and sat down next to me against the back wall.

"Hello," I said.

She didn't respond. She picked up a menu and flipped through the pages impatiently. I'd caught a lucky break. But she must not think much of me to stroll in here nearly an hour after we were supposed to meet. And to assume I'd still be here waiting for her after all that time.

"So, how are you?" I asked.

"I'm fine," she said without looking at me. She kept flipping through the menu without looking at it.

"So, did you do anything fun last night?"

She didn't respond. The waitress brought my burger. Liza ordered a bloody Mary but didn't get any food.

"So, I met with Callahan yesterday," I said.

She looked at me but didn't say anything.

"I went to RTG's headquarters. I've never seen anything like that place. I can see why you worked there all those years."

"I'm glad to be out."

"Why is that, Liza? I really would like to know what happened."

"Why, Ben? So you'll feel better? What does that do for me?"

"It's not for my sake. I'm supposed to be giving you legal advice. I can't do that unless we have a real conversation."

She looked at me and smirked. Such hostility. The waitress brought her drink. Liza stirred it and tossed the straw on the table.

"Ok, let's talk, Ben. Callahan invited you to the Crystal Palace. I'm sure you were impressed. Did you meet Bonnie?"

"Yeah. She's not the warmest person, that's for sure."

Liza stared at her drink and smiled ruefully.

"Ok, so listen, Liza. I know you'd like to get the contract wrapped up. Callahan's giving me all sorts of heat to move this along as well."

Liza snorted.

"Why is he in such a hurry, do you know?" I asked. "He said he doesn't want me running up my bill, but it's not like we've been spending a ton of time here."

Liza looked up at me. She looked back at her drink and took a sip. "I guess he just really cares about me," she said.

I was getting tired of her sarcasm. "Ok, Liza." I took the contract out of my backpack. "I'm dancing here. I asked Callahan to make a couple changes yesterday. But other than that, I've got nothing to work with, you know? So let's go over what they have to do and what you have to do. And then you can sign it and we'll be done with this. Ok?"

"I know what it says."

"Ok. Do you want to go over it one last time?"

She stared at her drink.

"Liza?"

She put her drink down and folded her arms across her chest. She wouldn't look at me.

"Liza, you've got to tell me if that's what you want."

She glared at me angrily. Then she spoke so softly, I could barely hear her.

"Just give me the fucking contract. I'm done with those assholes." Suddenly tears poured down her face. She wouldn't look at me.

The waitress walked up and saw Liza's tears. She turned and walked away. I watched Liza and waited.

"Listen to me," she said. "I don't ever want to see or hear from them again. I don't want to see you again. You're their fucking stooge and you don't even know it. Give me the contract and I'll sign it and you can tell Callahan he got what he wanted and he can go fuck himself."

She snatched the contract from me and fumbled around in her purse, looking for a pen. I pulled one out of my backpack and handed it to her. She flipped to the last page and signed her name. She shoved the contract at me, slid out of the booth and hurried out of the bar.

Everyone stared at Liza and turned and looked at me like I'd done something horrible to her. Maybe I had and was too dumb to know it. I poured ketchup on my fries and tried to look nonchalant.

I finished my burger and paid the bill. When I got up to leave, I noticed that Liza left her sweater on the seat across the table. I was tempted to leave it and just be done with the whole screwy situation. But despite her being rude as could be, I felt for her. Those tears just poured out of her. She was hurting and I was making it worse.

Still, it wasn't fair that she called me a stooge. I mean, I had tried over and over to get her to talk to me, and she wouldn't do it. So I'd done my job as well as I could. I'm not sure what else a good lawyer would have done, but if she wasn't interested in more from me, there really wasn't anything I could do. So I tried not to feel bad about letting her down.

I walked back to my office and typed a cover letter to Callahan saying the signed agreement was attached. I decided to send my bill to Callahan with the contract. The most I had ever been paid was nine bucks an hour, working at the desk in the fitness center in law school. I figured Callahan's real lawyers were probably billing him $700 an hour for their time. I typed up a bill for five hours of work at $150 an hour. That would pay my rent for more than three months. I hoped he wouldn't put up a fight.

I scanned the bill and the contract and emailed them to Callahan. I walked down to the street and dropped originals in the mailbox.

I thought this would feel good, but it didn't. I felt pathetic, but it was the best I could do.

13

I wandered back to my office. Joss's light was on, but it was quiet in there. I knocked on the door. No response. I knocked again, but still nothing. I think she was blowing me off.

I had nothing to do in my office, and decided to go down to the gym. There were no basketball games going, so I plodded a couple miles on the track and lifted weights. I might not have won over Liza, but at least I was in decent shape. That was something, right?

I went back to my building. I wanted to call Liza. I had this image of being friends with my clients, of them adoring me and being grateful for my help and exchanging Christmas cards every year. Liza was bitter and angry and I couldn't help her with that. She'd made it clear that she'd had enough of me.

I walked up to the second floor. Liza wanted nothing more to do with me, and neither did Joss. I was doing well. And then there was that weird thing with Lynn, whatever that was, and I'd let her down, too. I walked down the hall and Joss's light was still on. I could hear Annie Lennox playing on her stereo. I was pitiful, chasing after her. I leaned against the door and listened.

"Come in, Ben."

Shit. Busted.

I opened the door and walked in. "How'd you know it was me?"

"I can see shapes through the door."

Shit.

"What's up?" she asked.

I sat down on her couch. She was in her running gear, black yoga pants that went half way down her calves, and a white tank top. She was in her desk chair, and pivoted to face me. She waited.

"Not much," I said. "Just busy disappointing everyone. As usual. I pissed you off, and my only client can't stand me. Other than that, everything's great."

"How come she can't stand you?"

Did Joss just emphasize "she"? As in, how come her also? Not sure.

"I don't know. Her company sent her to me, so she never wanted me as her lawyer. At first she was cold. Well, she was always cold. Now she's downright hostile. Angry and unwilling to talk and thinks I'm a joke and wants nothing to do with me or the matter I was hired to help with."

"So you're popular, huh?"

"I am. Just not with clients. Or psychologists, apparently."

We sat in silence.

"Anyway," I said, "that's my day. Stumbling through, as usual."

"Stop it, Ben."

"What?"

"Stop being a victim. Stop being afraid to try."

That made me mad. I stood up. "What does that mean? You don't know what I'm up against. I'm a year out of law school and I'm dealing with this huge corporation with an enormous law department and the most powerful corporate lawyer in town and a client who won't talk to me. She won't even give me a chance…"

Joss jumped out of her chair and got right in my face.

"Stop it, Ben. Now listen to me."

"What did I do?"

"Stop and listen. You're not incompetent. You're smart and kind and have an intuitive feel for people and that's all you need. You can do anything you want, if you only have the balls to try. Stop being afraid and go get what you want. Do you hear me?"

She was inches from me and looking up at me with those beautiful brown, passionate eyes that just absorbed me. She tucked her hair behind her ears and all I could think of was kissing those soft lips.

"Have faith in yourself, Ben. Trust yourself. You'll be amazed if you try."

I put my hands on her shoulders. She didn't pull away.

"Would it be ok if I kissed you, Joss?"

"Ben! I can't believe you asked me that."

She stood there, watching me. Wait, what did that mean? Did that mean of course I could kiss her, why was I asking? Or did that mean I was crazy, how in the world could I think she would ever want to kiss me?

Why in the world would she want me to kiss her? I dropped my arms to my sides. She tapped me twice on my chest with her fist and walked behind her desk and sat down.

"Ok, Ben, I've got work to do."

My head was spinning. I had no clue what she wanted from me.

"Ok," I said. "I guess I'll let you get to it."

I took a deep breath and started to walk out.

"Ben?"

"Yeah?"

"Dinner."

"Oh? That would be great. Tonight?"

"No." She shook her head at me. "Take dinner to your client. Something warm. Like spaghetti all heated up and a bottle of red wine. And a baguette. Don't call. Just show up at her door and offer it to her and tell her you hope she's doing ok. And then leave. She's suffered a trauma, and right now you're just adding to it. And don't say a word about her work situation. She needs to see that you're not pushing her to bad places. Until she believes that, you're just part of the problem."

I stood there and stared at Joss. She looked up at me.

"Got it?" she asked.

"Yeah, I got it."

"Ben?"

"Yeah?"

"Don't you dare spend the night there."

"There's no chance Liza would want that, Joss."

She shook her head at me. "You're missing it, Ben."

She went back to her paperwork.

I walked out and went up to my apartment. Every time I got near Joss she bolted. Maybe she was just a tease. Or more likely, it meant exactly what she was doing – she bolted because she wanted no part of me. All I knew was that the rejection was getting old. I ached for this woman. And I had no clue what to do about it.

14

I fell asleep on my couch and got up around 4:30. Joss's suggestion about dinner for Liza was not something I would ever have thought of. But she was a shrink, and had a way with people that was beyond me. I had nothing else to do, so I figured I might as well try.

I walked across the street to Dave's, the grocery store everyone in the neighborhood used. How hard could it be to make spaghetti? I bought some hamburger meat and a big jar of Ragu. I couldn't believe how many pasta choices there were. They're just noodles. Anyway, I went with curly ones, and bought a couple cans of mushrooms and a cheap bottle of wine. And one of those long French bread things. What the hell, maybe I could call this "expenses" and bill RTG for it.

I went home and cooked the meat and mushrooms, boiled the pasta, threw them all together and dumped the Ragu on top. Maybe I could be a chef somewhere. This seemed pretty easy. And I was undoubtedly better at it than the lawyering gig.

I covered the big pot of spaghetti and wrapped a towel around the pot. I grabbled the wine and bread and Liza's sweater and drove to her house. I didn't like showing up unannounced. I'm sure she wouldn't like seeing me outside her door. What if she had someone over, or had one of those crazy parties going? Ugh, I hated this. But what the hell. I was going to trust Joss.

Liza's neighborhood was quiet. Peaceful, protected by century old trees. Her house was small, but striking, with thick brown timber casings holding white plaster panels, and French windows, all locked shut, with black iron panels bracing the glass. Really nice place. I wondered how she afforded it. Course, she'd been working for 20 years, and got all those bonuses. She was probably really good at saving her money.

I walked to the front door. There was no screen, just a castle-looking, solid mahogany door with steel strap hinges that looked like something from medieval times. There was a black lead knocker on the door. I took a deep breath and banged the heavy knocker on the metal plate behind it. Three short knocks that echoed through the house.

A minute later the door opened a crack.

"Who is it?" Liza asked from behind the door.

"It's me. Ben. I wanted to drop this off for you."

The door opened a bit more and Liza peeked around the corner. She saw me and swung the door open. Then she folded her arms and looked at me. She was in socks and plain grey sweats, with her hair tied back in a ponytail. That surprised me. She had always worn such expensive clothes, and I imagined her that way all the time. I guess there was no reason to wear heels and makeup and pressed blouses at home.

"What's going on, Ben?"

"Hi, Liza, sorry to stop by unannounced. You left your sweater at the restaurant. I'm sorry things weren't real pleasant earlier. So I made some spaghetti and got a bottle of wine, and figured I'd drop them off for you to enjoy." I held out my arms. "Careful, the spaghetti's still hot. Take the towel, too.

"You made this?"

"Yeah. I'm a man of many talents. Not many of

them useful. It's no big deal. Here, just take these and I'll be on my way."

Liza stared at me and then gave me a big, beautiful smile. Where did that come from?

"This is so nice of you. Here." She reached and took the spaghetti from me. She knocked the door open with her hip and walked into the hallway and placed it on a table. She came back and I handed her the wine and bread and her sweater.

"Ok, Liza, I need to run. Sorry again about before. Have a good evening." I turned and started to walk back to my car.

"Hey, Ben. Have you eaten? We could share this."

I stopped and turned. "I don't want to intrude. You should just enjoy it."

"No, no. Come on, let's eat together. I can't believe you did this. It's so sweet of you."

I walked back to the house and went inside. Liza shut the heavy door behind me. She bolted it and latched the chain.

Her house was warm, covered with knick-knacks and framed pictures. It didn't fit the barren sense I had of her. The house had to be at least 100 years old, and the floors were made of some kind of stone. But she had plush white rugs in each room that made them feel warm and welcoming.

"Your house is beautiful," I said.

"Thanks. I've been here eight years now. It's my safe haven."

"I like it! Warm and cozy."

We walked into the kitchen. It was spotless. She placed the spaghetti on a center island and dished it out onto a couple of plates. She cut the bread into pieces and threw them in a bowl. She opened the wine and got two glasses from the cupboard.

"C'mon," she said. "Let's go sit in the living room."

We walked through the kitchen into a small living room. There was a fireplace with a raging fire going. The wall around it was brick, and the sidewalls were all bookshelves, stuffed with books and pictures.

"What a room!" I said. "You must love to read."

"I do. It's how I escape."

I looked at the pictures and books. "What a great place to sit with a book."

"This is my sanctuary. I sit in front of that fire and lose myself in a good story, forget about everything and let a writer take me somewhere better."

She sat cross-legged on the couch facing the fire. I sat next to her at the other end of the couch. There was a wood chest in front of us and we put our plates on it. Liza poured two glasses of wine.

We ate and talked about Liza's love of books. I would never have guessed that she liked to read. I told her about being an only child, how my parents died when I was young. It was a really nice chat. Liza was engaging and surprisingly funny. We finished our spaghetti and Liza poured us each a second glass of wine.

We wound up talking for almost two hours and didn't once discuss RTG. I kept thinking that Joss was a genius. She had such an ability to read people and discern what they needed. Unlike me, she was clearly in the right profession.

When we polished off the wine, I stood and stretched.

"Ok, Liza, this was great. Really fun. I should get going and leave you to your night."

She got up and we walked to the front door.

"Thanks for doing this, Ben. It was a nice break."

She gave me a curious smile and I suddenly had the thought that she was being suggestive. If that's what she needed, maybe I should stay? No, Joss told me to get the hell out of here.

"Ok, Liza. You be well. I'm sure we'll be talking."

I left and walked to my car. I couldn't help but think I was letting her down by leaving. I could go back. I didn't want her to be disappointed in me. But there was a storm in there somewhere, and the safe thing was to get away from it. Joss's advice had been perfect. The night was great, and now was the time to end it.

I opened my car door and looked back at the house. I saw Liza's door shut and heard the bolt turn. My first real legal matter was done.

15

I waited in my office for Lynn on Wednesday morning, but she didn't show. I was kind of glad. There was something exciting about this woman offering to spend time with me. At the same time, she scared me, and I had enough to deal with. Probably best that she forgot about me.

I wandered down to Joss's office. Her light was on, but the door was closed. I could hear voices. She was probably with a patient.

I sat at my desk and opened my laptop. There was an email from Callahan. My stomach went right to my throat. I immediately started trying to figure out how I'd screwed up. I was such a wuss. Panicking because of an email.

It was all for nothing. The email simply attached the agreement, which Callahan had signed on behalf of RTG.

I forwarded it to Liza with a note saying that the deal was now done; RTG had signed the contract. Ten seconds later, my phone rang.

"Ben! It's Liza. I'm ecstatic. I'm coming by - we should celebrate."

Twenty minutes later there was a knock on my door. Liza was beaming. I thought she was going to hug me when she saw me, but she crossed her arms instead.

"This is such a weight off my shoulders," she said. "I can't tell you. To finally be done with them! I feel like the clouds have parted for the first time in a year."

She sat down in the chair across from my desk.

She was wearing a soft yellow skirt that opened on the side and showed off her legs when she crossed them. I flipped through the contract and showed her Callahan's signature.

"It's official," I said. "We're done."

"Let's get a glass of wine and celebrate," she said.

"Absolutely!"

"Great. Let's go to The Fairmount."

We walked down the hall just as Joss was pulling her door shut. She put her backpack down on the floor and locked the door.

"Hi, Joss," I said. "How are you doing?"

She fumbled with the lock without looking up.

"Joss, this is my client, Liza Allen."

Joss shot me a look. They shook hands. "Nice to meet you," Joss said. She looked annoyed. She probably thought I'd spent the night with Liza.

"Liza just stopped by my office to get some paperwork," I said.

"Do you two work together?" Liza asked.

Joss shook her head. "No, but if you know this guy, we probably should."

Liza gave me a quizzical look.

"Joss is a psychologist. I think she was suggesting to you that she needs legal help."

Liza laughed. "I doubt that. She obviously knows you well. Hey, we're heading over to The Fairmount for a drink. Care to join us?"

Ok, I love my client. Best client ever.

Joss looked at her watch and smiled at Liza. She opened her door and tossed her backpack on the couch. Joss and Liza walked down the hall side by side. I followed them. My worlds collide.

As we walked out of the building, I saw Lynn parking on our street a few cars down. I told Liza and

Joss to go ahead and I'd meet them in a minute.

I walked up to Lynn's car. A silver Mercedes convertible. Nice. She was fussing with her makeup in the mirror and didn't see me. As she got out of the car, I said hello and she practically jumped a foot.

"Sorry, I didn't mean to scare you."

She had her back to me while she locked her car.

"Hey Lynn, sorry I can't hang out. I thought you were coming by earlier. I have to go meet with some people across the street at The Fairmount."

She was fumbling around in her purse. "I need my sunglasses," she said.

It was drizzling and we were supposed to get rain all day. "You might be better off with an umbrella."

She didn't respond.

"I have a baseball hat I could lend you."

Lynn sighed and looked down. She turned and faced me. Her left eye was black and nearly swollen shut. Holy shit.

"Oh my god, what happened?"

"Nothing worth talking about."

She stood and looked at me. I threw my arms around her and hugged her. She stiffened, and then gave herself to me, leaning her head on my shoulder.

After a minute she straightened up. "I have to go, Ben."

She started walked towards our building. I walked with her. We got to the steps in front of the door and stopped.

"What can I do, Lynn?"

"Nothing."

"There has to be something. I'm so sorry. Do you want to talk?"

"I'm going to see my counselor. I'll see you

later."

And with that, she was gone. Holy cow. That poor woman. That put my pathetic little life in perspective.

I wandered to The Fairmount. Liza and Joss were sitting in the booth in the back, and were hitting it off like they'd known each other for a decade. I went to the bar and got drinks. I couldn't get the image of Lynn's battered face out of my mind. I lingered and made small talk with the bartender, a guy named Hal who I played softball with from time to time, trying to get myself back together. I kept glancing back at Joss and Liza. Joss had such an incredible way with Liza.

"Look at them, Hal. She's got her laughing like a schoolgirl. I wish I could do that."

"Laugh like a schoolgirl?"

"Yeah. That's what I meant." I went to the table and passed out the drinks.

As usual, Liza was sitting with her back to the wall on the aisle, facing the restaurant. Joss was sitting next to her on the inside. I slid in across from them. I felt like an outsider. Course, I always felt that way.

"Cheers," I said. We all clinked glasses. "You two seem to be getting along great."

"She's my type of woman," Joss said. "Smart and not willing to take shit from anyone."

"Especially her lawyer," I said.

"Hey, you got the deal done, right?" Liza said. "That's what I always used to hear from those assholes at RTG. 'Get the deal done. Be a closer.' And you did. So don't put yourself down. You should feel good about this."

"So is that the standard?" Joss asked. She turned in the booth and faced Liza. "Just get it behind you?"

I finally got a compliment, but Joss wouldn't let it stand.

Joss looked at Liza. Liza looked down at her drink. Joss kept staring at her.

Joss leaned towards Liza. "Let the sharks keep swimming? It's enough to get out of their water?"

Liza folded her arms across her chest and sat back. She was getting that glazed look again.

"Ben's such a sweetheart, Liza. Do you think he did his job with them? They got what they wanted, right? They're all guys, right?"

"Stop," Liza whispered.

I looked back and forth from Liza to Joss. Liza was sinking deeper into herself. Joss wouldn't let up.

"I'm sure it's good to be out of there, after enduring everything for a bunch of assholes who act like they own the world. Act like they own you, right?"

Liza was fighting back tears. This poor woman who'd been an ice queen was melting before us.

Joss reached over and touched Liza's arm. To my surprise, Liza didn't pull away. Joss stroked her arm, ever so slowly. Liza put her face in her hands and began sobbing. Joss slid closer to her and stroked Liza's hair. She put her arm around Liza, and Liza buried her face in Joss's chest. Joss rocked back and forth with Liza, whispering something that I couldn't hear. Then Joss leaned back and said, "We could cut it off, you know. That would put a stop to it."

Liza sat back and laughed through her tears. She picked up her napkin and dabbed her mascara to keep it from running. Joss glanced up at me. I mouthed the words, "Should I go?"

Joss ignored me. She whispered to Liza, "You didn't do anything wrong."

"I feel like I did."

"But you didn't. You know that."

Liza wrapped her arms around herself and rocked back and forth. She leaned forward, her face just inches from the table. I could see her tears dropping onto the wood.

"They raped me."

"Who did?" Joss asked.

"Nick and Jerry."

I was afraid to move. Liza put her forehead on the table.

"Tell us what happened," Joss said.

Liza sat up. She took a deep breath, but couldn't get the words out. The tears were just pouring out of her. Joss waited patiently. Finally Liza took a deep breath and said, "We were at a Board dinner. In Paris, last fall, at the annual meeting. Everyone was drinking. I didn't want to be there, but Nick insisted. This was just after he transferred Robby to Brazil. I was really mad at Nick and wanted nothing to do with him. But the Board was going out, and I was expected to be there.

"We had dinner at a restaurant in Paris. The restaurant only seats 20 or so, and we had the whole place. I don't remember much about what happened. All I know is that after dinner, Nick kept chatting with me. He has this way about him. He followed me up to the bar and leaned in real close and gave me that sexy smile. I told him to cut the shit and leave me alone. I told him I'd had enough of his games. He stepped back and told me that was fine. Let's at least share a drink. And the next thing I know, I'm in my hotel room and Jerry Greyson, our Chief Financial Officer, is on top of me. He was *in* me."

Liza wrapped her arms around herself again and started rocking, staring at the table. She took a deep breath and slowly let it out. "I was so confused.

I didn't know where my clothes were. And I kept thinking that I was going to puke. I looked over and Nick was sitting on a chair next to us. He didn't have any clothes on. It was crazy. I thought he'd help me. I said his name, and he said, 'Shut the fuck up.' I must have passed out, because next thing I knew, I woke on the floor. They were gone. My head was pounding and I started throwing up. I had dried blood on me, in front and in back. I hurt so much.

"I climbed on the bed and wrapped myself in the quilt. I woke up later when there was knocking on my door. I'm such an idiot. I kept thinking it was Nick, coming to make sure I was ok. But it was the hotel clerk. I was supposed to check out that morning and it was mid-afternoon. He wanted to know if everything was ok. I told him to go away. That I wouldn't be leaving that day. Those bastards flew home and left me there. I locked myself in my room for two days."

Liza stared at the table. She wrapped her arms around herself and rocked back and forth. Joss looked up at me.

"Get us another round of drinks, Ben."

I went to the bar and asked Hal for another round.

"Everything ok over there, Ben?" he asked.

"Peachy," I said.

"You sure have a way with women."

I went back to the table, but they didn't seem to notice. "I thought about calling the police," Liza said, "but I was in Paris. And I guess the truth is, it wasn't that. I felt like it was my fault. I knew what those guys were like."

The people at the table next to us got up. Liza waited until they left. She sighed. "I never would have imagined that they would rape me. But they're drinkers and treat women as playthings. They're like frat boys at RTG, all these privileged white men who always get what they want. The secretaries were fair game to them. They picked us for the Pool based on our looks and hopes of who knows what. They used to make jokes about guys who were 'in the Pool,' or were 'swimming.' So I felt like it was my own fault for being in that situation. I shouldn't have gone to the dinner. And who would ever believe me, my word against the word of the CEO and the Chief Financial Officer, guys who make millions a year? So I just tried to convince myself that it never happened, tried to pretend it was no big deal."

"It sounds like Rohypnol," Joss said, "the date rape drug. Did you see a doctor?"

"No. I had bruises. But I just didn't want to deal with it. I was embarrassed. I just wanted to disappear. It sounds stupid, but I kept thinking if I acted like nothing happened, I would be ok. Just do everything like usual and things would go back to normal. But I couldn't sleep. I was afraid to turn the lights out. I kept having panic attacks. I called the doctor a few weeks later and told him I was having trouble sleeping because of stress at work. He called in a prescription for Prozac, which I took for a few weeks. But I worried about getting addicted, and it made me foggy, so I just quit."

"Your doctor prescribed Prozac without seeing you?" Joss asked.

"Yeah. He's one of the RTG doctors. They pretty much hand out whatever you ask for."

Joss scowled. She looked at me and raised her eyebrows. I wasn't sure what she wanted. She nudged me with her foot under the table and raised her eyebrows again. Oh.

"So why'd they fire you, Liza?" I asked.

Liza looked at me wearily. She sighed. "These guys own the fucking world. Everything changed after that night. Even though Nick was CEO, I'd always had a certain power with him. He was after me from the day we met. He always pestered me to travel with him, even though he's married. And because Nick was interested in me, in a certain way, I had an elevated position with the other Chiefs."

She paused, and we waited in silence.

Liza sighed. "I stayed away from work for a week. And when I came back, everything was different. Instead of being treated with respect, the Chiefs treated me like I was trailer trash. I know that Nick and Jerry talked about me. The Chiefs made comments about me. They're such idiots. The Pool secretaries have access to their emails, and the things they wrote about me were horrible.

"So it was a struggle everyday. I was trying to pretend nothing had changed. Everyday was a marathon. You know, if I can only make it to 10 o'clock. If I can only make it to noon. I spent a lot of time in the bathroom, locked in a stall, sitting there crying. At the end of the day I'd race home and just collapse. I was in bed by eight, not wanting to face going back to work the next day. But I kept struggling through it, you know? I kept thinking it would get easier. I looked for other jobs, but who would pay me what I was getting at RTG? The reality is, Nick had taken care of me. He paid me a ton, gave me bonuses. I felt like this horrible thing was there no matter where I worked, so what good would it do to leave for another place for half the pay? So I just kept pushing through, trying to keep it together, trying to get through just one more day.

"It hasn't gotten better. I keep doing desperate things that I'm not proud of, drinking too much and other shit. Somehow I thought I could force Nick to talk to me. It just made things worse. I'm so isolated."

Liza stared at the table, her arms folded across her chest. Joss put her arm around Liza, and gently stroked her hair. We waited.

"A couple Fridays ago," Liza said, "there was a big rush because the company had a securities filing. And Nick sent an email to Greyson about getting a document back to the lawyers. Greyson responded that he didn't have Pool support to turn the document around, and asked if he could 'give it to the cunt' to type it up." Liza made air quotes. "And then Nick responded that he should go ahead and 'give the twat' the work. And I'm sitting there reading these horrible emails, as was Bonnie.

"So Nick walks up to me and orders me to get to work on Greyson's document. It was the first time he'd talked to me in nine months since that night in Paris. I was just so angry, but I didn't want to make a scene. So I whispered, how dare he, after what he did. And then he just snaps at me. 'Goddammit,' he said, 'get off your ass and do what I tell you if you know what's good for you.'

"I just exploded. I jumped up and got in his face and told him that if he knew what was good for him, he'd treat me with some decency or he'd find himself in jail. He didn't respond at all. He just walked away like I didn't exist. He's so fucking arrogant. I was starting to lose it, and got out of there. I couldn't stop shaking and crying. The next day when I got to work, Callahan called me into his office and told me I was fired. When I asked why, he told me that refusing to do work when they had a filing deadline was inexcusable. He said my attitude was unacceptable. And then that prick told me not to worry, the company would give me a generous severance package and I would be fine."

"Did you tell Callahan what Nick and Jerry did to you? Or about their emails?" I asked.

Liza shook her head. "What was the point? Callahan is Nick's stooge. He's made his career running around after Nick and sucking up to him. The joke around RTG is that if you need a tissue, ask Nick to sneeze, and Callahan will come running with one."

The three of us sat in silence.

"How are you?" Joss asked.

Liza sighed. "It feels good to get it out. I've been torturing myself about this for so long, trying to pretend it never happened. I haven't talked to anyone. I'm so pathetic."

"That's the farthest thing from the truth, Liza," Joss said. She stroked Liza's hair. "You would not believe how many women this happens to. I know it doesn't feel like this to you, but you are an incredibly strong, brave woman who did nothing wrong. Those guys are criminals. I know you don't feel this way, but you should hold your head high for weathering this as well as you have. And you should know that we believe you completely."

Liza started crying and leaned into Joss. How did Joss always know the right thing to say? I wish I had said those things. When Liza looked up at me, I said, "I'm behind you completely. You don't have to worry about that for a second."

Liza looked at Joss. "What happens next," Joss said, "is whatever you want. You're in complete control. If you never want to talk about it again, that's your choice. I hope that's not what you choose, but it's entirely up to you. If you want to go to the police, that's your call and Ben and I will march right over there with you. If you want to take your time and think about it, then that's fine, too. When this happens, women feel a loss of control, and the first thing I want you to focus on, now that you got this out, is that it's completely up to you where we go from here.

Liza nodded. And then, finally, the light bulb went on for me. Liza had signed the settlement agreement and the deal was done. There was a non-disclosure clause, and Liza had promised not to say anything disparaging about RTG, Nick, or any of the employees there. I couldn't remember what it said, but I know there were stiff penalties for Liza if she breached that promise, something like having to return her settlement and owing them five times what they paid her. Shit. Liza had needed a good lawyer. Instead, she had me. I decided this was not the time to bring it up.

We sat there for another hour. Joss was amazing. She just chatted away about nothing, really, moving to safe topics and making jokes and keeping us both laughing. It was her way of taking care of Liza. When we finally got up to leave, Joss insisted that she would ride back to Liza's house with Liza. I offered to follow in my car and drive Joss back to the office.

We got to Liza's and Joss stood in front of the door with Liza and talked for a few minutes. Then she hugged Liza and held her.

Joss walked back to my car and sat next to me.

"How did you know?" I asked. "Do you work in this area?"

"No. Won't touch it."

"Well, that was amazing. I know I'm an idiot, but I've talked to her for hours and I had no clue. You knew the minute you saw her. You knew before you met her, didn't you? That's why you had me take her dinner last night, right?"

"Well, you are an idiot. But you're a good guy, and she wouldn't have talked today without feeling she could trust you. So you did well. You should feel good about yourself. Although I don't think that bit of self-charity is in your arsenal."

I just grinned at her. This woman was scary.

16

I went back to my apartment and lay on my bed. I was doing a slow burn. I fell right into Callahan's trap, dreaming of working in the Crystal Palace, getting the big bucks. He had picked a dope like me for Liza to make sure nothing happened, so she would sign the contract and they would be home free. That's why Liza had said I was Callahan's stooge. A more experienced lawyer would have found a way to get Liza to share what had happened, and fought to get her something fair for what they'd done to her. And worse, those bastards had to be laughing at how they played me to make sure they got away with it. I mean, come on. Callahan was never going to hire me, an inexperienced clown who finished at the bottom of his class. Everyone knows I'm not RTG material. And his worry about me running up a bill was ridiculous. What I was going to bill RTG was peanuts to him. A few hundred bucks. He must be paying the real lawyers at the big firms a fortune. I should have known what was going on. I mean, RTG has over 100,000 employees, and a guy at Callahan's level so involved with the firing of a secretary? What was wrong with me?

Now I was pissed. The thought of Callahan taking advantage of me drove me nuts. I'd been played for a fool. Callahan knew it. Liza knew it. Everyone knew it. And I had no idea what to do about it.

And now Liza was done. She signed the contract, giving up all claims she had against them forever, in exchange for a year's pay. What would a good lawyer have gotten her? Why hadn't I pushed more? At least I wouldn't feel like I was played for a sucker. I was so sick of feeling that way.

It was Wednesday, and I had no work. I decided to go for a run around the Shaker Lakes, three small tarns nestled in the woods a mile or so up the road. I plodded along, barely breaking a sweat, more loosening up than really putting myself out. The little bit of exercise didn't make me feel any better about myself.

The next morning I went down to my office at noon. Joss's light was on, but her door was closed and I could hear talking in there. I looked down the hall, and there was some dude sitting on the floor outside my door. He stood up and handed me an envelope, and asked me to sign a form attesting that I had received it. I took the envelope and went in my office.

I opened it and there was another envelope addressed to me inside the first one. It had RTG's logo and Callahan's return address on it. There was a short cover letter saying the "original, fully executed settlement agreement" was enclosed. I glanced at the document. It had Liza's signature on it and Callahan's in bright blue ink. I tossed it on my desk.

I still had the problem of figuring out how to pay my rent. I dug into the envelope from Callahan, and saw that there was a check to me from RTG for 750 bucks. He'd paid my bill right away. Yippee.

There was a knock on my door. I opened it, and Liza was there with Joss. These two were becoming a regular couple.

"Hello, ladies. What's up?"

Liza walked into my office without saying anything. She sat in the chair across from my desk. Joss hopped on my desk and swung her legs back and forth. I stood and waited.

"Joss and I have been talking," Liza said. "Now that I've gotten this thing out in the open, I'm not sitting still. I'm furious with those fuckers. And the more I think about it, as Joss points out, I can't be the only one they've done this to. There have been so many women at RTG who have left suddenly over the years and then just disappeared. And what scares me is that if I keep quiet about this, they'll do it to someone else. I couldn't live with myself if I let that happen. So I want to fight. I want to sue those bastards. I don't have my settlement check yet, so can we back out of the deal?"

"No chance," I said. I picked up the signed contract. "You know we got an email with the signed contract yesterday. Callahan had the original delivered to me just a few minutes ago. And there's non-disclosure requirements in there, so you can't talk about this with anyone. You can't say anything bad about them. So it's signed and done, Liza. I'm really sorry about that, but there's nothing we can do."

"Oh, come on, Ben," Joss said. "You're a brilliant lawyer, right? There's got to be a way out. Liza wants to file criminal charges, too. They can't stop her from doing that, right?"

"I'm sorry, but she promised not to say anything bad about RTG or any of its employees, and not to talk about the settlement or what led to it. If she does, she has to return her settlement money and pay them five years of pay on top of that as a penalty. Are you in a position to risk that?"

"Of course not," Liza said.

"I'm sorry, Liza, but we're stuck."

"Not acceptable, Benny," Joss said. "We're headed to the Cleveland Heights police station in a few minutes. I know a detective there who's always happy to see me." Joss smiled and winked at me.

"You're going to have to figure something out."

"Hold on, wait. Just hold on." Now I was worried. "This is going to cause a huge mess. Listen to this language." I picked up the contract and paged through it. "Wait. I know it's here somewhere."

Liza rolled her eyes. "It's paragraph 7."

Argh. "Right, that's it. Listen: Non-Disparagement and Non-Disclosure:

"Employee agrees that she shall not make any communication of any kind, either directly or indirectly, to any person, organization, or governmental entity, which in any way disparages or reflects negatively on RTG, any of its current or former employees, board members, or representatives, at any time from the date of this Agreement into perpetuity. She further agrees not to disclose anything whatsoever about this Agreement, the events that led to this Agreement, to anyone other than her lawyer, doctor, and financial advisor, into perpetuity."

I looked up. "Perpetuity is a long time. I'm sorry."

Joss shook her head at me.

"That's just too bad," Liza said. "I'm not playing their game. I have to do something about this or I'll go crazy."

"Isn't there some other way to deal with this?" I asked. "You're going to get into huge trouble. What about counseling? That would be healthy and wouldn't cause RTG to come after you. Joss is a great counselor. Why not start some sessions with her?"

Joss kept swinging her legs. She looked down and shook her head. "Not my area."

"Look," I said. "If you have to go to the police, what if you tell them what happened, but don't give them any names for now? Don't tell them where you work or who was involved. Don't even tell them your name. Don't say anything that can be attributed to anyone at RTG. Just talk to them generally, and see what they have to say about it."

Liza and Joss looked at each other.

"Maybe," Liza said. "I can start there. What I really need to know is what they'll do about it. I need some answers."

"Ok," I said, "but you have to be really careful. If you file charges, RTG and Callahan will come after you in a second. So really, no names, ok? This could be a huge minefield you're walking into. Do you want me to go with you?"

"No," Liza said. "Joss and I will go."

Ouch. I looked at Joss. She was shaking her head at me like I let her down. But what else was I supposed to do? Liza signed the contract, and it said what it said, and there was no way around it.

We agreed to meet at Nighttown at 7:30, after Joss finished with her patients and their meeting with the cop.

I took a shower and paced around my apartment until 7:20. Finally, I hurried down to Nighttown. Joss and Liza were at the bar. Liza had obviously been crying. Joss asked the bartender if he could get us a private spot. He led us to a back room where we had a table to ourselves.

"What happened?" I asked.

Liza teared up and didn't say anything. She folded her arms across her chest and started retreating into herself.

"That prick," Joss said. "I know this detective. Long story. But the whole time we're there, he just seems amused by what we're telling him. He kept asking why Liza waited this long to say anything. He wanted to know why she didn't go to the Paris cops. He said even if this actually happened, only the Paris cops would have jurisdiction, because the crime was there, not here." She stopped and looked at me.

Damn, I should have thought of that. Of course Nick and Greyson couldn't be prosecuted here for something they did in France. Even I should have known that.

"He wanted to know if Liza had pictures of her bruises or whether there were bloody sheets or doctors' reports. And he kept asking over and over whether she had a boyfriend. They always ask that, those assholes. They know nothing about these crimes."

"Did you mention any names?" I asked.

"No," Joss said. "No names. And when Liza told him that she kept working there for nine months, he completely checked out. I tried to keep my mouth shut, but finally got fed up. I asked him how many reports of acquaintance rape they get. He said they get plenty of reports, but they never investigate them. He couldn't remember a single one. He said that they have to prove that the woman said 'no,' that she meant 'no,' that the guy believed that the woman was saying 'no,' and that even though the guy knew she meant 'no,' he had sex with her anyway. He said it's just too hard to prove, and it's not one of their prosecutorial priorities.

"It makes me sick," Joss said. "I said that if they get all these reports, doesn't that suggest that there's a real problem out there? What could be a higher priority than rape? And his only response was to ask again whether Liza had a boyfriend. He said that lots of women cheat on their boyfriends, and then claim it's rape so they don't feel guilty. Can you believe that? Or they get pregnant and then convince themselves it's rape so they don't feel guilty about getting an abortion.

"He was infuriating. He said if we're really set on pursuing this, we should do it with the police in Paris."

Liza reached into her purse and put on her movie star sunglasses. "I'm not talking to the fucking cops. Not here, not Paris, not anywhere." She spoke so quietly we could barely hear her. "I don't need any more of this shit. I have no interest in fighting with people who are supposed to help me. Who are these men who laugh at women who are attacked? Who think we're making up stories? Why won't anyone fight for me?"

She took off her sunglasses. She looked at me, her face pale and drained of hope. Tears were running down her cheeks, dragging her mascara in crooked lines. It broke my heart.

"Listen, Liza," I said. "I believe you. Completely. I know you did nothing wrong and what they did is horrible. And I'm going to make it right for you. We're going to take you home tonight and you can relax, because I'm going to fix this. They're going to pay for what they did."

Liza looked at me. Then she put her head in her hands and bawled. After a minute she looked up at me. She wiped her eyes and said, "Thank you, Ben. Thank you so much." She reached over and took my hand and squeezed it.

Joss sat back and shook her head at me. She saw right through me. I was so desperate to give Liza just what she needed, I'd promise her anything. But how the hell was I going to do it? Joss saw that, too.

17

I got up early Friday and walked to Starbucks. I was going to spend the day brainstorming, trying to come up with some way Liza could go after Nick Stanton and those bastards at RTG. I sat at a table in the back and pulled a yellow pad and pen out of my backpack. And then I sat there for nearly half an hour without a single thought coming to mind. Shit.

I decided that maybe a workout would help my creativity. I went down to the gym and pumped weights and then ran for nearly an hour. It felt great, but I had this gnawing guilt all the while. Liza was waiting and I was coming up blank. And Joss was watching.

When I was getting dressed I kept thinking that there had to be a way out of the contract. I didn't really remember much of anything from my contracts course first year of law school. I decided that maybe some time in the library would help.

I went to the law library and found an old treatise. Corbin on Contracts. I guess he was some famous dude who must have led a hideous life learning everything there ever was to know about contracts. It was 16 volumes. Ridiculous. Can you imagine dinner with this guy? Anyway, I started paging through the books.

I woke up with a start. Someone was shaking my shoulder. "Excuse me, sir, but you're snoring and people are complaining."

Lovely. I looked at my watch. It was nearly 3 o'clock. I'd done nothing with the day. I went back to the book and realized that it would take me about a century to get through it. And I just couldn't concentrate on what had to be the driest subject in history.

I decided to come back on Monday and dig in.

After a weekend of softball and beer and nachos with Bobby and the guys, I was back at the library first thing at noon on Monday. I decided that getting through the book was impossible, and focused on the table of contents instead. It was only 117 pages.

The only thing I saw that might possibly help Liza was the idea that some contracts are not enforceable because they violated public policy. I guess if you sign a contract to kill someone, and then refuse to kill the guy and get sued, the courts won't enforce the contract because killing someone is against public policy. So the question was, could I show that Liza's settlement with RTG was so outrageous, given that they had raped her, that a court shouldn't enforce it? That she should be free to talk openly about what they did to her and sue them, even though she signed a contract promising that she wouldn't?

Unfortunately, I couldn't find a single case that said that her contract was unenforceable. There were only two possible ways out. The first was that if Liza were subpoenaed to testify in someone else's legal matter, she could testify truthfully, even if that meant disparaging RTG. That didn't help her, though, because she still couldn't file her own lawsuit.

The other possibility was if Liza didn't understand what she was doing when she signed the settlement agreement. If RTG was taking advantage of her by having her sign something she couldn't be expected to comprehend, then the courts might void the contract.

But of course, that was exactly why RTG insisted that Liza have a lawyer review the contract with her. The courts were clear, if someone received the advice of counsel, the courts would never consider an argument that the client didn't know what she was signing. Callahan knew exactly what he was doing when he got me involved; he guaranteed that Liza couldn't attack the validity of the contract later.

I kept hoping that there would be some exception if the lawyer was completely incompetent. Like say, for example, the lawyer had finished last in his class and really only wanted to play basketball or softball and had no clue what he was doing on legal matters. Unfortunately, there were no exceptions, even for morons like me. And it wasn't an entirely appealing idea anyway, asking some judge not to enforce Liza's agreement because she had the great misfortune of having me as her lawyer.

I was at a dead end. I went back to my office. Joss's door was open, and I poked my head in.

"Counselor!" she said. "How's it going?"

"Hi, Joss." I plopped down in the chair across from her desk.

"You don't look happy. Having trouble playing superman for Liza?"

"Yeah. I've been digging through law books for days, trying to find some way out of that contract. I think she's screwed, so to speak."

"Should you get some help? Maybe someone with more experience in this area?"

Ouch. "The contract is airtight, Joss."

"What if you just called RTG and said you couldn't care less what the contract says. Liza's going to the police and going public with what they did to her unless they make this right?"

"But why would they do anything? Callahan will say they made it 'right' by giving Liza a year's pay."

Joss leaned back and folded her arms across her chest. "So, Ben, why'd you tell Liza you'd make this right?"

"Because she was so sad. I wanted to help her."

"Giving everyone what they want is unhealthy, Ben. Ask any college girl." Ouch.

"Have you thought about going to the press?" Joss asked.

"The press? Oh god, no. What would I tell them?"

"Liza said there were those awful emails that she and the other secretary saw."

"But how do I get the emails? RTG won't just give them to me. I'd have to sue them to get my hands on them, and I can't sue them because Liza signed the agreement."

Joss put her feet up on the desk. She put her hands behind her head and looked at me.

"What about one of the secretaries?" she asked. "Maybe they'd be willing to print the emails and give them to you."

"Maybe. But then what? I just don't see a fix here."

"Well, Counselor, it's your job to figure it out." Joss looked at me. "That's why they pay you the big bucks."

I snorted. "Yeah, I'm rolling in it."

Joss watched me. She was wearing a beige floral dress that buttoned down the front. It was plain and simple, but she filled it out just right. There was something so damn provocative about her. She got up from the desk and walked behind me and began rubbing my shoulders. Man she was strong. And she had touch, too. I sat back in the chair and closed my eyes. Luckily my shirt was long and untucked. I think she noticed the effect she was having on me anyway.

"So, Counselor," she said, patting me on the shoulder, "I think maybe you'd better go."

"Really? Why?"

"Because I'm starting to like you."

"Wait. What? You're starting to like me, so you want me to go?"

"Yup."

"I think you've got things backwards," I said.

"I usually do. But that's how I roll."

She mussed my hair and walked back around her desk. I sighed and got up.

"Maybe you could roll with me," I said.

She grinned at me. "See you later, Ben."

I sighed and walked out. A minute later I poked my head back in her door.

"You're really starting to like me?"

"Don't get your hopes up, Counselor. Now get out of here. I've got other wackos waiting for me."

18

My plan was to call Liza Monday night and break the bad news to her. I was at a dead end, and we were stuck with the deal she signed. But the idea of disappointing her made me feel ill. I attacked the conflict the best way I knew how: I fell asleep.

I woke up at 10 in a panic, worrying about what I would say to Liza. I could only think one thing: she had the wrong lawyer. Maybe Joss was right – someone more experienced should try to figure this out. Someone smarter, too. I called Rett.

Rett was still in her office working, but said she'd be happy to talk about it. She told me to meet her Tuesday at 7:30. In the morning.

We met downtown at a diner in the Terminal Tower, the iconic building in the center of Cleveland across the street from Rett's office. Only Cleveland would name its beacon of the city "Terminal." In any event, I walked into the diner, and Rett was waiting for me in a booth. She was a ball of fire, as usual. She jumped out, gave me a hug and slid back into a booth. She wanted to know what was going on as I sat down across from her.

"Coffee," I said. "I need coffee. How do you get going so early?"

"You're a slug, Ben. I've been in my office for an hour. So what's up?"

"Ok, well it's that case we talked about before. So here's the deal. My client didn't want to pursue things. She refused to talk about what happened to her. She insisted she just wanted to sign the severance offer and be done with it. So last week she signed the contract. And then I'm out with her and this woman to celebrate, this psychologist I know. And Joss, that's the shrink, she's really unbelievable. You should meet this woman. I've never met anyone like her. She's the whole package, Rett. Smart, beautiful. She's a complete mystery to me, of course. She's like you, only nice."

"The client, Ben. Tell me about the client."

"Oh, yeah. So Joss just has this way, you know? She spends a few minutes with Liza – that's my client – and Liza starts bawling and tells the whole story. And it turns out her boss, the company's CEO, and some other big shot there, raped her. Can you believe it? Those bastards raped her. And then like nine months later they fire her when she finally decides to speak up about things."

"Wait," Rett said. "The CEO and another management official raped your client?"

"Yeah, after a dinner with the Board of Directors."

"Holy shit. That's fucking unbelievable. Do you believe your client?"

"What? Of course."

Rett rolled her eyes at me.

"What?" I asked.

"You trust everyone. Your judgment is worthless."

"Thank you."

"You're welcome. Now keep going."

"Well, so here's the thing. Joss gets Liza to start talking, and it all comes pouring out. And so now that Liza has finally opened up about what she's been through, she's all fired up and wants to go after those bastards. But she's signed the settlement agreement. The contract waives all her rights. It's got a non-disclosure clause, and she can't disparage them. So she's completely out of luck."

"What did you tell her?"

"I told her I would make this right for her."

"Of course you did. What the fuck is wrong with you?"

"You should have seen her crying, Rett. It was heartbreaking."

"You're pathetic, you know that?"

"Yeah, I know. I didn't come here for reminders."

"Well, you are pathetic. And a moron. You're lucky you're so damn adorable or I wouldn't be here."

"Yeah, I know. You tell me that every time I see you."

"Only because it's true."

"Rett, I need help. Is there anything I can do for Liza?"

"How old is she?"

"What?"

"How old is she, you dipshit?"

"She's 38, why?"

"Oh, damn."

"Why?"

"Because of the OWBPA."

"What's that?"

"Oh my god, Ben. Did you really pass the bar? The Older Worker's Benefit Protection Act."

"Oh, of course. The OWBPA. What's that?"

"The OWBPA says that if you've signed a release of your rights under the age discrimination laws, you have seven days to change your mind and revoke the contract. But the age discrimination laws only apply to people 40 and older. So if your client's 38, it's probably not a help here."

"What do you mean, 'probably'?"

"Ok," Rett said. "First things first. I shouldn't

be helping you if my firm represents the company. But if those fuckers raped your client, then I'm helping you. So we never had this conversation, right?"

"Right. Never saw you, never talked to you. I don't even like you."

"Ok, so everyone uses forms for everything. Nobody creates a contract from scratch. All the employment settlement agreements have standard waivers of all rights as part of the settlement."

"Yeah, they gave us a form agreement for Liza."

"Ok. So Liza gets paid some money, and in exchange, she waives all her rights to sue and has to agree to keep quiet forever. But most of those forms are all-inclusive. What I mean is, they waive every possible right in the world, including rights under the age discrimination laws, even though the age laws don't apply to your client because she's under 40. But sometimes when the employee is under 40, lawyers forget to take those provisions out of the contract even though the age laws don't apply to them."

"So why does that matter?"

"Here's why, genius. One of the requirements of the OWBPA is that if you sign the contract and waive your rights, you can change your mind and revoke your signature, as long as you do it within seven days of signing it."

"Ok. But Liza is 38."

"Right. But here's the thing, Ben. If the company used a form contract, then its lawyers may have left the age language in there. Even though there was no need to because Liza is under 40, they may have left the language in there giving her the right to revoke her signature. That happens all the time. I'm constantly warning the partners at our firm to get that language out of there, but they're pussies and afraid to change the form."

I reached into my backpack and yanked out Liza's settlement agreement.

"Wow," Rett said. "You actually brought it with you. Very impressive."

"Shut up."

I flipped through the contract. Right above Liza's signature, there was a paragraph in all capitals. It said:

> THIS AGREEMENT CONTAINS A RELEASE OF LEGAL RIGHTS, INCLUDING RIGHTS UNDER THE AGE DISCRIMINATION IN EMPLOYMENT ACT. EMPLOYEE UNDERSTANDS THAT EMPLOYEE MAY REVOKE THIS AGREEMENT WITHIN 7 DAYS FROM THE DATE OF SIGNING BY DELIVERING A WRITTEN REVOCATION TO WILLIAM CALLAHAN, RTG CHIEF LEGAL OFFICER, 22300 PARNELL ROAD, GATES MILLS, OHIO, BY HAND OR CERTIFIED MAIL. EMPLOYEE UNDERSTANDS THAT IF EMPLOYEE REVOKES THIS AGREEMENT, EMPLOYEE WILL NOT RECEIVE THE BENEFITS CONFERRED HEREUNDER.

"It's in here Rett! That bastard Callahan, he's their Chief Counsel, he screwed up! This is great."

"When did Liza sign it?"

"What?"

"Ben, you're a fucking idiot. She has seven days to change her mind and revoke her signature. When did she sign it?"

"Oh." I looked at Liza's signature. Under it she had written the date: June 3rd, exactly seven days ago.

"She signed it a week ago today."

"What time?"

"I have no idea."

"Ben!" Rett stood up and walked around the booth. She swung her hip into me and moved me over and sat next to me. She put her arm around me and whacked me in the back of my head. "Don't be an idiot. Did you email it to the lawyer after Liza signed it?"

"Oh. Damn. Yes." I pulled out my phone and searched for Callahan's name. I had sent it to him last Tuesday at 9:15 a.m.

Rett sat with her arm around me, reading over my shoulder.

"Is that it?" she asked. "9:15?"

"Yeah, that's it."

She looked at her watch. It was a few minutes after 8:00. "You've got barely more than an hour. If you're going to do this, you've got to hurry."

I looked at Rett. I put my arm around her and kissed her on the cheek. "I love you, Rett! You're amazing."

"I know." She slid out of the booth and let me out.

I grabbed my things and Rett grabbed my arm. "Hey Ben, you have to call me today."

"Why?"

"Because you're in love. I need to hear about this shrink."

Damn. Nothing got by Rett.

19

I jumped in my car and raced through Cleveland towards Liza's house. I called her on my cell, but she didn't pick up. Shit.

I got to Liza's house and banged on the door with the old knocker. It was already 8:25. Liza finally opened the door. She was in a bathrobe.

"Liza, I figured it out. Well, a friend did. Listen, we can get out of the contract. But we have to do something now. We don't have much time."

She stepped aside so I could come in her house. "What's going on?"

I followed Liza into her kitchen. "There's a way to cancel the settlement, but we have to do it by 9:15. This morning. I have to get a letter to Callahan. I'll have to drive it there."

"Can you email it?"

"No. The contract says I have to hand-deliver it or send it by snail mail."

"So if I cancel, then what happens?"

Shit. I hadn't thought about that. "Well, then we have all the options before us. You can go to the police."

"I told you, I'm not doing that."

"Ok, well you can go to the press. You're free to say whatever you want about those guys."

"And if I go to the press, and tell them that Nick and Jerry raped me, then what?"

"I don't know. I haven't thought it through."

"The press will call Nick, and he'll say that I'm a bitter, misguided employee who lost her job and I'm trying to get money out of the company. I've seen it a thousand times. Then what?"

"I don't know, Liza. Will any of the secretaries give us the emails?"

"I doubt it. I haven't heard from anyone since they fired me. I'm sure they were told not to talk to me. Can't you get the emails?"

"The only way I can get them is if we sue them. Then they have to give me all the documents."

"Then let's sue them."

Oh, man, that made me sweat. I'd never sued anyone in a real case. I'd been in little small claims court on a few landlord-tenant disputes, and that was it. I was going to take on RTG and its army of mega-firm lawyers?

I looked at my watch. It was 8:35. We were down to 40 minutes. "You understand, Liza, that if we revoke this, you get no severance? If we sue them, it could be years before we have a trial."

"I'll get by."

"Callahan's going to be really mad about this."

"Do you think I care?"

"Do you have a computer and a printer?"

"Yeah."

There was a small countertop space under a cabinet in the corner of her kitchen that she used as a desk. She had an old PC there. I opened a Word document and typed:

> Dear Mr. Callahan:
>
> As permitted by my agreement with RTG, I am revoking my signature and the agreement.

We printed it off, and I had Liza sign it and date it. I had her add the time as well. It was 8:50. I had 25 minutes to get it to Callahan.

126

I ran to my car and raced through the suburbs to RTG's headquarters. My heart was pounding. What was I doing? I wish I had more time to think it through. Shit, was I going to get into a fight with Callahan? I'd get killed. Shit, there were a million stop signs weaving through these suburbs. The clock was ticking. I had to run a few stop signs, and a very slow red light, but I finally got there at 9:13. The same guard stopped me at the gatehouse.

"Can I help you?"

"I need to see Mr. Callahan!"

The guard grinned at me. "I remember you. Is Mr. Callahan expecting you?"

"No."

"Then I can't let you through."

"How about Bonnie? You know, his secretary?"

He shook his head at me. "I can't let you in unless they've approved it."

I slammed my hand on the wheel. Shit. I was screwed. I'd fucked up again.

"Is there a problem?" the guard asked.

"I need to get him this letter. It's urgent."

"If you have a delivery for Mr. Callahan, I can accept it for him."

"Really? Oh my god. Here!"

I handed him the letter. "Wait! Sorry!"

I pulled out my phone and took a picture of the guard with the letter. It was 9:14.

"You'll be sure he gets it?"

"It's my job."

I backed out and drove home. My heart was racing. I was hoping I'd feel good about myself. But I couldn't. Whatever was coming next scared the crap out of me.

20

I went back to my office, hoping to bump into Joss. I couldn't wait to tell her that I'd found a way out for Liza.

I went into my office and dumped my backpack on the couch. As I started to leave, the office phone rang. I grabbed it.

"Ben Billings here, lawyer excellante!"

"What do you think you're doing you little prick?"

"Pardon me? Who is this?" There were too many candidates to know.

"Goddamn it, Billings, you just made the mistake of your life."

Oh. Shit. It was Callahan. He was shouting at me at the top of his lungs. So much for his suave demeanor. I didn't like how he was talking to me.

"What happened to class and professionalism, Mr. Callahan?"

"You fucking little punk. You're going to pay for this. If your slutty client thinks she's ever going to work in this city again, she's got another thing coming. I don't know where you think you're going with this, but your client's a whore, and if you've got any brains at all, which I really doubt, you'll walk away from this right now. There's a bunch of ways you can go with this, and all of them are horrible for you. So walk away if you have any common sense. Surprise me, Billings. Let's see if you have any intelligence."

He slammed the phone down.

Nice. I wondered if he'd still be willing to offer me that job.

21

Liza was a wonderful client. She was anxious to sue RTG and make them pay for what they did to her. She wanted to make sure that no one ever had to endure what Stanton and Greyson had done to her. But when I told her I would need a couple of weeks to prepare the paperwork for a lawsuit, she was fine with that. She didn't pressure me, and gave me time to try to figure things out.

Rett was great, too. I gave her the details about what happened, and she got all fired up. Or, I should say, even more fired up than she always was. Turns out her firm didn't represent RTG, so there was no conflict. She gave me forms I could use to draft the lawsuit. I laid out what happened, what our claims were, and what we wanted in the case. I spent about two weeks working on it, and sent it to Rett to get her feedback.

I hadn't heard from Callahan since he screamed at me on the phone. I'm sure he thought he'd scared me into going away. It pissed me off, though, the way he used me. I mean, I know I'm not Clarence Darrow, but he pretty much told me that the only reason he sent Liza to me was because he thought I was a complete screw up. I don't know much, but I know you don't treat someone like that. Not cool at all.

Rett and I finished the lawsuit. We named RTG, Nick Stanton, and Jerry Greyson as defendants. I laid out what happened, that Stanton and Greyson drugged Liza and raped her. And then, when she complained about what they had done and how they treated her, they fired her. So we had three basic claims. First, assault and battery for the drugging and rape. Second, sexual harassment for the "unwelcome physical contact." And third, retaliation, for firing Liza when she complained about how they treated her. We asked for damages in an amount over $25,000, which was all we had to say. We also asked for damages for the emotional suffering they caused Liza, and for punitive damages because of their outrageous behavior.

I went over the document with Liza line by line to make sure it was accurate. She was worried about people turning on her when this got out. I assured her that she had nothing to worry about. I told her that it would take a week or so for the document to be served on RTG, Nick, and Jerry. Then they would have at least 30 days to respond to it. After that, we'd have to meet with the judge to set a schedule for the case, so there was really nothing to do but wait for the next couple months. I assured her things would be quiet and we'd have plenty of time to get ready.

I had to sign the papers when they were done. That made me anxious, putting my name at the end of the document. I was telling a judge that the men running one of the biggest companies in the world had done some really horrible things. It was kind of like declaring war, and I felt like I was putting a really big target on my back. But people filed lawsuits every day, right? It was just part of the process. So I signed my name and drove downtown to the county courthouse and filed the papers.

I went back to my office and collapsed on the couch. This whole process stressed the hell out of me. I dozed off, but was awakened by knocking. I was hoping it was Joss, and threw open my door. Lynn stood there scrolling through her phone. She looked up.

"Hello, Ben."

"Hi. Boy, I didn't expect you. Uh, how are you?" I hadn't seen her for a couple weeks, since she had that awful black eye. You'd never know, looking at her. I couldn't tell if it was makeup or what, but she looked good.

Lynn slipped by me and into my office. She walked around and stopped in front of my plants, and then walked up to my desk.

"This is nice," she said, stroking the leather insert with her perfect fingers. "Your office has character."

"If only I did."

She looked at me. "Do you have some time, Ben?"

I looked at my watch. I had nothing scheduled for the next few hundred days. "Sure. What'd you have in mind?"

"Come with me. I want to talk, but not here."

"Uh, sure. Ok."

We walked out of the office and down the hall. Joss's office was dark behind her door. Lynn wore blue jeans and a grey button-down shirt, which looked casual and expensive at the same time. She walked quickly in front of me, down the stairs and out onto the street. It was a beautiful Cleveland summer day, 75 and sunny and not a hint of humidity.

Lynn beeped her silver Mercedes that was parked on the street in front of our building. She slid into the driver's seat and lowered the roof. I had never been in a convertible before. I stood watching from the sidewalk as she looked in the rear view mirror. She puckered her lips and painted them with gloss. She looked up at me. "You coming?"

Something about her intrigued me. And scared me. Her world was completely foreign to me. "Sure."

I slid into the passenger seat.

She roared out of her spot and made a U-turn across the busy intersection, darting in front of an SUV and up Fairmount Boulevard.

"Where are we headed?" I asked.

"Somewhere we can talk."

We raced up Fairmount. She was going nearly 70 on a 35 mph road. The wind made talking impossible. Lynn weaved around traffic and roared eastward, jamming the clutch down and shifting gears, jerking us back and forward, accelerating further into the suburbs, past houses that grew larger and larger as we zipped away from the city. Soon we were in one of the Metroparks, a massive reserve of trees and streams and hiking paths that form a horseshoe around Cleveland, with both tips ending on the shores of Lake Erie. Lynn turned onto Chagrin River Road, a narrow winding street that cut through the forest. She made a hard turn left into a parking area and skidded to a stop. She jerked the emergency brake up and got out of the car.

I sat there looking at her. She kicked off her expensive heels and slipped into a pair of sandals. She tossed the heels into the back seat. "C'mon, Ben, let's walk."

We walked down a dirt path and suddenly were in a different world. Wildflowers everywhere, eight feet high on both sides of the path. Waves of green and yellow and red and purple. The luxuriant smell of plants and grass. As we walked, I could hear running water growing louder. We made our way down to the Chagrin River. It was about 100 feet wide and moseyed lazily downstream. I stopped at the bank and skipped a few stones.

Lynn started walking on a path along the river and I hurried to catch up to her. "This is a great spot,"

I said.

"It is. No one around for miles."

She seemed to know where she was going. This was no casual stroll. We followed the path around a bend in the river. She strode purposely onto an old stone bridge, about four feet above the water with tunnels cut in it for the river to flow through. She kicked off her sandals and sat, dangling her feet above the water. I stood next to her, enjoying the spot, wondering why I was here.

She patted the ground next to her. "Sit with me, Ben."

I sat.

"So, Lynn, are you ok? I've been so worried about you since I saw you. Did your husband do that to you?"

Lynn didn't respond. I waited. Finally, I said, "Lynn, why don't you leave this guy?"

"Maybe you're the exception, Ben, but you know that lawyers are scum, right?"

"He's a lawyer?"

"No. But I'm stuck with him because of bad lawyers."

"Oh boy. Why's that?"

She sighed. "We got married right out of school and jumped into our careers. We were both doing well. And that's when the jealousy started. He didn't like me spending time with other men. I mean, he could do all those things that business guys do. He could go to dinners and golf outings and business trips and parties. But if I did any of that, he'd pepper me with hours of questions. 'Who was I with? What does he look like? Who'd you sit with at dinner? What'd you talk about? Did you go for drinks afterward?'"

Lynn swung her feet back and forth over the bridge. "It was miserable. It got to the point that I dreaded doing the things I needed to do for work. I mean, I loved what I did. I was good at it. I was moving up at my company faster than he was at his. Sure, I'm not naïve. I have no doubt some of the men had ulterior motives, because men are pigs." She paused and looked at me. "Well, most of them. But I just couldn't stand it at some point. And one night, after we'd been married a couple years and he'd been interrogating me for days about a trip I had with some clients, I just said, 'Fuck it, I'm done.' And I quit."

"I'm sorry," I said. "That's so unfair."

"Yeah, well the unfair thing is that we have a prenup, and it says that if one of us asks for a divorce, the one asking gets half of our assets, or what the asking one earned during the marriage, whichever is less. So since I quit working after just a couple years, I get pretty much nothing if I demand a divorce."

"So what? You can't live with this. He beat you. My god, Lynn, don't stay with that."

"It's not the first time."

"That's all the more reason to get out. Nothing's worth that."

"I have nowhere to go, Ben. I'd have nothing. My parents are gone. I have no family."

"Come on, Lynn. Anywhere is better than living with that. You can move in with me. Seriously, you can have my bedroom. I'll sleep on the couch."

She leaned into me and sighed. "You're very sweet, Ben."

We sat for a time. "So this is a lawyer's fault?" I asked.

"Yeah. My husband cheats on me. He doesn't even bother to hide it. In his sick mind, it's somehow my fault that he's cheating on me."

"Lynn, why would you live that life? Just for the money? That's crazy. Just get up and leave."

"Yeah, well here's how the lawyer screwed up. The prenup says that if one of us commits adultery, him in this case, then I get half of our assets, or what I earned during the marriage, whichever is more."

"So there you go," I said. "Just leave him and take half. What's the problem?"

"The problem is that the prenup requires that his adultery has to be proven in a court of law, by testimony under oath."

"So sue him for divorce. People do that all the time."

"Yeah, but that's how the lawyer screwed up. Because there's boilerplate language at the end of the agreement that all disputes related to the prenup must be resolved through mediation. I've been to five different lawyers about this, and they all said the same thing: I can't take him to court. My only option is settlement discussions with a mediator. So I'm stuck. There has to be testimony under oath that he cheated, but I can't go to court to get testimony that he cheated."

"Holy shit, that's ridiculous. Have you thought about suing the lawyer?"

"Yeah, but it's too late. I waited too long."

I was glad I wasn't that lawyer. He really screwed up. Or maybe he did it on purpose, protecting her husband all along.

"Lynn, I know I can't know what your life is like, but seriously, you can't stay with a guy who beats you and cheats on you. Why live like that? It's not worth it. Just get out. You're so beautiful and smart. You've got a whole lifetime ahead of you. Just start over. Your future will be wonderful, whatever you want it to be."

She rested her head on my shoulder. "Thank you, Ben. It's so nice to hear that."

I was a little uncomfortable. I stood and picked a stone off the bridge and lobbed it into the water. It made a healthy kerplunk and a circle rippled out. I took another stone and tried to toss it right in the middle of the circle. "Bingo!" I said.

Lynn looked at me and grinned. That frown as a grin. "You're such a child, Ben."

"Sorry, I can't help it."

"It's endearing. Don't apologize. Whatever you do, don't be the fool I was when I was your age."

"Why'd you marry him?"

She sighed and stroked her hand through her hair, pulling it back. It fell perfectly in place again.

"I had a vision of the life I wanted and I let that vision blind me to reality. I let my dreams distort my perception of who he was."

"Who is he?" I sat back down next to her.

"Do we have to do this? I like you because you help me forget him. You're just what he's not."

"Ok," I said. "Who am I?"

She frowned/grinned. "You're kind. You want to enjoy people, not use them. And you make me feel good about myself. You're naïve, in an innocent sort of way, wanting to see the best in everyone. There's a lightness about you."

"I'm a lightweight, no doubt about it."

She leaned into me with her shoulder.

I threw a stone into the water. "C'mon," I said. "Give it a try. See if you can throw a stone into the center."

"You are a kid."

She stood and tossed a stone. She had a good arm, but missed.

"Here, I'll show you." I stood and threw a stone into the center of her circle. Bingo!

"Showoff," she said.

She threw another stone, and then another, then another. Finally, she hit the mark.

"There you go!" I said. I turned and gave her a high five. She reached up and slapped my hand.

She stepped toward me. "Bet I can hit this mark," she said. She swung her hip into me, and knocked me towards the edge. I tumbled and fell into the water. Damn, it was cold! And deep too, luckily.

"Hey! Not fair!"

She jumped after me and did a cannon ball.

"Nice!" I said.

She paddled to me. We drifted closer to shore, where we could stand. Lynn stood in front of me, frown/grinning. I went under for a second and came up with both hands on her hips. I picked her up and tossed her so she landed on her back. She laughed and floated on her back.

"Oh shit!" I said. I reached into my back pocket and pulled out my cell phone. It was ruined. "Not good."

"Don't worry," she said, breast stroking her way to me. "I'll get you another."

I pulled my wallet out of my other pocket and held it and my cell phone in front of me. She stood in front of me, close, inside my arms. She smiled up at me. I thought she was going to kiss me.

Suddenly she turned and dove into the water away from me. She swam for the riverbank and climbed out. "Come on, Ben!"

I waded through the water, holding my wallet and phone above my head, and climbed up the bank. I followed her away from the water and into a small clearing surrounded by the tall flowers. She sat and stroked her hair behind her head. Her shirt clung tightly to her. I looked down at my phone.

"Are you still worried about that stupid phone?

Here," she pulled her car keys out of her pocket and tossed them to me. "Go put your things in the car and forget about it. I've got a towel in the trunk. Go grab it and bring it back."

I walked back to the car. The top was down and I didn't know how to raise it. I put my phone and wallet in her glove box and locked it. Damn, I wish I had one of those waterproof phones. I got the towel out of her trunk, and worked my way back through the tall grass toward the clearing. When I got back to the edge of the clearing, I stopped short. Lynn was lying in the sun on her stomach, buck-naked. Or butt naked. Her clothes were stretched out at the edge of the clearing.

She turned her head and rested it on her arms, looking back at me. "Gotta let those clothes dry, you know."

She was a stunning woman. She could have passed for a college girl.

"Why don't you join me?" she said.

I sat next to her, leaning back on my hands.

"Take your clothes off, Ben. They'll never dry unless you spread them out."

I stood and pulled off my shirt and laid it on the ground by hers. I hesitated.

She stood and stepped up to me. She was lean and strong. Her nipples seemed to be reaching for me. She put her hand on my chest. "Your pants need to dry, too." She reached down and tugged on my belt.

She looked up at me while she worked on my pants. She got down on her knees and pulled off my flip-flops. Then my pants. She stood back up and held me to her, feeling the V of my back with her hands. She reached down and gripped my butt, pulled me against her. She started kissing my neck.

"You want me, don't you, Ben? Tell me you

want me."

I didn't know what to say, so I started kissing her. Man, she was just voracious. Her mouth was all over me. I pulled her tight against me, and she practically devoured me.

My head was spinning. Suddenly, I felt alone. I didn't know Lynn at all. I mean, she was a really good person, and I felt so bad for her, but we were being so much more intimate than our relationship called for. I took a step back.

"What?" she asked.

"I'm just worried, Lynn. Are you sure about this?"

She looked down, and then back up at me. For a minute I thought she was going to cry. Then she stepped up to me. "Don't you find me attractive, Ben? Don't you want me?" She ran her fingernails down my chest. Down my stomach. She reached down and started stroking me.

"I think I have my answer," she said, frown/grinning at me.

She pulled me down on top of her. "Tell me you want me," she said.

Suddenly it hit me that this strong, smart, accomplished, beautiful woman was desperate for affection. For kindness. I felt a million miles away, but she was so hungry for a connection.

"Of course I do," I said. You're incredible."

She wrapped her legs around my back and pulled me into her.

I went through the motions, so to speak, and she seemed to lose herself in our fun for a time. When we were done, we lay in the sun. After awhile she said, "C'mon, Ben. It's time to go."

We wiggled into our clothes, which really weren't dry yet, and walked back to her car. She closed the roof and turned on the heat and suddenly became surprisingly chatty.

"This is such a beautiful day, isn't it? I just love this city. Don't you love it, Ben? To be able to go to the most beautiful theaters in the world? The greatest museums? And Severance? I think that's the most spectacular concert hall I've ever seen. And then to be able to drive for only 15 minutes and have an entire metropark to yourself? Don't get me wrong. I love to travel. I would move to Paris in a heartbeat, if circumstances were right. But you just can't beat Cleveland, even though everyone makes fun of it.

"I'm playing tennis tonight. I group of my friends play a couple times a week. Tennis and then dinner with lots of wine. It's a really great combination. Exercise and friends. Do you have good friends, Ben? I don't have friends like I did in college, but it's still nice to have people to be with."

"Do they know what's going on with your husband?" I asked.

Lynn looked at me and frowned. "No. God no. None of us talk about our husbands. Who wants to hear that? We get together to forget about them."

We pulled up to my building. "Do you want to come in?" I asked. "My apartment is a dump, but you're more than welcome."

"No. I need to go."

"Ok, Lynn. Thanks for today, that was amazing. Will I be seeing you soon?" I didn't really know what to say. Was I supposed to kiss her goodbye?

She reached over and patted my leg. "Go."

I got out of the car and shut the door. She drove off.

I stretched. Time for a nap. I looked up and saw Joss watching from her office window. Damn.

Damn! Wait, why would I feel guilty? Anyway, all that happened was that I got a ride to the office. Well, that's all Joss knew. In dripping wet clothes.

I walked up to the second floor and stopped in front of Joss's office. The light was off. I knocked, but there was no answer. Shit.

I went down to my office and plopped down on my couch. What a day! I would have thought I'd feel good about myself.

22

I was starting to doze off, when I noticed that my message light was flashing. Had Joss been trying to reach me? I stumbled to my desk and hit the button. There were over twenty messages. Must be those damn political robocalls.

So all that time I thought I'd have before having to worry about RTG? Boy was I wrong. What I didn't realize was that there are courthouse "reporters" who apparently have nothing better to do but hang out at the courts and dig up juicy stories for the papers and blogs. Some sell the info to the law firms, which are scavenging to get cases. Most of the messages were from some guy named Jonathan, who was working on his blog. One call was from a reporter for the Cleveland Times, Cleveland's only daily paper. And one was from Liza. She was a complete wreck and asked me to come by as soon as I could. Just a few hours after filing the lawsuit, I was already in over my head.

I drove to Liza's and knocked on the door. Liza opened it and turned her back on me and walked into the kitchen. She was wearing white sweatpants and a loose gray sweatshirt. She poured herself a cup of coffee. She stood there sipping it and wouldn't look at me.

"Mind if I have a cup?" I asked.

She didn't respond. I poured a cup and leaned against the counter next to her.

"So, I'm guessing the press called you, too?" I asked.

She walked over to her phone. It was mounted

on the wall. She pushed a button, and it said, "You have four messages." She hit the play button.

The first two were from Jonathan, the courthouse reporter. He asked her to call him as soon as possible. The third was from a reporter at the Cleveland Times. Liza skipped that message.

The last call was from some guy who didn't identify himself. It sounded like he was on the speaker and too far from the phone. He launched into a diatribe, getting angrier as he went on. "You really screwed up here. What the hell do you think you're doing? You just opened a door that you're going to be really sorry about. Because when the truth comes out, you're going to wish you never worked here. Your life is over. How stupid are you? You'll never work again. The whole story's coming out now. This lawsuit is going to bankrupt you and you're going to be sorry you ever fucking lived. Look over your shoulder, because here comes hell you fucking bitch."

I leaped across the kitchen and hit the "stop" button.

"Who is that? Do you know who left that message?"

"I'm really not sure."

"It's got to be someone from RTG. Is that Nick?"

"I'm not really sure. It could be, but I can't tell."

"Do you have caller ID?"

She nodded.

I picked up the handset and found the caller ID. The first two were from the same number, which must have been Jonathan's. The third one said "Cleveland Times." But the last one said "Caller ID Blocked." Dammit.

Liza played the third message from the

Cleveland Times. "Ms. Allen, this is Andrew Lally from the Cleveland Times. I'm writing a story about the lawsuit you filed today, and would like to know if you have any proof of your claims. Why did you wait this long to raise these allegations. I understand that you never reported this to the police. What you filed contains no proof. Please call. I intend to file my story online and for tomorrow's paper by 7pm tonight. I can be reached at 216-395-5555."

Damn. Lally was obviously in RTG's pocket. Even I knew that when you file a lawsuit, you don't provide the evidence for your claims. That comes later. All you're supposed to do is state generally what your claims are.

I looked at Liza. She put her coffee down and stared at the floor. She wrapped her arms around herself. I stepped up to her.

"Liza." She didn't respond. I put my hand on her shoulder, and she recoiled like I shot her. She spun and mumbled something I couldn't make out and walked out of the room. I put my coffee down and followed her.

She walked into her bedroom and collapsed on the bed. She pulled the covers up and turned her back to me, curled in a fetal position. I stood at the side of her bed and waited. And waited.

"Listen, Liza, I'm sorry I didn't anticipate this. I had no idea the media would be snooping around. But we knew we were in for a fight. We're just going to keep our heads down and plow through this, ok? The truth is on our side, and we're going to hammer away until it comes out. So let them say what they want. Let them scream and holler. We'll just slug our way through it until this is made right."

She didn't respond. I waited.

Finally, she rolled over. Her mascara was

streaked from her tears. "Promise me," she whispered.

My instincts screamed that I shouldn't. One of my professors had said that litigators should never promise their clients anything. I mean, no matter how great your case, there's so much that can happen that you have no control over. The judge who's assigned to the case can dictate who wins. Some judges let cases linger forever, rather than deal with it. Shit, it just occurred to me that I hadn't even looked to see which judge was assigned to our case.

But there was Liza, so distraught, begging me for comfort. "I promise, Liza. You can count on it."

She reached out and held my hand. She squeezed it and then let go.

"Are you ok?"

She nodded.

"Ok," I said. "I've got to go deal with this. But listen, don't talk to anyone about this. Don't call the reporters back. Maybe you should get rid of your landline and just use your cell from now on. No conversations with anyone. Ok?"

She nodded.

"Ok," I said. "I'll talk to you soon."

I let myself out, and made sure the door locked when I pulled it shut. Liza just suffered another wound, and I felt terrible. But as I drove back to my office, something was nagging at me. It was something that guy said on the message. What did he mean about the "whole story" coming out? What wasn't Liza telling me?

23

I got to my office and thought about calling the reporters back. It made me sick to my stomach. I had never talked to a reporter, and had no idea what I would say. But Rett had told me that the paperwork we put together was solid, and I thought it would be easier just to let it speak for itself. It saved me the stress of dealing with the press.

The next morning, I woke up at 6:30 when my laptop dinged. There was an email from Rett. It said, "You're famous!"

That worried me. I showered and went down to my office. I took a deep breath and pulled the Cleveland Times up on my laptop. There was a front-page story about the case. The headline was "Disgruntled Employee Files Unfounded Claims Against RTG." Wonderful. What ever happened to objective reporting? The article was short. It said:

> "Part of the cost of doing business, especially for large and thriving companies, is expending valuable resources on frivolous lawsuits," said RTG Chief Counsel, William Callahan. "Unfortunately, unscrupulous lawyers often think they can make a quick buck by making claims against successful companies. RTG doesn't play that game with extortionists."
>
> Yesterday, Benjamin Billings, a 26 year-old lawyer who graduated law school

last year and finished at the bottom of his class, filed a claim against RTG that prompted Mr. Callahan's comments.

Mr. Billings represents Elizabeth Allen, a former secretary at RTG. Ms. Allen was fired for refusing to work. Mr. Billings then filed suit against RTG, making vague allegations about wrongdoing by the company that allegedly occurred nearly a year ago. Neither Mr. Billings nor his client raised any suggestion of wrongdoing by RTG at any time until after she was fired.

This reporter attempted to reach Mr. Billings and his client to obtain information about their assertions, but they refused to take or return my calls.

"Unfortunately, at the end of the day, all of us in society pay a price for these frivolous claims," Mr. Callahan said. "It makes company employees stop doing their vital tasks to address nonsense like this. That inefficiency ultimately results in higher prices for all of us. It uses up judicial resources, and maybe that's the biggest tragedy, because instead of our talented judges devoting their efforts to important societal matters, they have to spend their time on these falsehoods. And meanwhile, society's real issues don't get the time and attention they deserve."

Mr. Callahan indicated that the

company would vigorously oppose the lawsuit and was confident of a prompt and successful resolution.

This may have been the most embarrassing moment of my very embarrassing life. There I was, front and center, and labeled as a bottom dweller for all to see. And there was not one mention of Liza's claims. I mean, we could not have been more clear that Stanton and Greyson drugged and raped Liza. And that she complained about it and was fired for complaining. RTG clearly had the Cleveland Times in its back pocket.

My message light was flashing. I couldn't bear to listen. It was probably some other reporter calling to verify that I had really finished last in my class. Or checking to see if I really passed the bar. I decided to get out of there and walked down the hall to head for Starbucks. Joss's door opened as I approached it and one of her patients stepped out. It was some 50 year-old fat guy in a suit looking miserable. He looked at me and blushed and hurried off towards the steps.

I poked my head in the office. Joss looked up at me. "Hello frivolous lawyer who's out to make a quick buck."

Shit, she had read it. I hope.

"Hi. Nice way to start the day," I said.

"You know what they say: all publicity is good publicity. Right?"

I just rolled my eyes.

"Hey," Joss said. "Did you get a new client?"

"No, why?

"Oh, I thought I saw you with a new client the other day. Someone with a fancy car."

Oh, damn. "Well, it's someone having some marital issues, and she's in a bad spot because of her lawyer. I don't think I can do much for her."

Joss watched me. She didn't say anything.

"So," I said, "I'm going for coffee. Wanna come?"

"Hmmm. Ok, Ben. I've got an hour between patients. You look like you could use some company."

We walked down the hall. "Hey," I said, "how come your patients always look so miserable?"

"Because if they're not miserable, they don't come to see me."

"But aren't they supposed to get less miserable after they see you?"

"That's the idea, if you believe in psychotherapy."

"Don't you?"

"Sure, to a limited extent."

We got in line at Starbucks, and Joss started talking away. It occurred to me that she was trying to distract me from my own misery.

"A lot of us are just programmed a certain way," she said. "I mean, come on, do you really think something dawns on someone after counseling and suddenly they're happy-go-lucky? Most of what forms a personality is genetic or so deeply ingrained from early childhood that there's no chance of meaningful change." The people around us were listening to Joss, but she didn't seem to care.

"Your job sounds as bad as mine," I said.

We were at the counter and placed our orders. We walked to the "pick up" counter and waited.

"It's about expectations, Ben. If the goal is for my clients' lives to be just a bit more manageable, then you might be proud of what I do. But if you expect my clients to have endless orgasms after seeing me, then I'm failing every time."

"Maybe I could hire you and see if we can fix

your failure rate."

She laughed. We got our drinks and walked to a table. Joss's hair was pulled back in a ponytail. Those big beautiful brown eyes swallowed me whole. Joss smiled at me.

"What?"

"You poor boy. At least they didn't put your picture in the article. If they had, they wouldn't serve you here anymore."

"That day may still come. It's just a matter of time."

She burst out laughing. A deep, hearty laugh. I loved that laugh, even when it was at my expense.

"Poor Benny," she said.

"I'm glad you find my plight so amusing."

"You'll be fine. Just probably not without some scars."

"I can only hope. There's nothing like public humiliation. Just a little whipping in front of friends, colleagues, and unbearably sexy psychologists."

Joss gave me a huge smile. "You could use a distraction, Counselor."

I looked at Joss. Maybe too hopefully.

"Not that distraction. I've got a patient coming in at 10. Wanna get out of here at 11?"

"Sure, that would be great." Best news I'd heard in a long time. "What did you have in mind?"

"Beats me. I'll knock on your door when my next miserable patient leaves."

We sat and looked at each other. There was an unsettling yearning in my sorry old heart. And elsewhere, too. I felt untethered, swamped by unlimited possibilities when I was with Joss, entirely lacking in control and at her mercy. It was enthralling and miserable at the same time.

We walked back to our offices. If I were smart,

I would use the hour to work on Liza's case. But the next step was RTG's answer to my claims, and that was a month down the road. And usually defendants get an extra month to file it. So it would probably be two months before anything happened. And given that I really wasn't sure what I should be doing, it was easy to procrastinate.

In any event, I was excited about spending time with Joss. Man, I was smitten by this woman. She was five leagues above me, though. So smart and so beautiful. And so at ease with herself. I wish I had that kind of confidence. She was such a mystery, though. It seemed like every time I started to get near her, she turned away.

What I really wanted was to just bowl her over. To have her so enamored with me that she just wanted only me and cared about nothing else. That look that my dog, Halle, always gave me when I was a kid when she saw me. That unconditionally-devoted-unbounded-joy-at-seeing-me look. I wanted Joss to love me like a golden retriever. I really am pathetic.

I didn't know what to do with my energy. I started doing pushups. Sets of 20. It felt good. I wanted Joss to want me. I may not be the sharpest crayon in the box, but I'm in pretty good shape. If not for my wit or charm, at least maybe she'd find me physically desirable. I'd take what I could get.

My message light was still flashing. I took a deep breath and hit the button. To my surprise, it was Lynn: "Ben, I want to see you. I'll come by or call you back."

Uh oh. I checked caller ID, but it just said "Private Number." I felt bad, but was kind of glad I didn't have her number and couldn't call her back. I mean, Lynn was an intriguing woman, and I felt awful for her and the miserable position she was in.

Yesterday's fun in the metropark was really something. But I worried about what she wanted from me. I was feeling overwhelmed with everything coming at me all at once. It was too much.

There was a knocking on my door. I opened it to Joss's beautiful, beguiling, smiling face.

"You ready?" she asked.

"You bet."

"C'mon." She had a gym bag slung over her shoulder and walked down the hall to the elevator. "Do you have a bathing suit in that apartment of yours?"

"Yeah, but it's way too big for you."

We got on the elevator and I pressed 4. We went into my apartment. She looked around. "My god, you live like you're a freshman in college."

She was right, of course. I had boards resting on cinder blocks for shelves. And an old box spring and mattress on the floor that I'd picked up at a garage sale. My clothes were thrown all over the bedroom, which she could see from the entranceway. She laughed and looked at me. "How old are you? Go put on a bathing suit and get a towel. Hurry up. I've got to change, too."

I went into my bedroom and dug out a pair of shorts that worked as a swimsuit. The bathroom was off my bedroom, and I went in and changed. I left my t-shirt on. "Ok," I said, coming out of the bedroom. Your turn."

I stopped. I thought Joss would change in the bathroom after I did, but there she was in the middle of my living room with her back to me, wearing a pair of bright red running shorts, and pulling a white tank top down over her shoulders. No bra. My god, she was gorgeous. She turned and smiled at me. "Ok!" she said. "Are you ready?" She pulled a t-shirt over her tank top.

"For what?"

"Ha. C'mon." She threw her work clothes into her gym bag. She grabbed the bag and walked out of my apartment.

We drove down to the Flats, a development in downtown Cleveland on the Cuyahoga River in the valley that divides the east and west sides of Cleveland. There were bars and restaurants, office buildings and condos on the banks of the river that fed into Lake Erie. We went into Bilbo's Pub, got a table outside overlooking the water, and ordered burgers and beer. It was great, sitting in the warm sun, watching boats and tankers cruise by, an endless stream making their way into the huge lake to the north.

After a bit, Joss said, "Finished?"

"Yup."

"Ok, let's go."

I followed her out of the restaurant. We walked down Old River Road, parallel to the winding river. Joss went into a boat rental shop and told the guy we wanted a Jet Ski. I offered to pay, but she waved me off. Thankfully.

We walked down to the edge of the water and got five minutes of instructions and warnings from the guy in the boat shack. Joss took off her t-shirt and stuck it in her gym bag.

"Come on, stud, let's have that shirt," she said. I pulled off my shirt and handed it to her.

She looked at me and gave me a whistle. "Not bad. For a lawyer, anyway." She stuffed my shirt in her bag and asked the boat guy if we could leave it with him. He put it inside his shack. He asked if we wanted to wear life jackets, and I said I thought we should.

Joss hopped on the Jet Ski, and patted the seat behind her. "Come on, Benny boy, let's go!"

I climbed on behind her. There was nothing to hang on to but Joss, so I put my hands around her and her life jacket, which covered her waist and chest. I should have turned down the life jackets. Damn.

Joss roared out of the dock like an old pro and raced down the river toward the lake. The water was choppy inside the canal, and we bounced all over the place. Suddenly the canal burst open and we shot out onto Lake Erie. It was immense, stretching north, west and east as far as I could see. Joss blasted straight north, away from the city, and then cut sharply to the east. We were about 500 yards out, riding parallel to the coast.

A motorboat passed nearby, and Joss turned to go over its wake. We hit the wave we went airborne a few feet. This was one of the things the instructor had told us not to do, of course. But it was a blast. Joss leaned back into me and told me to hold on. She circled back and hit the wake again at full speed. The Jet Ski lifted off the water and angled upward. It flew forward in a smooth arc, and as it did I flew backward in my own arc. I let go of Joss so I wouldn't pull her off and landed head first in the lake. I came up and tried to clear the water out of my nose. Joss pulled up, laughing her head off at me. I climbed back on.

"So this is fun for you, huh?" I asked.

"This is a fantastic! What do you think these things cost? Really, I should get one of these."

Joss took off again, and scoured the coast, looking for waves to hop, trying to set new records for height off the water. It scared the crap out of me, but I loved that huge smile on her face, the unbridled, reckless fun she was having, and mostly, the feel of her wiggling and bouncing against me.

154

Eventually we cut the engine and just drifted, sitting side by side on the seat. We took our life jackets off and basked in the afternoon sun. Joss was such a treasure. She never talked about herself, and I really knew nothing about her. But we just talked, chatting about anything and everything; the huge houses on the water's edge, the boats going by, the pace of life in Cleveland. We made up stories about the people we saw. Talked about how good it felt being out on the water, what we lost by being stuck in buildings day after day. Time disappeared when I was with Joss. Suddenly it was nearly 6 o'clock, the deadline for returning the Jet Ski. We cruised slowly back to the boat shack. Joss leaned back into me, nestled against my chest. I wrapped my arms around her waist, warm and comfortable, and nothing could make me put those life vests back on.

We returned the Jet Ski and got Joss's bag. I drove back to the office, and pulled into the parking garage. We got out and walked to her car.

"Thanks for that, Joss. That was great. Just what I needed."

"Yeah, that was a blast."

"So," I hesitated. "Any interest in coming up to a tastefully decorated college-like apartment?"

She was standing close to me, looking up at me, and I was fighting the urge to reach down and kiss her. But she wasn't backing off, and maybe that's what she wanted.

She tucked her hair behind her ears. "I'd love to, Ben. But I have to get home to someone. I promised to cook dinner tonight." She reached up and mussed my hair. "Gotta run. Thanks for a great afternoon."

The day ended about as well as it started.

24

The next day I wandered down to my office late in the morning. I had nothing to do and no motivation. I could not believe that Joss had a boyfriend. I had no clue what was going on with her. Was she a shameless tease? Was she just toying with me for her own amusement?

I had the nagging thought that Joss was a grown woman and I had no idea what that meant. I mean, she was 35 years old, almost a decade older than me. I still think of myself as a teenager. I can't even imagine being 35. So maybe I just have no clue what adult relationships are like. Maybe by the time I'm ten years older, I'll feel free to flirt and enjoy people without it being anything other than that. I mean, I'm perfectly comfortable sitting with someone and having a cup of coffee. Maybe in another ten years, the range of things that will be comfortable will be so much broader. Maybe in 20 years doing what Lynn did with me will be like having a cup of coffee. Maybe that's what life is like for grown ups. All I knew was that what I felt when I was with Joss didn't fit with her having a boyfriend. And knowing that she was going home to someone else reminded me how bitterly alone I was. All the time.

So Joss had just been messing with me. But every time she gave me that inviting smile, laid her suggestive hand on my arm, looked at me with those hungry eyes, I felt a longing that paralyzed me, a yearning for intimacy and bonding that I never felt before. And while the universe spun wildly off its axis for me with new promise, for her it was turning as mundanely as it always did, dull and constant, another day sipping coffee.

She had a boyfriend.

I couldn't focus. I wandered down the hall to the bathroom, hoping I'd bump into her, but her office was dark. Katrina's office was next to Joss's, and her door was open, which was rare. I leaned in the doorway and knocked. She looked up from her computer.

"Oh. Ben! How are you?"

"Good. I was just saying 'hi' since your door was open. Is this a bad time?"

"No, no. It's good to see you. How have you been? I've got a patient in 15 minutes, but this is nice. Come, sit."

She pointed to her couch. It was brown leather, with three sections, and seating pads that wouldn't stay in place. I sat down on the edge of the couch, and the back of the pad flipped up. I wound up on my ass on the floor. Katrina laughed out loud.

"Sorry, Ben. That happens to everybody. Really. I keep thinking I should replace that awful couch, but it amuses me to no end."

I stood and she picked up the pad and shoved it in deep, firmly under the back of the couch. I sat down again, this time further back.

"How long have you been in this office?" I asked.

"Going on 18 years now."

"Wow. Has it always been shrinks on this floor? How long have Joss and David been here?"

"David's been here five years longer than I have. Joss moved in three years ago. Well, into her current office. She used to share a suite with Richie, but that didn't work out. So for the last three years, it's been just her there."

"Richie? Is that her boyfriend?"

She looked at me and grinned. "Richie? No. Well, I mean they were spending time together at one point. But that didn't last, and they couldn't keep a practice together. Eventually he moved to Seattle and she stayed here. She's with Westy now, you know."

She looked at me with a knowing smile.

"Westy?"

"Yes. Westy."

"I don't know Westy."

"Everyone knows Westy," she said.

I looked at her questioningly.

"You know, Taylor Westbrook?"

Oh shit. You've got to be kidding me. Taylor Westbrook was the running back for the Browns, their one superstar. Despite the Browns' woes year after year, Westy was their shining light, a perennial pro bowl player. He was the "heart of the team," as the coaches called him. He was basically a human wrecking ball, a beast of a man, impossible to tackle and built like a god. He was in about 1,000 commercials. Last year he was on the cover of ESPN's Body Issue, this huge guy with rippling muscles and piercing blue eyes.

"Westy is Joss's boyfriend?"

"I thought everyone knew that. They've been seeing each other for a year or so now."

I was so depressed. I lay down on Katrina's couch.

"Well, they must be quite the couple," I said, trying not to let my disappointment show.

Katrina looked at me and smiled.

"What about you, Katrina? Are you dating anyone on the Browns?"

She laughed. "I'm happily married, Ben. 32 years now."

"A coach?"

"You're funny, Ben. A really good guy."

"And we know where good guys finish."

"Nonsense," she said. She looked at her watch. "I hate to do this, Ben."

"I know, I know. It was nice chatting."

"It was. Stop by more often. I like talking with you."

I wandered back to my office. Lovely. Not only was Joss taken, but she was with the hottest bachelor in the NFL. I must be a joke to her.

I went back to my office and shut the door. Now I really didn't want to see Joss. What would I say? She'd obviously been humoring herself at my expense.

I sat at my desk and put music on my cell. Someone slipped an envelope under my door. I went and looked at it. It was from Stallon Moore, the largest firm in town. In fact, it was the largest firm in the world, headquartered here in good old Cleveland.

I opened the envelope. There was a very formal looking letter. It was addressed to me, and said,

Re: Allen v. RTG, et al.; Case No. CV-16-325748

Dear Mr. Billings:

The undersigned and this firm have been retained to represent the Defendants in the above-referenced matter. Hereafter, all communications regarding this matter should be directed to the undersigned.

I have attached Defendants' Notice of Plaintiff's Deposition and Document Request. We expect to see you and your client on the referenced date, barring a judicial order to the contrary. Please confirm your attendance.

Sincerely,

Alexander Sebastian Shaw, Esq.
Stallon Moore

I looked at the attachment. This clown with three names had scheduled Liza's deposition for 9 o'clock in their offices on Friday, just two days away. Shit.

I thought I was going to puke. Two days! I had never seen a deposition, and had no clue what went on there. A lot of people took litigation practice courses in law school, but I never bothered. Shit.

I called Rett. As usual, she was pressed for time.

"What's going on?"

"Got lunch plans today?"

"No time today. Can't do it."

"You have to," I said. "Really, Rett. I need you."

"You suck, Ben. Fine. Meet me outside my building at noon." She hung up.

Ok, now I was breathing a little easier. I called Liza and told her she was being deposed on Friday. She wasn't happy about it, but we agreed that she'd come by my office Thursday afternoon to prepare. Then I sent an email to Alexander Sebastian Shaw to let him know that Friday would be fine and we would see him at his office at 9:00.

I pulled out the local court rules on depositions, and they didn't say much of anything, just that lawyers should conduct themselves professionally. I'd have to try to figure out what that meant.

It was a beautiful, warm day, and I decided to ride my bike downtown to meet Rett. I thought the exercise and fresh air might help with my stress level, which was off the charts. She was waiting impatiently for me outside her office at Public Square, a big open grassy area at the heart of downtown.

I hopped off my bike. She walked up and hugged me.

"Careful," I said. "I'm sweated up from the bike ride." She didn't seem to care.

"Come on," she said. "Let's get something and sit."

There were about a dozen food trucks lining the square. We picked out one that had gyros, Rett's favorite. She got the "Monster Gyro," which looked big enough for four people. It was amazing she stayed so skinny. I got the "Regular Gyro."

We sat on a bench in the square. "Thanks for coming out, " I said. "I'm glad you could get away."

"I'm bored out of my fucking mind, Ben. I've been at Warner Levitt for 18 months now and all I do is write briefs and memos. Most of my firm's partners aren't very bright. They're only there because they started there 30 years ago. Most of them have never even tried a case. My job is to do all the work and act impressed by them.

"But I don't have time to bitch. What's going on?"

"Well, you know my case?"

"Who doesn't?" She chuckled.

"Yeah, well I know now that your firm isn't on the other side, so you don't have to worry about that. They hired Stallon Moore."

Rett laughed.

"What's so funny?"

"Oh, nothing. Who's on the case?"

"Some guy named Alexander Sebastian Shaw."

Rett burst out laughing.

"What?"

"You're so fucked! Shaw is the head of their worldwide employment group. He's probably the most accomplished litigator in the whole city. He's considered the 'Dean' of employment litigation. But don't fool yourself thinking he's the only one on the case. They'll have a whole team on this. That's why the average partner at Stallon Moore makes over two million a year. Shaw's rate is something like $1,250 an hour. And they'll probably have four other lawyers on the case, charging anywhere from $350 to $750 an hour."

"Are you kidding me?" And I thought I was so slick, getting Callahan to pay me $150 an hour for five hours of work. He must think I'm a complete joke.

Rett chomped on her gyro.

"So listen, Rett. They're taking my client's deposition on Friday."

Rett stopped eating and stared at me. "What do you mean, they're taking her deposition on Friday?"

"I got the notice today. They scheduled it for Friday."

"But you just filed your complaint Monday. They haven't even filed their answer, right?"

"Right. Their answer isn't due for 30 days."

"Ben, you know that I love you, right?"

"You always tell me that, and it's always followed by something awful."

"I love you, Ben, but you have to get co-counsel on this case. Someone with experience, any experience at all."

"I think I can handle it."

"So, did you agree to the deposition?"

"Yeah, I talked to Liza and we're both free on Friday."

Rett put down her sandwich and started pacing. She walked over and stood above me. "You poor, poor boy. You're in so far over your head. You're really fucked.

"Listen, Ben. You shouldn't let them take your client's deposition until after they file their answer. But now you're stuck because you confirmed that you're available. How do you know what their defenses are? Maybe they'll file counter claims against Liza. How can you prepare her without knowing those things? You shouldn't let them depose her until they've responded to your discovery requests and produced documents. Did you file discovery requests with your complaint?"

At least I knew what discovery requests were. They were requests for the other side to provide their documents and answer written questions under oath. But I had no idea I could send them out when I filed the lawsuit.

"No," I said.

Rett rolled her eyes. "You should never let them depose your client so early. Who's your judge?"

"Oh, I keep forgetting to check that."

"Oh my god, Ben." She pulled out her phone and pulled up my case on the court's electronic docket system. She stared at her phone and shook her head.

"You're so fucked," she said. "You pulled Christopher Williams. He'll throw out your case at the first opportunity. No point in trying to delay the deposition. He'll never agree. He'll let Shaw do whatever he wants."

I sat there and stared at my feet. I could work at the dry cleaner's. I'm sure I could.

"Do you have time to prep your client for her

depo?"

"Yeah. We're meeting tomorrow afternoon. But would you mind telling me what happens at a deposition?"

"Jesus Christ, Ben! Are you fucking kidding me?"

"How would I know? I've never been to one."

"How did you get through law school?"

"By leaning on you. Come on, Rett. I'm dying here. I have no one to train me. Help me out, please."

"Ok. Here's the deal. You don't see much about depositions in the movies, but they're the most vital things in every case. When witnesses answer questions at trial, it's really the second time they've given testimony under oath. The deposition is the first. You sit in a conference room at a table. There's a court reporter. The witness is sworn in and has to answer questions from the other side's lawyer. It's his only chance to learn what your client will say at trial. But it's way more than that, because everything your client says is used for the rest of the case. If the other side files a motion to dismiss the case, which you know Stallon Moore will, and your client said something dumb, then they'll use her testimony to show that the case should be thrown out. Or if there's ever a trial, and your client gets up on the witness stand and says something inconsistent with what she said at her deposition, that snake Alexander Sebastian Shaw will show the jury what she said at her deposition, and that her testimony has changed. This proves that your client is a liar. So what happens at her deposition is crucial. Your entire case hinges on it."

Now I felt really sick. I threw my gyro in a trash bin.

"You look like you're going to puke, Ben."

"I am."

"Well, maybe there is one positive in this. By taking your client's deposition now, Shaw doesn't have much time to prepare. And he only gets to depose her once. He hasn't been able to see her documents yet. Does Liza have any important documents?"

"I don't know. She said there are some good emails, but the company has them. Shaw's deposition notice included a list of documents she's supposed to bring with her."

"What's she supposed to bring?"

"It just said all documents related in any way to her claims and damages."

"You know what he's doing, don't you?" Rett asked. "If there's a document that you don't bring on Friday, he's going to say that you're barred from using it because you failed to produce it. So he's catching you with your pants down and stopping you from ever pulling them up again.

"Listen to me, Ben. Your case is two days old and you're on the verge of losing it. You've got to get help on this."

"How about you?"

"You know I can't do that. My firm would never let me take a plaintiff's case. There aren't really any good plaintiff's employment lawyers in town, but you've got to find someone."

"You could quit. Be my partner. Fifty-fifty. We're a perfect team, Rett."

"Yeah? I'm making $140,000 a year. And I've got $200,000 in student loans. What would I make with you?"

"Half of everything we bring in."

"If I'd been at your firm last year, what would my half have been?"

"Almost $2,000."

Rett stared at me. She sat down and stretched her legs. "You know what, Ben? I actually think you'd make a great trial lawyer. That schoolboy innocence makes you so damn likeable. People are drawn to you. And if you ever get the balls to use that brain of yours, you'd really be something. It would be fun to work with you. But with all my student loans, there's no way."

"Come on, Rett. You're not happy at your firm. And think about how good we are together. It'd be like being back on the basketball court. We'd be great."

She sat down and leaned against me. "We would be great. But I can't do it. Not until you're in a better position to bring in real money. Look, I'm bored out of my mind at my firm, and my clients are weasels, always turning to us to clean up their messes. And even though I was valedictorian, there's no disguising that I'm their token African-American in the Cleveland office. Those fuckers put me front and center on all their promotional materials, and never invite me to any of the social events with clients. I sit there writing memos all day and don't get to do real lawyering because the male partners want all the credit. But I'm learning and they're paying me a ton. Anyway, all your money comes from landlord-tenant cases, right? Doesn't that bore the shit out of you? I'd go nuts doing that."

"What about my case against RTG, Rett? Those bastards raped Liza. Doesn't that interest you? Don't you want to help someone who deserves it?"

"Do you believe your client?"

"Of course I do."

Rett didn't respond. Then she got up and began pacing again. "Yeah, it interests me a lot. More than you know. I'd love to help Liza. I want to work for people who need my help in important ways. But I'm skeptical, too. I'd have to spend time with her before I would ever take on a matter like that."

"You'd like her, Rett, even if she's a mystery to me. Course, all women are. But think, if this case goes well, we could make a lot of money. We could go into employment law full-time. People are always losing their jobs and needing help, especially when the economy is bad. We'd be recession-proof."

"Well, you're right about that. But you've got to establish yourself. You can't find clients until you make a name for yourself."

"Hey, I was in the paper yesterday!"

Rett patted my leg. "I would love working with you. But these are desperate economic times for me, and it's too risky. Go win this one and prove me wrong, ok?"

She was challenging me like she used to on the basketball court. If only I was playing hoops against RTG and Alexander Sebastian Shaw. If that were the game, I'd destroy them. In this game, I was lost.

"Ok, Rett. You have to get back to work. And I have to figure out how to beat these clowns. Someday when I'm a big shot I'll convince you to be my partner."

She rubbed my head, mussing my hair. "Hey, at least we can still share monster gyros made in trucks."

And with that, she was gone.

25

Friday was here faster than I could bear it. A mushrooming panic enveloped me, to the point I couldn't eat or sleep. I wanted time to slow, to keep me from that dreaded day, and when suddenly Friday was upon me, I'd have done anything to make it fly by.

I met with Liza for an hour Thursday afternoon. The only document she had was her invoice from the Paris hotel, but nothing responsive to Shaw's document request. The only relevant documents she could identify were the emails from work, which of course she didn't have. She was a basket case herself, angry at having to go through this. She quickly became the ice queen. She was impatient and angry and withdrawn.

We agreed that I'd pick her up at 8:30 Friday morning to drive downtown to the deposition. I stopped by my office to gather my things, and Joss walked in.

"Hello, Counselor! What are you doing here so early?"

She had obviously just finished a run. She was wearing her bright red shorts and a white tank top, and was covered in sweat. Damn she looked good. But I was tired of the game with her. She was dating the biggest star on the Cleveland Browns, and I was just an amusement for her.

"Sorry, Joss. I'm getting ready for Liza's deposition. I really can't talk now." I turned back to my desk and began placing pens and markers and yellow pads in my backpack.

"Are you ok, Ben?"

"No, to be honest. But I've got to focus here."

"Ok, I'll leave you to it. But Ben?"

"Yeah?"

"No matter what, the sun's going to rise tomorrow." She smiled at me and walked out.

I felt guilty, because she was just being nice. But she was so damn provocative, always saying exactly what I needed to hear, always making me yearn for so much more, and then vanishing like smoke when I reached for her.

I picked up Liza. We were both in suits, which made me more nervous. She was wearing the movie star glasses.

"How are you doing, Liza?"

She didn't respond. We drove downtown in silence and pulled up to Stallon Moore's offices. They had an entire twelve-story building to themselves, if you can believe it, right down by the lake, overlooking the waterfront. We parked in the garage below the building and took the elevator up to the 8th floor. The receptionist called someone, and a secretary came out and led us to a huge conference room. It was ridiculous. The table was gigantic, an elongated oval, big enough to seat about 50 people. There were huge leather chairs all around the table and expensive leather writing pads on the table in front of each chair. Liza and I sat next to each other in the middle on the side near the window.

A few minutes later an attractive 30-year-old woman in a business suit came in carrying a large rectangular briefcase. She sat at the head of the table without saying anything and began unpacking. She set up a laptop computer, and then a tiny typewriter on a stand.

She came over and introduced herself and gave

me her card. She was the court reporter. I didn't have a card. I wrote my info on a piece of paper and handed it to her. She gave me a condescending grin and went back to her seat.

Liza hadn't said a word all morning and didn't seem interested in making conversation. A few minutes later, the door opened and a flood of people poured in. The only one I knew was Callahan. He seemed glued to the hip of a tall, distinguished, gray-haired dude who was wearing what looked like a $10,000 Armani suit. I stood up, but none of them paid any attention to Liza or me. Finally, the distinguished guy walked around the table to me. He stuck out his hand and introduced himself as Alexander Sebastian Shaw. He actually used all three names. He handed me a stack of cards, one for each person in the room. He just dripped of sophistication. There were two other lawyers from RTG there with Callahan, and five lawyers from Stallon Moore. So all in all, they had eight lawyers, all facing across from little old me. I could only imagine how Liza felt. Shaw sat down next to the court reporter at the end of the table. Callahan sat next to Shaw. I sat back down next to Liza. I kept my game face on, but thought I was going to puke.

I looked at Liza. Her arms were folded across her chest. She was staring at the table in front of her. She looked like she had turned to stone.

"Before we get started, can I get anyone a beverage?" Shaw asked.

No one responded.

"Ok. We have coffee and water and soft drinks on the credenza. If you want anything, just help yourself." He looked at me and waited.

There was an uncomfortable silence. I had no idea what he was expecting. Finally, he said, "Ben?"

"Yes?"

"You and your client need to sit by the court reporter. Your client should be next to the court reporter, and if you would like, you can sit next to your client."

Everyone on the other side laughed. I was off to a great start. Liza and I picked up our things and moved to the end of the table so that Shaw was directly across from us.

Shaw looked at the court reporter and nodded. The court reporter asked Liza to raise her right hand and asked her to swear to tell the truth. Liza said that she would.

Shaw said in a kind, fatherly way, "Now, Liza, we haven't met before. My name is Alexander Sebastian Shaw, and I represent the defendants in this matter. I'm going to be asking you some questions today, and you must know that you are required by law to answer my questions. Do you understand that?"

Liza nodded her head.

"You must state your answer."

One of the RTG lawyers leaned over to Callahan and said, "Yeah, the court reporter can't type the sound of rocks rattling around." Callahan laughed, as did everyone on his side except Shaw. Shaw shook his head and they were quiet.

"You must respond verbally," Shaw said. "Do you understand?"

"Yes."

"Do you understand that you are required by law to answer my questions?"

"Yes."

"Do you understand that you are under oath, and that if you lie today in answering my questions, you will be committing the crime of perjury, which is a felony?"

"I guess so."

Shaw slammed his hand on the table. I nearly jumped through the roof. "Not good enough!" he barked. "Do you understand? Perjury is a felony! Do you understand?"

"Yes."

Shaw asked Liza a bunch of questions about whether she was capable of giving her best testimony, whether anything prevented her from doing that, whether she was on drugs or taking medication that would prevent her from remembering. He asked where she lived, and if she had any plans to move. I wrote furiously on my yellow pad to get everything down. Shaw kept glancing at me.

"Now Liza, you worked for RTG for 20 years, correct?"

"Yes."

"Ok. We're going to talk about your last day at RTG later. But now, I want to talk about your entire time at RTG from your first day until the day before you were fired for insubordination and refusing to work, ok?"

"Ok."

Liza was still staring at the table in front of her. She wouldn't look at Shaw or anyone else in the room.

"You were fired for insubordination and refusing to work, right? That's what RTG told you and that's your understanding, right?"

"Yes."

"In the entire time you worked at RTG, up until the last day when you were fired because you refused to work and were insubordinate, you never once claimed that you were raped, correct?"

Liza sat in silence. I looked at her and watched that beautiful, flawless face start to melt. Her eyes grew red, and then she started sobbing. She put her head in her hands and just bawled. She got up and ran out of the room.

I stood up to follow her.

"Off the record!" Shaw barked. The court reporter stopped typing. "Mr. Billings, your client is in violation of the rules of court. If she won't comply, this case will be dismissed and the court will sanction you. You will be fined and may see jail time. Now get your client back here and tell her to answer my questions. Do you understand?"

"Just give me a minute."

I found Liza by the elevator in the hallway. "Are you ok?"

"I feel like I'm getting raped all over again. Why does he get to order me around like that?"

"That's the way it works. This is his only chance to talk to you. So he gets to ask you his questions. We'll have our chance to question their people. But we have to get through this day. Just this one day."

Liza turned and looked at me desperately. I felt so bad for her. She was a wreck. Her mascara had run all over her face.

"I don't think I can do this," she whispered.

"You have to, Liza. If you want to get them, you have to. And we're going to get them. We're going to make them pay. Just remember, the truth is on our side. You just need to say what happened. So how 'bout you go into the bathroom and wash your face, and then we'll plow through this?"

She got that vacant look on her face again, and nodded. I walked her to the bathroom, and a few minutes later she came out with the stone demeanor.

We went back into the conference room and sat down. Shaw nodded at the court reporter.

"Liza, you understand that you're still under oath?"

"Yes."

"Do you regret filing this lawsuit?"

Liza shrugged.

"State your answer. As you sit here right now, you regret filing this lawsuit, right?"

"Yes."

"You received a request to bring all documents related to your claims to this deposition, correct?"

"Yes."

"Do you have any?"

"No."

"Did you give any to your lawyer?"

"No."

"That's because you don't have any. None exist, right?"

"Right."

"Mr. Billings, do you have any documents responsive to our request filed with the deposition notice?"

I jumped. "Uh, no. No. I don't."

"There are none, correct?"

"Not that I know of."

"Liza, prior to your last day of work on May 23rd, you never once filed a complaint against anyone at RTG about any matter, right?"

Liza nodded.

"State your answer!"

"I never did."

"You never complained of rape, correct?"

"Correct."

"You never complained of assault, correct?"

"Correct."

This just didn't feel right. "Um, excuse me Mr. Shaw. I'm sorry. But you're not letting Liza explain what happened."

The lawyers across the table laughed. Shaw put his pen down and stared at me. Finally, he said, "They're called leading questions, Ben. They're permitted by Evidence Rule 611(c). You know that, don't you?"

I turned about 12 shades of red. "Ok," I said. "Let's keep going."

Shaw turned back to Liza. "You never complained of a single thing in 20 years, not of someone being rude, or inconsiderate, or of an unfair performance review, or of a failure to promote you or give you a good enough raise or bonus or of anything whatsoever, correct?"

"Correct."

"In fact, just a few months before you were fired for refusing to do your job, you received the best bonus of your career, correct?"

"Yes."

"The company and its employees never did anything, in all those years, that caused you to go to Human Resources or any management official and complain that you were treated unfairly, correct?"

"Yes."

"You know that there were some employees at RTG who filed complaints over the course of your 20 years, correct?"

"Yes."

"So you knew that if you wanted to file a complaint, you could do that, correct?"

"Yes."

"And you never did, correct?"

"That's right."

"Now, Liza, you're familiar with Howard Morley, correct."

Liza did not respond.

"Elizabeth Allen!" Shaw said, slapping his hand on the table. Liza jumped. "Did you hear my question?"

"Yes."

"Howard Morley is the Chief of Human Resources at RTG, correct?"

"Yes."

"You know where he lives, don't you?"

Liza nodded.

"Liza, you know better. Speak."

Liza's hands were in her lap, and she stared at them. "Yes," she mumbled. "I know where he lives."

"This past February, just a few months ago, you went home with him, correct?"

"Yes."

Oh shit. Where was this headed?

"He owns a condominium in Little Italy, and you told him that you would like to see it, didn't you?"

"Yes."

"And while you were at his condo, you had sex with him. You chose to have sex with him, didn't you?"

"Yes."

"Are you claiming that he raped you?"

"No."

"It was completely consensual, right?"

Liza wrapped her arms around herself and started rocking back and forth. She was staring down at the table. "Yes," she said softly.

"This was after you claim you were raped by two RTG executives, correct?"

"Yes."

"You chose to go back to Mr. Morley's place after work and have voluntary, consensual intercourse with an RTG executive, right?"

"Yes."

"In fact, you knew that he was married, right?"

"Yes."

"And you knew that his wife was out of town, because you had made her travel arrangements for her and bought her tickets, correct?"

"Yes." Liza seemed only semi-conscious, like she wasn't really here.

"Were you in a relationship with him?"

"Who?"

"Howard Morley. You know that we're talking about Howard Morley, right?"

"Yes."

"Were you in a relationship with him?"

"No."

"This sexual escapade you had with him, where you went home with him after work after making arrangements to have his wife away, and then seduced him and slept with him, was that just a one-time sexual escapade?"

Liza nodded.

"Speak."

"Yes. One time."

"Now the day before you were fired, Mr. Stanton asked you to prepare a document that needed to be filed with the Securities and Exchange Commission that very day, correct?"

"Yes."

"You understood that this was an important filing that had to be filed that very day, and Mr. Stanton and his team were rushing to meet a deadline, correct?"

"Yes."

"And your job was to help prepare documents for filing, correct?"

"Among other things."

"Was I correct?"

"Yes."

"And you objected to doing your job, correct?"

"I didn't like how I was being treated."

"And because your boss ordered you to get your work done, you refused to do the paperwork?"

"I didn't refuse. He wasn't treating me right."

"Did you do what you were asked?"

"No."

"And then after refusing to do your assignment, you left your place of employment before the workday was over?"

"Yes."

"In fact, you left your place of employment without doing the work that was asked of you, and without getting that important document filed, correct?"

"That's right."

"And the next day, you were told by RTG that you were being fired for insubordination, for refusing to do the work you were asked to do, correct?"

"That's what I was told."

"You were never told another reason for your firing, correct?"

"Correct."

"So as far as RTG goes, there was no other reason for your firing, correct?"

"I guess so."

"Ok, now after you were fired, you went to the police and made the assertion that you were raped, correct?"

Liza looked up. "Who told you that?"

"You're here to answer my questions. You made that assertion to the police, correct?"

"Yes."

"This was more than nine months after you

were supposedly raped, correct?"

"Yes."

"And this was after a lawyer, Ben Billings, got involved, right?"

"Yes."

"So you only went to the police after you were fired, and after you started working with a lawyer, correct?"

"I guess so."

"Did you ever make a personal visit to a doctor for injuries related to rape?"

"No."

"There is not a single doctor in this universe, to your knowledge, who could verify that you were raped, correct?"

"I guess not."

"In fact, there is not a single person in this universe who could verify that you were raped, correct?"

"Well, Nick Stanton could. And Jerry Greyson."

"Let's put them aside for a minute. There is not a single person, other than Mr. Stanton and Mr. Greyson, with a shred of evidence to support your claim that you were raped, correct?"

"I guess so."

"And if Mr. Stanton and Mr. Greyson testified that they never raped you, that you are lying, then you would agree that there is no evidence whatsoever in the entire universe to support your claims in this case, correct?"

"I'm not a lawyer."

"I know that. But prior to being fired, you never told anyone that you were raped, correct?"

"Correct."

"Did you ever put anything in writing stating

that you were raped?"

"No."

"So if Mr. Stanton and Mr. Greyson testify that they never raped you, there is no legal basis whatsoever for your claims against RTG and the defendants, correct?"

"I guess so."

Shaw paused to look at his notes. I looked over at Liza. She looked like she had been kicked in the gut. I needed to give her a break from this. Plus, my hand was cramping from writing so much.

"Um, excuse me, Mr. Shaw. I need a bathroom break. Would that be ok?"

"Of course."

I walked out with Liza. She had that blank expression on her face.

"He's twisting everything," she said.

"I know."

"Can't you do something about it?"

"Unfortunately, no, he gets to ask you his questions."

Liza looked up at me. Her eyes told me that I failed her. That she had just been pummeled yet again.

"Are you ok, Liza?"

She glared at me. "What the fuck do you think? You're supposed to take care of me."

"I know. Come on. Let's take our bathroom break and keep fighting our way through this."

The court reporter came out of the bathroom. She came up to me and said, "I see you're trying to write everything down that's said in there."

"Yeah," I said. "I want to make sure I keep track of everything."

"You know that I'm taking every word down. Literally, every word. That's my job. And you can get a copy of the transcript from me in the next few days."

I looked at her and blushed. She grinned and patted me on the shoulder. She went back in the conference room. Liza shook her head at me. Lovely.

We went back to the conference room. I poured water for Liza and me. "Would anyone else like some?" No one responded. I poured a glass for the court reporter, even though she hadn't asked. She looked uncomfortable, but I thought I caught a glimmer of appreciation in her eyes.

I took a deep breath and sat down. This was agony. Liza was being tortured, and Shaw was just killing us, getting testimony to convince the Judge that we had no case. And we were only 30 minutes in. I couldn't stand the thought of going through this for an entire day.

Shaw was paging through his notes. "Ok," he said. "We're almost done here."

Wow! I wanted to jump on the table and dance. I thought he'd keep us until dinnertime. I could see Liza's face brighten.

"Ok, back on the record," Shaw said. "Liza, you went out with Nick Stanton many times, right?

"We traveled many times for work."

"That's not what I'm asking. You dated him, correct?"

"What's that got to do with this?"

"Answer my question! You dated him, correct?"

Liza glared at Shaw. "Yes."

Oh shit! I couldn't believe it. Are you kidding me?

"You dated him on and off for eight years, correct?"

"That sounds about right."

"You dated him willingly, correct?"

"Yes."

"No one forced you to date him, correct?"

"Yes."

"No one ever conditioned your job or your benefits on dating Nick Stanton, correct?"

"That's right."

"And while you dated Nick Stanton, you slept with him, correct?"

Liza stopped and looked at me. "Do I have to answer this," she whispered?

"No talking with counsel!" Shaw snapped. "You're under oath and must answer my questions. Now Liza, you dated Nick Stanton and you slept with him, correct?"

"Yes."

"And by that, you mean that you had sex with him, correct?"

"What does that have to do with this?"

"Everything, Ms. Allen. Everything. Now answer my question. You had sex with Nick Stanton while you were dating him, correct?"

"Yes I did."

"And while you were dating Nick Stanton, you willingly had sex with him, correct?"

Liza didn't respond.

"Liza," Shaw said, "you had sex with Nick Stanton willingly, correct?"

"Yes."

"How many times would you say that you willingly slept with Nick Stanton?"

"I have no idea."

"More than once?"

"Yes."

"More than ten times?"

"Yes."

"More than 50 times?"

"I guess so."

"Eight years is almost 3,000 days, right?"

"I don't know. I guess so."

"So in the more than 3,000 days you dated Nick Stanton, you had sex with him probably hundreds of times, right?"

"Probably."

"Maybe 1,000 times?"

"I don't know."

"I'm not asking for an exact number. You would estimate that in the 3,000 days that covered the time you dated Nick Stanton, you may have had sex with him 1,000 times, right?"

"I doubt that."

"But it's possible that you had sex with him willingly 1,000 times, correct?"

"It's possible."

"Is that 'yes?'"

"Yes."

"You had sex with him in hotels, right?"

"Yes."

"You had sex with him in his house when his wife was away, right?"

"Just one time."

"You had sex with him in your house, right?"

"Yes."

"You had sex with him in his car, right?"

"Yes."

"You had sex with him in his office, right?"

There was a long pause. I couldn't look at Liza. Why hadn't she told me any of this? I was afraid to breathe. Finally, I looked at Liza. She was glaring at Shaw.

"Liza," Shaw, said, "you filed this lawsuit. Now you have to answer my questions. You had sex with him in his office, right?"

"Yes."

"You even performed oral sex on him while he was on a conference call with the Board of Directors, right?"

Liza folded her arms across her chest and didn't respond.

"Am I right?"

Liza nodded.

"State your answer!"

"Yes."

"In fact, that was a little game with you, right? When he had a call with the Board, you would go in his office, shut the door, and perform oral sex on him while he was on the call. Correct?"

"Not every time."

"Numerous times?"

"Yes."

"And when Mr. Stanton was in his office on the phone on a work call, you walked in and pulled down his pants, hiked your skirt up, and straddled him while he was on his call, right?"

"Once."

"And when you were done, you laughed about it, right?"

"I don't remember."

"If Mr. Stanton testified that you did laugh, would you have any evidence to refute it?"

"No."

"There were many times when, as a Pool secretary, you accompanied members of the management team on business trips, correct?"

"Yes."

"You went willingly?"

"It was my job."

"You went willingly, correct?"

"Yes."

"And during those business trips, you often went out for drinks with Mr. Stanton and members of the management team, right?"

"Yes."

"And many times, probably too many to count, you then returned to the hotel and had sex with Mr. Stanton, correct?"

Liza nodded.

"Speak!"

"Yes."

"And you had sex with him in hotels after work meetings willingly?"

"Yes."

"Let's turn now to the night you refused to work and left your job early. That night, you emailed Mr. Stanton a video, right?"

Liza didn't respond.

"Ms. Allen, you are under oath. That night, you emailed a video to Mr. Stanton's personal account, correct?"

"Yes."

"Describe that video."

"It was just a video of Nick and me."

"In fact, Ms. Allen, it was a video of you and Mr. Stanton having sex, correct?"

"Yes."

"And you had secretly made that video without his knowledge, correct?"

"I never discussed it with him."

"You had secretly set up a camera in your bedroom, and you filmed the two of you without his knowledge, correct?"

"That's right. So what? Lots of people do that."

"That video showed Mr. Stanton without any clothes on, correct?"

"It showed both of us."

"Yes, both of you without any clothes, correct?"

"Yes it did."

"That video showed you performing oral sex on Mr. Stanton, and then having more traditional sex, correct?"

"I don't know."

"Well, Liza, how many films of Mr. Stanton did you make?"

"Just one."

"Did you make movies of your other lovers?"

"No!" Liza said.

"Did you make a video of you having sex with Howard Morely?"

"No."

"Usually, when you weren't having sex at your house, or in the office or his car or his house when his wife was away, you had sex in hotels, correct? I'm talking about you and Mr. Stanton now."

"Yes."

"But one time, you insisted on going to your house instead of a hotel?"

"I don't recall."

"And when you went back to your house with Mr. Stanton instead of a hotel, you video taped the sexual encounter?"

"I already said I did."

"Are you claiming that Mr. Stanton raped you that night?"

"No."

"The night before you were fired by RTG, you sent Mr. Stanton an email, and you attached the video to the email?"

"I may have."

"And in the email, you wrote, and I quote, 'You'd better be careful.' Is that correct?"

"It's possible."

"I'm showing you what I'm marking as Defendants' Exhibit 1. I will not be including this on the record until we obtain a Protective Order. Will you agree to that Mr. Billings?"

I jumped. I wasn't sure what he meant. "Uh, sure, of course."

"Ok." Shaw slid a document to Liza. "That's an email from you to Mr. Stanton, correct?"

"Yes."

"You sent it from your personal email address, dated May 22, at 8:43pm, to Mr. Stanton's personal email address?"

"Yes."

"It includes an attachment, correct?"

"Yes."

"That attachment is the sex video that you secretly recorded without Mr. Stanton's knowledge, correct?"

"I guess so."

"By this email, you intended to threaten Mr. Stanton, correct?"

Liza stood up and yelled, "I was telling him he couldn't get away with treating me that way. I was telling him he was not immune. I was telling him…"

Shaw slammed his hand on the table and stood across from Liza, glaring at her. Liza stopped.

"Now you listen," Shaw said. "You must answer my question. Sit down this minute."

Liza sat down and crossed her arms.

Shaw sat back down. "By sending this email to Mr. Stanton, you intended to threaten him, correct?"

"Yes, I did because…"

"Thank you," Shaw interrupted. "How many copies of that tape exist?"

"Just the one."

"Who has it?"

"I do."

"Ok. Now I have one last question for you. Prior to being fired, you never once filed a complaint or told anyone that any of your sexual encounters with Mr. Stanton or Mr. Greyson or anyone was rape, correct?"

"That's right."

"Ok, I have no more questions." Shaw turned to the court reporter. "Roberta, I'll need a copy of this transcript first thing Monday. Will that be a problem?"

The court reporter said it would not, and asked if I would like a copy. I told her I would, just because Shaw was getting one so it seemed like I should.

"Ok," Shaw said. "Good day."

He got up and walked out. The entire team followed him.

"C'mon," I said to Liza, "let's get out of here."

We packed up our things and went to the elevator without talking. We rode down to the garage in silence. When we got in my car, Liza broke down. She bawled with her head in her hands like a baby. For the first time, I had no interest in reaching out to her.

26

I got back to my office and my head was spinning. Liza had lied to me. If she lied about dating Nick, she'd probably lied about everything. Maybe Callahan and Shaw were exactly right. Maybe Liza had refused to do the work, they fired her for it, and she made the whole thing up to get even. Shit.

It occurred to me that I should try to track down Bonnie to see if she had seen those emails that Liza told me about. But my heart wasn't in it. If Liza was playing me, why would I waste my time on this?

As if he were reading my mind, just then I received an email from Shaw with a letter attached. It said,

> Dear Mr. Billings:
>
> As you well know, I represent RTG and the individual defendants in this case. As the company's legal representative, I am writing to remind you that you may not contact any current or former RTG employee. If there is any current or former RTG employee with whom you would like to speak, you must contact me to discuss procedures.
>
> Sincerely,
>
> Alexander Sebastian Shaw, Esq.

Yeah, fuck you Alexander Sebastian Shithead. I felt completely deflated. I had no clue whatsoever what I was supposed to do. It was like I was being asked to create engineering designs for a jet engine. And this sophisticated, smooth operator Shaw with 40 years of experience and unlimited resources at his disposal was picking me apart at every turn.

I had two softball games over the weekend, and it was a relief to hang with Bobby and lose myself in the games. I made a few diving plays at shortstop and hammered the ball a bunch of times. I wasn't much fun to be with, but it felt good to do well at something.

First thing Monday morning, the transcript arrived, along with a bill for 400 bucks for "Printed Transcript and Expedited Services." Shit. I couldn't even get myself to read it. I called Rett.

"Hey there, Ben. How'd it go?"

"I'm dying, Rett. Meet me for lunch, please?"

"Christ, Ben, you sound awful. I can't today. The associates here have a mandatory lunch so we can tell the head of our office how much we admire him."

"Please?"

She laughed. "You poor boy. I can't. But listen. I'm coming your way. I have a training session on the east side at three. It should take an hour. How 'bout I swing by when I'm done?"

I thanked her and decided to head down to the gym. I could use a workout and maybe some basketball to get my frustration out. Or to deal with the gnawing pain in my stomach. I changed into my shorts and t-shirt. Before I left, I started thinking that maybe I could find a different job. I would love to coach. Maybe high school basketball. Or baseball. I think I'd be really good at that. I know a lot about sports, and I'm good with kids. Maybe they would respect me, and I'd have a blast with them. I spent the day scrolling through the Internet, looking for job openings. Nothing I was qualified for, of course.

I was in my office, wearing shorts and a t-shirt and waiting for Rett. The song "Girl from the North Country" was playing on my laptop. Joss stopped in.

"Got a minute, Counselor?"

She sat in the lounge chair by my door. She was barefoot and wearing a powder blue summer dress. When she sat and crossed her legs, it fell open to her thighs. I was determined not to notice.

"How's your day going?" she asked.

"Trust me, you don't want to know."

"That bad?"

"Worse."

"Well, I was just wondering if you're mad at me. You've barely spoken to me since jet skiing."

I'd had enough of her teasing and flirting. She had a boyfriend. I was a joke to her, not that I blame her. I mean, come on, she's dating Westy. I couldn't compete with that. I was nothing to her, and that felt like yet another slap in the face. I'd had enough of those lately.

"You know, Joss, I kind of feel like we're in different places, looking for different things. And with all that I'm dealing with, I really don't need that frustration. I'm sorry for saying that, but I feel like I need to channel all of my energy into this miserable case that I've got. And you scare me, to tell the truth. I feel like I could really lose my way with you. I'm just a silly kid to you. I'm overwhelmed right now, and you don't take me seriously, and I understand that. I mean, I don't take myself seriously, either, so I respect you for that. But I don't need another reminder that I don't have what it takes, you know?"

Joss just sat there looking at me. Was I boring her? I got up and walked to my door and opened it.

"I'm sorry, Joss, but I need to get to work."

She stood up and walked up to me. She stood

within inches of me, and I thought she was going to kiss me. I was surprised, and waited.

"Where's this headed, Ben?"

"What do you mean?"

"Look, you're off with your college girls, with your Mercedes girl, and who knows how many others. And you're expecting what exactly from me? Tell me what it is you want."

I wanted to disappear. Joss was right there with a spotlight on me, and there was nowhere to hide. "I don't know what you want, Joss."

"I'm asking what you want, Ben."

"I... I have no idea. I just really like being with you."

"But you're angry with me. Because I made dinner for someone? You're off with other women. So why are you angry?"

I had no answer to that. My head was swimming. I was pouting and knew that wasn't fair and god I didn't want her to be mad at me and I didn't want to do anything wrong and it killed me to think I was disappointing her but what was I supposed to do? I just wanted her to like me. I wanted her to yearn for me. I wanted to throw my arms around her and hold her and let her feel how good I could be for her. She was so close, looking up at me with those hungry eyes. Damn, I wanted to kiss her. She had to know that. She had to feel that. Can a person sense that? Her eyes are full of yearning, but maybe I'm way off base. Every time I think she's drawn to me I'm wrong. But still, she was inches from me and her mouth so close and it felt like she wanted to kiss me.

I was about to ask Joss if it would be ok if I kissed her, and my office phone rang. I let it go to voicemail, and we could hear the caller leaving a message: "Ben, it's Lynn. I really need to see you. I'll keep trying."

Damnit!

Joss shook her head at me. She turned and walked towards my door.

"I have a patient. See you, Ben."

Before she got out my door, I blurted out, "Joss! Can we get dinner tonight? Just you and me?"

"I've got work, Ben. I've got work for an hour." She left.

Well, what did that mean? We'd be going to dinner? Or no, she was going to get to work, and that was that? This was maddening. What did she want from me? I had no clue how to navigate this. Or anything. She was asking me impossible questions, and I had no clue what I was supposed to do. There was nowhere to hide with Joss, she wanted me all out there, and I'd spent my life hiding in safe places. I sat back in my desk chair, and put my feet up on my desk and folded my arms across my chest.

It was a fitful sleep.

27

I woke to a persistent knocking on my door. I jumped up. Dinner with Joss? It had to be her! I rubbed the sleep out of my eyes and tried to look like I'd been working away. I opened the door. There was Rett, grinning at me in a navy blue business suit, looking far more professional than I ever did. I was confused for a minute. Damn, I forgot that she was coming by. I felt ridiculous standing there in my gym shorts and t-shirt.

"I'm glad you dressed up for work, Ben. Did I wake you?"

"Maybe. This is one of the many benefits of working for myself. I can do whatever I want. The boss doesn't yell at me. Well, not too much."

"Actually, that seems wonderful. I can't stand wearing this straight jacket every day. Even though I never see a client, I've got to wear these suffocating clothes."

She stepped by me and into my office. Then she looked at me. "Ok, I have to tell you, I love this place. What a great office! It's five times the size of mine. Did you put all these plants in here?

"No, that would require taste. They were the prior tenant's. He forgot to take them."

"Well, this is great." She wandered around the office and looked at my pictures. I had a ton of them from my biking trips. Really just random shots, but there was a common theme – railroad tracks heading away, leaving me. Something about that image hit home for me, that sense of being alone and lost, but with the vaguest hint of possibility if only I had the courage to wander into the unknown.

"Did you take these?"

"I did."

"You've got talent, my friend. These are good."

"Thanks. I took a photography course in high school and I've been hooked ever since. I've got a ton of these in my apartment upstairs. It's one of my many hobbies when I'm not raking in the big bucks."

"You live in this building, too?"

"Yeah, right upstairs on the fourth floor."

"Oh, man, am I jealous! I spend 45 minutes commuting each way, and 20 bucks a day on parking. That's sweet."

She kept walking around my office and saw the deposition transcript on my desk. "So, your first depo is done. That's great. No matter what, you've got one under your belt. It's got to feel good to know you've defended a deposition against one of the country's top lawyers."

"Defended?"

Rett looked at me and turned her head. "Very funny. Got an extra copy? I want to read this."

"Do you have to?"

"Come on, that's why I'm here, right?"

I sighed. "This is the only copy."

"So make another."

I couldn't think of an excuse to stall any longer. I walked down the hall to the copier that the second floor tenants shared. When I came back, Rett was sitting on the couch. Joss was in one of the chairs in front my desk, facing Rett. They were laughing uncontrollably, undoubtedly at my expense. My other worlds collide.

"So you've met?" I asked.

They just kept giggling. I looked from one to the other. Finally, Rett said, "Got the transcript?

Come on, were going for drinks and dinner. Bring both copies."

I looked at Joss and hesitated. "I'm sorry, Joss. I messed up my schedule."

She and Rett grinned at each other. "Joss is coming with us," Rett said. "Let's go."

I wasn't going to argue. I threw the transcripts in my backpack. I put a yellow pad in as well. I dreaded Rett reading what had happened. We walked to Nighttown.

We sat at a table in the back. We ordered drinks and I pulled out the transcripts. I gave one to Rett.

"I want to read it, too," Joss said.

"Is she allowed to see it?"

"Of course," Rett said. "The Judge hasn't issued a protective order, has he?"

"Not that I know of."

Joss reached across and snatched the other transcript out of my hands. "How is it that Rett knows these things and you don't?" she asked. "Didn't you go to school together?"

This was getting worse and worse. And now Joss was going to see how awful I was as well.

"We did," Rett said. "But I've been at this big stodgy firm where they don't know what to do with the new lawyers. So they give us endless training and bill our time doing nothing at outrageous rates. I've gotten a lifetime of lessons on the rules and know them inside and out, while dear old Benjamin here has been sitting alone day after day doing who knows what with himself. Well, I can guess what he's been doing with himself."

Joss giggled. I scowled at Rett and fidgeted while they read the transcript. When I couldn't bear it any longer, I went to the bar and talked sports with Todd, the bartender.

Finally, I saw them talking. I asked Todd to have our waiter bring another round of drinks. I went back and sat down.

"Jesus Christ, Ben," Rett said. "You didn't object a single time. You let Shaw walk all over Liza and your case."

"What was I going to object to? He's allowed to ask leading questions. Rule C-6, or something like that."

Rett shook her head at me. "Rule 611(c), you idiot. You need to object every time he asks a question that's not relevant. You need to object every time he asks a question that's ambiguous. You need to object every time he tries to intimidate or harass Liza. You can't let him badger her. You need to help her when his questions are confusing Liza. Now that you haven't objected, you've waived the right to argue later that the testimony is inadmissible. He took advantage of you."

I didn't say anything. My shoddy work was embarrassing enough. But to have it laid out in writing for Rett and Joss made it worse. I craved their respect more than any two people I knew. I'd be happy to coach middle school baseball. Maybe elementary school. It didn't have to be high school.

We sat in silence for a while. Finally, I said, "She never told me that she was involved with Stanton. The first I heard about it was when Shaw made her admit it."

"Lesson number one, Ben," Rett said. "All clients lie. They tell you what they want you to know. They want to convince you that you should be on their side. So they lie about all the bad stuff."

"Going to Morley's condo when his wife was gone is really bad," I said. "Damn, it's all bad. Do you think Stanton raped her?"

"How the hell would I know?" Rett asked. "That video's really bad. It makes it look like she's been trying to blackmail him all along. Like this lawsuit is part of her scheme."

Joss slammed down her transcript. I looked at her. I'd never seen her mad before. She shook her head at me.

"What? I'm sorry, Joss. It was my first deposition."

"Why are you doubting Liza?" Joss asked.

"It really bugs me that she never told me she'd slept with Stanton," I said. "Or that she dated him for eight years. Or that she threatened him. What credibility does she have? And why would Stanton rape her when he could sleep with her any time he wanted? It doesn't make sense. And if she'd been out drinking with him and sleeping with him so many times after work, how in the world is anyone going to believe that somehow this time was different?"

Rett nodded. "She doesn't sound like a victim. Stanton wasn't some crazy lunatic who broke into her room and attacked her. They were screwing for years. Maybe this is all about revenge. Stanton dumped her, she wouldn't do her job, they fired her. And there he is, rich as hell, and now she's trying to get a piece of his money to get back at him."

Joss sat back and folded her arms across her chest and glared at me.

Rett didn't slow down. "Why didn't she go to the police when this happened? Why didn't she tell anyone about it? How the hell will a jury feel sorry for her, given what went on? Who's going to believe her? I mean, come on, she's blowing him every time he has a Board call?"

"I think I need to get out of the case," I said. "Can I do that?"

"Sure," Rett said. "There are some issues to work through, but you could dump her. She's put you in a terrible spot. And this depo made the case unsalvageable."

I looked at Joss, but she wouldn't look at me.

"What do you think, Joss?"

"I want to see Liza."

"Why?"

"Because you two have no clue what you're talking about."

"How so?" Rett asked.

"Ever been raped, Rett?"

"No!"

"Well you're lucky. Did you know that 85% of all rapes are by an acquaintance? The fact that she knew Stanton means nothing."

"But Stanton's one of the big players in town," Rett said. "The guy's good looking and loaded. There's probably a line of women outside his door trying to nail him. Why in the world would he rape someone, much less someone he was sleeping with anyway?"

"It doesn't work that way. And the fact that Liza didn't go to the police means nothing. Few women do. Most are in denial. They don't want to accept that something this horrible has happened to them. So they try to act like nothing happened."

"But why didn't she tell me about her relationship with Stanton?" I asked.

"I want to talk to her," Joss said. She was determined.

I took a deep breath and sighed. "I guess that's up to Liza. I need to talk to her about where we go from here. Maybe I can arrange a meeting with her when you'll be around."

"That works."

"I want to be there, too," Rett said.

"Can you do that? I mean, with your firm and all?"

"We don't represent RTG. I want to meet her."

I couldn't tell if they wanted to get some answers, or were just trying to rescue me. I was drowning, and we all knew I had no capacity to do anything about it. I couldn't stand what they must think of me.

"Well," I said, "I'll see what I can set up. I don't know how she'll feel about it."

"Go find out," Rett said.

So that was it. Liza had scorned me and didn't respect me enough to tell me anything. All I knew was that we were getting hammered, I was floundering, and we were going to lose the case.

I went back to my office and there was another manila envelop from Stallon Moore under my door. The panic hit me again. Now what? I opened it. There was another terse cover letter from Shaw. He attached a motion he filed with the Court. I looked at it. It was a motion to dismiss our case, and for sanctions against Liza and me for filing a "frivolous, malicious" lawsuit. There were affidavits attached from Stanton and Greyson, stating that they had never raped Liza, and that Liza had been fired for insubordination for refusing to do her job. And there was an affidavit from Callahan accusing me of ethical violations for trying to get a job from him while I represented Liza.

There had to be an opening for a baseball coach somewhere.

28

I made arrangements for Liza to come to my office at 10 o'clock on Tuesday. It took some arm-twisting. At first she just said, "No." I tried to convince her that we needed to talk about where we go from here, but she didn't respond. I shared with her that Shaw had filed a motion not only to get her case thrown out, but also to have the court fine us and make us pay the defendants' costs. I told her we had to respond or we could really be in trouble, and she finally relented.

Liza showed up on Tuesday and barely acknowledged me when she came in. She walked right by me and plopped down in the chair across from my desk. She was wearing her movie star sunglasses.

Rett and Joss were waiting down the hall in Joss's office. I explained to Liza that Joss and a lawyer I knew might be helpful. I asked if it would be ok if they came in and joined us.

She looked at me with disdain. "Do I have any choice?"

"Yes."

"Whatever you want. I don't care."

"Look, Liza. I'm not doing this because it's fun for me. I think it's important for both of us. One of them is a lawyer with more experience in this area than I have. And you know Joss. We can use their help."

"Let's just drop the lawsuit and be done with it."

"At this point, I don't think we can just walk

away. Shaw asked the Judge to sanction us. We have to deal with that."

"Just settle it. I've had enough. I'll take the year's pay."

"I can try. But what if they refuse? Think about the message that sends to them. It tells them we think we have no chance in this case."

Liza didn't respond. I decided to take that as consent.

I went down the hall and got Rett and Joss. They marched in and sat on my couch across from Liza like they'd done it a hundred times before.

"Hi, Liza," Joss said. "This is Loretta Anderson. She's an employment lawyer with one of the big national employment firms."

"Hi, Liza," Rett said. "I read your deposition transcript and understand you've been through a miserable experience. Not just with Stanton and Greyson, but in this lawsuit.

"We'd like to talk about your case, and how you and Ben might go forward. How would you feel about spending 30 minutes with us?"

Wow. Rett had such a direct way about her. As always, she just exuded competence. Liza turned her chair to face them. I was in my chair behind my desk, on the outside as always. I kept my mouth shut and listened.

"Ok," Liza said. "Let's talk."

"You must be completely fed up with these men bossing you around all the time," Joss said. "But I think we can figure out how to take control of this situation. Maybe start moving forward in ways you would like."

"That would be a nice change," Liza said. Ouch.

"Ok," Joss said. "I assume you ended your

relationship with Stanton some time ago."

"Yes."

"And he's been horrible to you ever since."

Liza snorted.

"Hostile, condescending, scornful?" Joss asked.

"You can't imagine."

"Tell me about it."

Liza took her sunglasses off and laid them on my desk. "If you only knew. You really have to know this guy. He's just so smooth. He's smart, good looking, and charismatic. But he's crazy insecure."

"Most of the pretty boys are," Rett said.

"Yeah, he's a pretty boy all right. I didn't know him when RTG hired me. I was just a lowly 18-year-old secretary in the finance department. He was working out west somewhere. Then they moved him to the headquarters in Cleveland and eventually made him CEO. One day I was working out in the fitness room, and he came in to work out. I always worked out in the middle of the afternoon when it was less crowded. Anyway, he didn't say anything to me, but a week later I was invited to interview for an administrative assistant opening in the Pool.

"There were six of us women in the Pool. All young and good looking. And all thrilled to be part of this elite group. And all scared to death about ever offending one of these powerful men. It was a really schizophrenic place. Everyone miserable about possibly screwing up, but desperate not to lose our place.

"I was there about two months and barely had a word with Nick. He was always traveling. But at the Christmas party that December, right there in the Crystal Palace, there was a band and drinking and dancing. Nick asked me to dance. Those were really his first personal words to me. I was uncomfortable, but what was I going to say? We went out to the floor and he looked down into my eyes and gave me his big, sexy smile. Then he pulled me close and held me like we'd been in a relationship for years. It was completely inappropriate, but intoxicating at the same time. I mean, here I was, 30 years old, dancing with this 40-something man who was one of the most powerful guys in the world. He was charming and handsome. He has that Cary Grant look about him, you know?"

Joss and Rett nodded. I'd never seen Liza talk so freely.

"When the dance ended, he kissed me on the cheek. And that was it. Then he started stopping by my desk during the day to ask how I was. He was always joking. He wasn't the least bit funny, but the fact that he made the effort made me feel good. And then one Friday evening, I was the only admin there and he asked me out for a drink. And then it became our regular thing on Fridays. And then several times during the week if he wasn't traveling.

"It was just so pleasant being with him. He took me to the finest places. He always paid. He charmed me with his ability to let me do things I could never do on my own. And then in March we had a Board meeting. The meeting was in London, and the Chiefs brought two of the admins with them. We flew over on the corporate jet, which was unbelievable.

"Those meetings are a lot of work. In addition to making sure the Chiefs get the help they needed, the whole Board is there. So we're running around catering to these men all day. But the last day there, Nick invited me and the other Pool girl to join them for dinner. We ate in this gorgeous restaurant near Kensington Gardens. And afterwards, a minibus drove us all back to the hotel. Nick and I went down to the bar for a nightcap, and eventually wound up in his room.

"He told me he was married, but they were getting a divorce. Turns out that was a lie. There were always women in Nick's life, and his wife knew he was not faithful. So their marriage was awful.

"Nick and I cycled through a really intense and dysfunctional relationship. For the first couple years, we had fun. Then we moved to a different phase, where we were always breaking up because it was clear that he was with me for thrills and not much more. I kept telling him that the relationship was going nowhere. But he's a smooth operator. He'd say things like, 'Life is too short to ignore passion when it finds us. If we have a chance to have a special moment, we would be fools not to seize it. Otherwise, life is nothing but an endless dentist's appointment.'

"So we were on and off for years. It was passionate and intense and maddening. Finally, I'd had enough. His need to be perceived as the most impressive person in the room every moment of every day was pathetic, and just so exhausting. I mean, seeing him drunk and hung over, sprawled out in his underwear, changes things, you know? He wanted me to worship him one minute and then have nothing to do with him the next. Finally I put a stop to things. And then I met a really sweet guy. He was new in the finance group. We went out a few times, and Nick found out about it and went nuts. That made me really mad. I mean, here he was, married, and also seeing other women when it suited him, but he went nuts when he heard I had gone out with another guy. So next thing I know, they transfer Robby to our Brazilian operations.

"That was it for me. I mean, by this time I really knew Nick. He could charm the pants off of anyone.

But he drank all the time. He had to be the center of attention. He was fanatical about following what people said about him. He was just a narcissist, and it was everyone's job to make him feel special. It was pathetic. I was 37, and he was 50. Even though he was in good shape for a guy that age, he was getting old. He was no longer attractive to me, and he was increasingly jealous. One night he asked me to get drinks after work, and I just wasn't interested. This was about a year ago. But he insisted, and so I went. He spent the whole evening complaining about the CEO of some other company, who the Times described as Cleveland's top business leader. Nick was incensed. And listening to this grown man whining like a kid in middle school just made him seem like such a sad joke. He never had any interest in anything I had to say. Then he wanted to go back to a hotel to spend the night, and I wouldn't go. He wasn't used to that. I told him I no longer wanted that kind of relationship with him.

"His reaction was what I should have expected. He pouted like a child. But I stuck to my guns. He was drunk, and told me that I was nothing without him, and that he'd made my whole career. He shows his true character when he drinks. I'll never forget what he said to me. He told me he could break me in a second and I'd be just 'a poor, uneducated twat' desperate for a job.

"I knew he was hurt, and he was drunk, but it was so obvious to me - - finally - - what a fool I'd been spending so much time with this nasty human being, trying to keep him happy. I walked out of the restaurant and left him there, actually feeling good about myself and looking forward to moving on to better things."

Joss looked at me. "Go to Starbucks and get us

some coffee, Ben, if you don't mind."

I was in the way, as usual. "Sure," I said.

I got up and walked out. As I shut the door, I heard Joss say, "Take your time, Benny boy."

I came back about 45 minutes later. The women were giggling as I walked in.

"Speaking of pretty boys," Rett said. They all looked at me and burst out laughing. Lovely.

"You know we're just kidding, right Ben?" Rett asked. "You're really not that pretty."

"Yeah, thanks. Not even pretend flattery for this guy."

There was a pile of used Kleenex on my desk near Liza. I used my training in logic to deduce that they had not been laughing the entire time I was gone. Three years of law school and $180,000 of debt weren't for nothing.

"Listen, Ben," Rett said. "We've talked. There's going to be a new legal team on the case."

I looked at Liza. She was fishing through her purse. "You're firing me?"

Liza snorted without looking up.

"No, Ben," Rett said. "I'm working this case now."

I looked at Joss and she smiled at me.

"What about your firm, Rett?" I asked. "They'll never allow it."

"I'm leaving my firm," Rett said. "I'll fit in better with my new firm."

"What? Where are you going?"

"Billings and Anderson. You and me." She gave me a huge smile.

"You and me? Holy shit, are you kidding?"

"I'm game if you are, partner."

I walked over and hugged her. "Oh my god, this is fantastic," I said. I stepped back and looked at her. "You're ok with a 20 percent share, right?"

"Nice try," she said. "Give me a week to wrap up at my firm. Actually, I'll tell them tomorrow and give them three weeks' notice. They'll boot me out tomorrow, but pay me for three weeks. We'll start together on Monday."

I looked at Liza. "Are you ok with this?"

"Relieved, to be honest."

I couldn't blame her. I felt the same way. I looked at Joss. She jumped up and winked at me. "Gotta go," she said. "Can't let my patient lose patience. Let me know if I can help."

Joss left. Rett turned to Liza. "This is going to be a whole lot easier from this point on. We'll huddle in a couple of days and give you a call. We'll get a strategy in place."

"Strategy?" I said. "What's that?"

"Yeah, I'll explain it to you." Rett and Liza looked at each other and laughed.

This was progress. Right?

29

Rett and I met in my office at seven on Monday morning. She brought a slew of corporate papers she had drawn up over the weekend. She named us "Billings & Anderson" and split the firm fifty-fifty. I trusted Rett implicitly, and was happy to sign anything. We clicked our way through the Secretary of State's website to register our firm, and walked down to Starbucks to toast our new endeavor. I was thrilled. I had my first glimmer that lawyering might not always be walking barefoot on broken glass.

We came back to our office, and Joss came in a minute later with a bottle of champagne and hugs for us both. I hadn't talked to Joss since our weird confrontation last week, and I felt a little awkward. In addition to the swirl of insanity that gripped me whenever I saw Joss, somewhere below the surface there was always some level of sexual tension with Rett. She'd never shown any interest in me that way, except for a graduation party at law school where we'd both had too much to drink and got carried away dancing.

In any event, the three of us were in my office. Our office. Joss was in a summer dress, looking her usual beguiling self. Rett was wearing jeans and t-shirt that did little to hide her assets, celebrating her "new-found freedom" to dress as she pleased.

"So I have to ask," I said. "You sent me to get coffee last week, and when I came back, you were both fully in Liza's corner. Rett, you quit your job for a dolt like me, and Liza's acting like the three of you are long-lost sisters. What happened?"

"What happened," Rett said, "is that Joss is unbelievable. She put Liza at ease and got her talking. If her story's true, it's heartbreaking. And infuriating. And then suddenly Joss's got me talking about why I was here and what I wanted. And in minutes she made me realize it was foolish to keep postponing the work I want to do. I'm sick of defending people who are trying to justify mistreating others. I mean sure, most of the time my clients did nothing wrong, and the claims against them are bullshit, but I want to spend my time helping people who need help. People who deserve help. Help in a fundamental way. Help in a way that touches them here," Rett said, touching her chest. "I have no interest in helping companies with their bottom line. And I can't think of anyone I'd rather work with than you. I think this is going to be fantastic. So quit asking stupid questions before I change my mind."

I grinned at Rett. "What about that warning you gave me, that all clients lie? Are you comfortable that Liza's telling the truth?"

"What does your gut tell you, Ben?" Joss asked.

"I don't know. I want to believe her. But why did she hide her relationship with Stanton? She put me in a really bad spot. I don't know if I would have filed this case if I knew that."

"Maybe she needed to hide part of the story because that was the only way you would help her," Joss said.

Rett looked back and forth at us. "This is classic," Rett said. "There's nothing wrong with a guy being sexually active, right? He's a hero if he scores with some babe. But if a woman enjoys sex, she's a slut and gets what she deserved if she's raped. That's why I'm standing up for Liza. A woman should be as free as any guy to have her fun without being treated like an animal. No one would say a guy is fair game for anal rape because he enjoys sex."

I looked at Joss, who watched me intently. Maybe Rett just needed to believe in Liza, given the monumental changes she had just made to her career, but something still felt off to me.

The office phone rang. I ignored it. I didn't have nearly enough time with Joss, and I wasn't going to waste it. Rett was sitting next to the phone on my desk and looked at it.

"That looks like a court extension," she said.

"What do you mean?"

"It's a 443 number. That's a call from one of the judge's offices. You should pick that up."

I was nervous. "Let's let it go to voicemail."

Unfortunately, my phone played the voicemail tape for everyone to hear. My recording came on: "Hi! It's Ben! Tell me what's shakin'!"

Joss looked at me and burst out laughing.

"Very professional," Rett said. "We'll have to change that, you idiot."

We could hear the caller leaving a message: "Is this Mr. Billings? The lawyer? This is Michael Miller from Judge Williams' chambers. I'm calling about the RTG matter. The Judge would like a conference today at two o'clock to discuss RTG's motion to dismiss. Please call me at 443-1507 to confirm your attendance."

I looked at Rett and started to freak out. She just shook her head. "That prick," she said. "Judge Williams is our biggest problem in this case."

"Why's that?" Joss asked.

"He hates employment cases. He throws out every one of them."

"How can he do that?"

"Judges are graded on how quickly they resolve their cases. You'd think that would be a good thing, because you want cases handled efficiently. But Williams is stupid and lazy. He hates plaintiffs and blames them for giving him work. Especially employees. The quickest way to clear his docket is to dismiss their cases, and that's what he does."

"I thought Liza was entitled to a jury trial?" Joss asked.

"That's not completely right," Rett said. "The jury's job is to decide the facts. But there's a rule that if there are no material facts in dispute, then the judge can take it from the jury and decide himself. So RTG filed a motion asking the judge to rule that there are no material facts in dispute, and decide the case without a jury. And that's how Williams will get rid of this case."

"But there are facts in dispute," Joss said.

"Of course there are. But he doesn't care. He just wants the case gone."

Joss stood up. "Justice in America just isn't. Ok, I'll leave you guys to get ready. Sounds like you have your work cut out for you."

She left. I looked at Rett. "I'm so glad you're here. I have no clue what to do."

"Well, the first thing is our clothes. Do you have a suit handy?"

"I live upstairs. Remember?"

"I know. That doesn't mean you have a suit."

"Funny. But true."

"I'm going to have to leave some clothes in your apartment, partner. I'm going home to change. Williams is going to tell us he's throwing out the case if we don't settle it. Have you talked to Liza about what she wants?"

"Yes. She wants justice."

"Great," Rett said. "You can tell the Judge that we'll drop our case in exchange for justice."

Rett got back to my office at one o'clock. She looked like she belonged in a suit, which she filled out perfectly. She was just so professional and sharp. I felt like a softball player in the wrong uniform.

Rett sat at her laptop and filed a notice of appearance with the court. We agreed that she would take the lead at the hearing. She'd never argued a motion herself, but had prepared partners at her firm and sat in on a couple. "I finally get to be a real lawyer," she said, rubbing her hands together in anticipation.

I, by contrast, was a nervous wreck. I'd been at a couple landlord-tenant hearings, but never one where there was a lawyer for the other side. And my little disputes weren't before real judges at real courts – just the small claims court for a few hundred bucks. I felt guilty that Rett was carrying the entire load, but was thrilled she was here to do it.

"Ok," she said. "I'm going to spend the next 25 minutes reviewing their motion again. We should leave at 1:25. You're in charge of the car and getting us to the courthouse. That will give me more time to get my thoughts together."

"I can handle driving. I'm pretty good at it."

"That's why we're partners."

Glad I could contribute. I sat there while Rett paged through Shaw's motion, which I still hadn't read. She pulled a highlighter out of her briefcase and colored some passages. Then she turned to the affidavits.

"Did you ask Callahan for a job?"

"No! Well, I mean, when I met with him at their headquarters, I told him how amazing it was and I'd love to work at a place like that. He said something about discussing a job opening when Liza's case was over. But that was it."

Rett nodded and kept reading.

The phone rang, and I let it go to voicemail. I didn't want to distract Rett. After my childish greeting, we heard Lynn leaving a message: "Well, Ben, you're obviously screening my calls and avoiding me. I understand what you're doing. It's probably for the best. You won't hear from me again."

I lunged for the phone, but she had hung up. I checked caller ID, but as before, it said "Private Number," and she'd still never left her number. And regardless, she'd made a point of not asking me to call her, probably because of her thug for a husband. Still, I didn't want her to get the wrong idea. I really liked her, and felt sorry for her. Damn.

I looked sheepishly at Rett. What would she think of her new partner? "I think that was a wrong number," I said.

"Car," Rett said, without looking up.

"What?" I looked at my watch. It was 1:20. "Shit! Sorry. I'll meet you on the street." I hustled out, and half way down the steps realized I'd forgotten my backpack and something to write with. I ran back to the office and grabbed them. Rett just shook her head.

We drove downtown and Rett kept scribbling notes and reading through Shaw's motion. I kept quiet so I wouldn't bother her. I parked in the city lot next to the courthouse, and we hurried into the Justice Center on Ontario Street. The building housed the county jail, all of the county offices, as well as 27 courtrooms, not one of which I had ever been in.

"Do you have your attorney badge?" Rett asked.

"What's that?"

"Jesus Christ, Ben." Rett pulled out a county ID that had her picture and said she was an attorney. "If you don't have this, you have to get in line with everyone else and go through security. Hurry up!"

Rett showed a guard her badge and walked in. I got in line behind about a hundred people, mostly criminal defendants and their families, waiting to get searched and then skewered by our system of justice.

30

Rett and I took the elevator to the 23rd floor and walked into the hallway. There were four courtrooms on the floor, two on each side. Judge Williams' courtroom was 23B.

We walked into the courtroom, and it was empty. It was pretty ugly, to be honest. The building was built in the 60s, and it lacked the nobility of the older courthouses. No marble, no fine wood, no stained glass. The jury box, lawyers' tables, and Judge's desk were made of cheap, yellowed pine. There were four rows of faded plaid movie theater seats for the public. Despite the common-looking room, there was still something intimidating about the Judge's desk hovering above the lawyers, and the solemnity of the place. Serious things happened here.

I followed Rett in. She walked past the public seats, through the swinging wood gates and past the lawyers' tables, and up to the Judge's desk. Then she walked around it and opened a door behind it.

"Where are you going?" I whispered.

"To our meeting. The Judge's office is back here, dipshit."

I followed her through the door and into a long hallway. There was a plain room with a conference table for jury deliberations. Further down there was a reception area to the left. We walked in. A guy about my age sat at a cheap metal desk in front of a row of scratched, worn filing cabinets. It looked like a government office. A cop stood leaning against the wall talking to someone in a cheap suit, probably a prosecutor. In the hallway a bunch of lawyers sat quietly, waiting for their turn with the Judge.

"We have to check in," Rett said.

I followed her up to the desk where the law clerk sat.

"Loretta Anderson and Ben Billings representing the plaintiff for the two o'clock conference with Judge Williams," she said.

"Case number?"

"CV-16-325748," Rett said. How did she know that?

The clerk leafed through some papers and dropped a sheet on his desk in front of Rett. She wrote our names on the left side, and "Plaintiff" on the right.

"Are all parties here?" the clerk asked.

"I haven't seen defense counsel," Rett said.

"Ok, let me know when they're here."

We went into the hall and waited. Rett paged through her notes. I wondered if this would eventually feel like old hat to me. For now my heart was racing and I couldn't wait to escape.

A minute later Shaw strode up with a cadre of lawyers. He walked right by us and announced himself to the clerk and signed in. Then he came out into the hallway. All of the lawyers walked up to greet him. He cracked jokes with them as if he didn't have a care in the world.

He finally noticed me and came over to shake my hand. "How are you doing, Ben?" He acted like we were old friends.

Just then the clerk called out, "Elizabeth Allen versus RTG, et al!" Shaw turned on his heels and strode into the office. His lackeys followed. Rett and I went in last.

The clerk opened a door behind his desk and we filed into Judge Williams' chambers. It was a large office, with a humongous wood desk and conference table. There was golf paraphernalia scattered all over, and a putter and a bunch of golf balls on the floor.

"Please be seated, gentlemen," the clerk said, ignoring Rett. Shaw sat on the far side of the conference table, next to the chair at the head, which was undoubtedly for the Judge. His lackeys sat along the same side of the table. Rett sat down across from Shaw, and I sat next to her.

"Who are you, dear?" Shaw asked Rett.

"I'm Loretta Anderson, Ben's partner." Shaw made no effort to shake her hand.

"Have you entered an appearance?"

"Yes. This morning."

Shaw nodded and pulled a yellow pad from his leather briefcase. He pulled a Mont Blanc pen from his suit coat, one of those fat ones with gold trim that probably cost more than my car. We sat there in silence, five of them facing Rett and me, just two feet away across the table. Finally, after a few minutes, the Judge walked in from a door behind his desk. He was wearing plaid pants and a yellow polo shirt, stretched to its limit over his bulbous belly. We all stood as he came into the room.

"Sit," he said without looking at us. He scrounged around his desk, picked up an accordion folder, and with a big sigh plopped down in the chair at the head of the table between Rett and Shaw.

He may have been the most unpleasant looking person I ever saw. It's not just that he was hunched and overweight and had a greasy, stringy, dyed black comb-over that looked like it hadn't been washed in a month. He had a pained look on his face like he just drank sour milk.

He flipped through papers in his folder. We waited, listening to him wheeze through his nose, his stale breath sibilating through the room.

"This is RTG, right?"

"Yes, your Honor," Shaw said. "Stallon Moore representing the defendants."

The Judge didn't respond. He kept flipping through pages, but not reading them. Finally, with a heavy sigh, he shoved the folder away from him as if it were too much to bear. Without looking up, he said, "Who are you?"

There was silence for a minute, before Rett realized he must be talking to us. "I'm Loretta Anderson, and this is Benjamin Billings, Judge. We represent the Plaintiff."

"There's a motion to dismiss, right?"

"We filed it last week, your Honor," Shaw said.

"You've made outlandish claims here, Mr. Billings. You know you're talking about the CEO and CFO of Cleveland's largest company?"

"Yes, Judge," Rett responded, ignoring the slight.

"What proof do you have?"

"The Plaintiff was raped, and when she spoke out about how she was treated, they fired her."

The Judge picked up the folder and slammed it on the table. Rett and I jumped about a foot. "I said proof! What proof?" he hissed. He leaned on his forearms, about three inches from Rett's face, and glared at her.

For the first time I could remember, Rett was flustered. Or maybe he made her nauseous. I jumped in. "We have our client's testimony, Judge. We have witnesses who saw her object to the abusive treatment just before she was fired."

The Judge leaned back and looked at me. He reached with his middle finger and began digging in his nose. I thought Rett was going to puke.

"They have affidavits from top executives.

How do you expect to overcome that?"

"When we have the chance to talk with witnesses and see emails, I think the truth will come out, Judge," I said.

"The truth!" He practically spit the words. "Get out of here."

He glared at Rett with disdain. We weren't sure what he meant.

"Did you hear me? Get out. I want to talk to defense counsel. "

Rett and I picked up our things and walked out. We stood in the hallway outside his office.

"Are you ok?" I asked Rett.

"What a fucking prick. I can't believe he talked to me that way."

We sat in the hallway chairs and waited in silence. About fifteen minutes later, the Judge's door opened. We could hear laughter. Shaw said something I couldn't make out, and there was another round of laughter.

Shaw and his water boys walked up to us. "Your turn," Shaw said.

We went back in the Judge's office. He was sitting in his chair at the conference table. We sat back in our seats.

The Judge looked at us derisively. His nose whistled every time he exhaled. He began picking at something on his neck with his fingernail.

"You need to get out of this case," he said.

"We think we have strong claims, Judge," Rett said.

"You're going to lose the motion."

"Your Honor," Rett said, "we intend to depose witnesses who will confirm that the Defendants retaliated against the Plaintiff. Emails from the Defendants, which were read by a number of witnesses, confirm that the Defendants abused Ms. Allen. We have witnesses and proof that Ms. Allen was retaliated against and fired for opposing clearly illegal behavior. With all due respect, there are material facts in dispute. Whether our client was raped is obviously material to this case, and is in dispute. The reason our client was fired is in dispute. These are issues that should be decided by a jury, and in our view, granting the motion to dismiss would be clear error."

There was Rett. Precise and on the money. Her argument was irrefutable.

The Judge glared at Rett. "What's the matter with you? I'm telling you I'm going to grant their motion. Your case will be over. Do you have settlement authority? I can talk to Alex and try to get him to drop his claim for sanctions if you walk away."

He called Shaw "Alex." Like he was his best buddy. Wonderful.

"That will not be acceptable to our client," Rett said.

"Would she prefer to lose the case and owe legal fees? Would you and your boy here prefer to be sanctioned?"

Rett was flustered again. I knew she would have liked to smash this douchebag in the face. But if I remember, one of our law professors told us we shouldn't do that.

There was an uncomfortable silence.

"Did you hear me, Missy?" the Judge spat.

"Judge," I said, "we haven't had a chance to respond to their Motion. We just got it a few days ago. Hopefully we can prove to you that we have solid claims. Some really bad things happened that need to be addressed. We understand that we have to convince you and that we have our work cut out for us."

The Judge looked at me and nodded. He stood up and turned his back to us and dumped the folder on his desk.

"You have 30 days," he said. "No extensions." Then he walked out the back door of his office.

Rett and I sat at his conference table. We looked at each other. "That was fun," I said.

"Let's get the fuck out of here."

31

I loved Rett's reaction to Judge Williams' awful behavior. It just made her mad and want to fight harder. She told me that we were going to spend the rest of the day getting the office set up, and then, "tomorrow this case starts. Tomorrow we get to work. I'm going to crack that nut. He's going to love me before we're through. I'm going to have him wrapped around my finger."

We spent the afternoon rearranging the office. The landlord had some old tables in the basement he said we could use, and we grabbed one for Rett's desk. I kept the back wall by the window. Rett had the opposite wall next to the door. The couch was between us on the east wall, with the nerf ball hoop above it. Rett slid some of the plants on the west wall over and put the lounge chair across from the couch. She was mystified how I could function without file cabinets, and ordered two low, three drawer cabinets from Amazon and put them on her credit card, and said we'd figure it out later.

We finally finished setting up the office around five when Katrina poked her head in. I introduced her to Rett, and she invited us for drinks with the docs at Nighttown. Rett jumped up and turned off the lights. "Let's go!" she said.

We walked to the restaurant. Joss and David were already there, getting drinks at the bar.

We sat at a booth in the back. David and Katrina were across the table. I sat in between Joss and Rett.

"I'm sorry for being grumpy," Rett said. "We

had a hearing today with a judge and he was shameful. Treating me like I'm inferior because I'm a woman, and treating our case like it's worthless because we're plaintiffs. I've heard plaintiffs' lawyers whine about prejudice against their clients, and I thought it was bullshit. But today I saw it front and center. He was outrageous."

"Come on, Rett, don't be so sensitive," I said. "I don't think he treated you that way because you're a woman. I think it's because you're black."

"Oh, thanks. Now I feel better."

"Who is the judge?" David asked.

"Christopher Williams," Rett said. "Do you know him?"

"I do. The worst of the 'Infinite Williams,'"

"What's that?" I asked.

Rett slapped her palm to her forehead.

"There are six judges in our county named Williams," David said in his monotone. "The voters never know who they're voting for. Every election, someone named Williams runs and wins."

"They're all incompetent," Rett said. "They run for judge because they can't keep a job practicing law. We even have one judge who lost three elections in a row, and then changed his name to Williams and won. And once you're elected judge, they never vote you out. The incumbents are there for life."

"So much for an informed electorate," Joss said.

"Yeah, exactly," Rett said. "Most won't run for judge if they're going against a Williams. There's just no point."

"Well, you've got it particularly tough if you're in front of Christopher Williams," David said.

"How do you know about him?" I asked.

"I often testify as an expert. I've been before most of the state and federal judges in Ohio."

"What's your experience with Christopher Williams?" Rett asked.

"He's lazy. He hates plaintiffs. He never lets a case go to trial. In fact, the only times I've testified in his courtroom have been after he threw out a case, and the appellate court reversed him and ordered a trial."

"Do all of you work as legal experts?" I asked.

Katrina raised her hand. "Many times," she said.

"Not me," Joss said. "I wouldn't mind doing it if not for you lawyers. You guys make my skin crawl." Lovely.

"I do it all the time," David said. "It's important work."

Rett was animated. "What types of cases do you testify in?"

"All of my work with courts involves child custody issues," Katrina said. "I'm a guardian ad litem. I work as a court appointee, and my job is to recommend what's in the child's best interests. That let's me ignore pressure from the parents and social workers and do what's right."

"That must feel good," I said.

Joss and Katrina looked at each other and rolled their eyes. Joss reached up and mussed my hair. "You're so naïve," she said.

"Why?"

"There are no winners in child custody cases, Ben," Katrina said. "Everyone loses, especially the kids. Most of these cases involve physical abuse, and the kids usually wind up in foster care. When they do, the studies show that they have virtually no chance of success in their lives, by any standard. Most are incapable of forming secure emotional relationships as adults. Most repeat the pattern of abuse with their own children. They can't keep a job. Most wind up in jail. So we do what we can to keep them out of foster care, but often even that's better than leaving them in a known abusive family situation. So the real question in these cases is, which result is the lesser disaster?"

"That sounds horrible," I said.

Katrina raised her glass in a toast. "Such is my life. Working for lesser disasters."

We all raised our glasses. "To lesser disasters," Rett said. "Hopefully that's not the moniker for my legal career now."

"Thanks for the vote of confidence," I said.

Rett reached up and mussed my hair.

"So what do you specialize in?" Rett asked David.

"My practice focuses on the victims of abuse. But I testify in any case in which there's a claim for emotional suffering."

"Cases like sexual assault and illegal firings?" Rett asked.

"Frequently."

Rett looked at me and raised her eyebrows. I gave her a sheepish smile and shrugged my shoulders.

"You didn't know this?" she asked.

"Nope."

"David's being modest," Katrina said. "He's one of the country's top experts on sexual assault. He's the go-to guy."

Joss nodded.

"So, David," Rett said, "is it possible you might be willing to serve as an expert in a little case that Ben and I have going?"

"Possibly. We should talk and see whether it makes sense. If it does, and you can pay me, then I can serve. My rate for an expert report is $350 per hour. If I testify, it's $500 per hour."

"No problem," Rett said.

It dawned on me that my lovely partner hadn't reviewed our firm's accounts. They were empty. I hoped she had some spare cash.

Nighttown has live music a few nights each week, and a jazz combo was playing in the back room.

"No more work talk!" Joss exclaimed.

Katrina stood and turned to David. "Doctor, would you like to dance?"

David slid out of the booth without a word and walked out to the dance floor. Joss, Rett, and I watched them for a few minutes. They were surprisingly good, great, actually, doing all sorts of spins and twists like they'd been doing this for years.

"Are they just friends?" I asked.

Joss smiled. "Of course, my dear."

Joss slid out of the booth. "C'mon," she said. "We should dance."

I glanced at Rett uncomfortably. I didn't feel right leaving her by herself.

"What makes you think she was talking to you?" Rett asked.

I grinned and looked at Joss.

"I was talking to both of you. Let's go," Joss said.

We spent the evening dancing in different combinations. David and Katrina left around ten. Joss, Rett and I stayed and pounded down too many drinks. It drove me nuts that Joss seemed every bit as drawn to Rett as she was to me. We wandered back to our building around midnight. We agreed that Joss and Rett had too much to drink to drive. They both slept at my place, Joss and Rett in my bed, and me, unfortunately, despite my not-so-subtle suggestions, on the couch.

We were starting to make an interesting team.

32

Joss, Rett, and I took turns in the shower and got ready for work. I tried not to look like a pervert watching them stroll around without compunction in their underwear. These women were seriously beautiful, and far less self-conscious than I was. I mean, I was in decent shape, playing sports and working out regularly to accommodate my excessive lack of work. But still, I found them disturbingly attractive and felt a powerful sexual electricity in the room. Can an electrical current run in only one direction?

We went to Starbucks at 7:30 and sat in a booth sipping our morning caffeine. Rett was already going a mile a minute about what an arrogant prick Shaw is and Judge Williams is in his back pocket and we need to find a way to drive a wedge between them. Joss and I sat and watched and listened. Rett's passion was entertaining and comforting. My trepidation was paralyzing, and I was grateful to have her firepower on my side.

We went back to our building in time for Joss's 8 o'clock appointment. It was hard for me to fathom the endurance she had to see patients hour after hour. She said that it was just like running for her; she built stamina over time, and it was no big deal. And she had no choice but to work such a frantic schedule, "because every idle hour is a step closer to the poor house." We walked to the second floor and got to Joss's office. She gave Rett and me hugs, unlocked her door and went to work.

Rett and I went in our office and she jumped

right in. She drew a 30-day calendar on a yellow pad for the time we had to respond to Shaw's Motion. Then she began working backwards. She said she needed five days to write our brief. She needed two days after we took depositions to get the transcripts. We needed a week to take depositions. That meant we needed to get our deposition notices out immediately to ensure we could squeeze everything in.

The question, then, was who to depose? Obviously, we needed to depose Nick Stanton and Jerry Greyson. But who else? Rett wanted to depose Howard Morley, the head of HR, to see if other employees who were insubordinate had also been fired. If they weren't, that would support our claim that the real reason Liza was fired was for opposing Stanton's mistreatment of her. And Rett wanted to depose Callahan, since he fired Liza, to learn the reason he was told to fire her. I reminded Rett that Liza said that Bonnie had seen the emails that caused her to get so upset. But Rett said we should just call Bonnie and talk with her instead.

"But Shaw said if we want to talk to employees, we have to make arrangements with him since he represents the company."

"That's horseshit. It's a game defense lawyers play. They tell you that you can't talk to witnesses, and you idiot plaintiffs' lawyers believe them. The reality is, we can talk to everyone we want, as long as they're not represented by counsel. Why would Bonnie hire a lawyer? She has no need. Shaw can't tell us to stay away from witnesses."

"So we'll just call her?"

"Yup, we'll just call her. Call Liza and get Bonnie's number, and we'll call her at lunch."

"Are you sure? I don't want to get in trouble."

"Grow a pair, Ben! How do you think Shaw

would react if we announced that he needed our permission to talk to witnesses? He'd tell us to fuck off. So here's what you do. Call Bonnie. Tell her you represent Liza. Ask if she's represented by counsel. She'll tell you that she's not. Tell her that if she was privy to any privileged information, she shouldn't share it with you. And then talk to her. Find out everything you can."

"Me? You're not going to call her with me?"

"I've got enough on my plate. Just pick up the phone and call her."

"Shit. Ok. Can I meet with her?"

"If she's willing. Why?"

"I'm better with people face to face."

"If she'll meet you, have at it. If she's cooperative, and has valuable things to say, ask her if you can write up her statement in the form of an affidavit, and if she'll sign it. Then we can use it in our brief opposing Shaw's Motion."

Wow, I was going to do real lawyer stuff.

Rett prepared the deposition notices, since I had never done it, and emailed them to Shaw. She set the depositions for the following week in our building. There was a small conference room at the end of the hall for the second floor tenants, and I reserved it for the week. Monday would be the first depo, and it would be of the company's email custodian. That would allow us to learn how they stored emails and what was there for us to see. Tuesday would be the company's HR Chief. Rett set Callahan's depo for Wednesday, Greyson's for Thursday, and Stanton's for Friday.

Rett had never taken a deposition before, but had observed some and had been to a dozen training sessions. She had also written the scripts for partners who were taking depositions, and had read hundreds of transcripts. She couldn't wait for her chance to run the show.

I got Bonnie's cell number from Liza, and called Bonnie at lunchtime. She was not happy to hear from me. She told me she had not hired a lawyer, and that no one had shared privileged information with her. I asked her if I could take her out for a drink after work and talk about Liza. She said that she'd like to help Liza, but didn't think she should get involved. I suggested that we just chat and figure out what she's comfortable with, and if nothing else, we'll enjoy some good wine. She finally relented.

I met Bonnie at the Cedar Creek Grille, a classy spot a safe distance from RTG. I was a nervous wreck. She was waiting at a table in the back when I showed up. All of the arrogance I had seen when we met at RTG's headquarters was gone. She was nervous and fidgety.

I sat down. She didn't shake my hand. I noticed that she was sitting with her back to the rest of the restaurant. She was going out of her way to make sure she wasn't seen with me. Her legs were crossed, and her top leg was swinging back and forth a mile a minute like she was trying to put out a fire.

"Thanks for coming out, Bonnie, I really appreciate it. It means a lot to Liza, too."

Bonnie nodded. She was already polishing off a glass of red wine. I needed to find a way to break the ice with her. She was wearing a sleeveless summer dress, and despite being probably 40 years old, she was just ripped. There was no fat on her, and you could see the muscles in her shoulders and arms when she moved.

"You look like an athlete," I said. "Do you play sports?"

"Tennis, yoga, and golf."

Ok, I don't know much, but yoga and golf aren't sports. I thought it was best not to point that out. "Wow. I've played some tennis. Nothing serious. Have you been playing long?"

"Yeah, since I was a kid."

This was going to take some doing. "Well you look like you could play on the professional tour. I hope you don't mind me saying that." Flattery will get you everywhere.

"Thanks. I make plenty of use of the RTG exercise facility. Five days a week. I run three days a week, and lift weights the other two."

"Ok, now I feel like a wimp. That headquarters is quite the place."

"That's one way to put it."

"Liza said the same thing to me. That it looks like heaven there, but it comes with a heavy price."

"She would know, the poor woman."

"Are you ok if we talk about it for a few minutes?"

"Sure."

Bonnie was recovering her swagger. I ordered a beer and got Bonnie another glass of wine. I waited for the server to leave.

"Did Liza talk with you about what happened in Paris?"

"I know everything about what goes on there."

She was a real mother hen. It was hard to tell what was real and what was ego. "When did she talk with you?"

"About a month after the trip. She missed some time from work. I can't remember how much. But when she came back, something was really off with her. She's typically chatty and funny. That's how we passed the days. Not when the Chiefs were around, but most of the time it's just the Pool girls there. Liza and I kept each other laughing, making wisecracks about the Chiefs. But after she came back, she barely spoke at all. When she did, she was mad."

"Mad at the Chiefs?"

"Mad at everyone. And I kept asking her if everything was ok, you know? And she just kept snapping at me."

"Were you guys good friends?"

"Sure. We'd both been at RTG a long time. I'd been working with the Chiefs longer, and was an Executive Assistant, a higher position than hers. But we did this a lot," she said, lifting her glass and pointing to it. "Lots of drinks. Lots of talking about the Chiefs and their affairs."

"Affairs?"

Bonnie gave me a condescending grin. "These guys didn't get where they are because they're choir boys, Ben. They take what they want."

I nodded.

"Anyway, Liza was spending a lot of time away from her desk, and one afternoon I went into the bathroom after her. She was sitting in a private area crying, and I told her I wasn't leaving until she told me what was going on. She said she'd been struggling since she got back from Paris. She mumbled something about Nick."

"Did she say anything about Jerry Greyson?"

"No."

"What did she say?"

"Well, I knew all about her and Nick. Everyone did. I had been with Nick for a couple months before Liza started up with him, and as things dragged on with them, I encouraged her to dump the asshole. There's nothing healthy about being involved with Nick Stanton."

"What did Liza say about what happened in

Paris?"

"It was obvious that something happened. But she wouldn't talk about it. She was crying, and told me she wouldn't talk in the Crystal Palace. So we left work and went out. She said she was done with Nick forever, but she wouldn't say more."

"And that was it?"

"I wasn't going to pry. Nick's a scary guy, trust me. And Greyson is scum, a real pervert. I'm sure they gave her a bad time. But all Liza said was she's done with Nick, and I told her that was a good idea, the sooner the better."

"How did you guys leave it?"

"We drank a lot of wine and talked about other things."

"Did you ever talk about it again?"

"No. With time, Liza had more good days. More days where she seemed almost like her old self. But most days she just kept to herself. Something changed. The Chiefs didn't like it, because Liza was hostile. You know, these guys think of us as their toys, and they want us to have orgasms at the prospect of interacting with them. And Liza quit playing the part."

"Were you there when they fired her?"

"Yeah. But she was in Callahan's office, so I couldn't hear anything."

"Did anyone talk about why she was fired?"

"Well, Callahan came into the Pool the morning she was fired, and told us that they had to let her go because she refused to help with the 10-Q. I think we all knew that was their excuse to get rid of her."

"Why would they need an excuse?"

"Because everyone knew about Nick and Liza's relationship. Everyone knew that something ugly was going on. I mean, Nick has lots of women, you know?

But most of them are just amusements for him. Like I was." She polished off her wine. "But Liza was much more involved with him. That must have been threatening, somehow. Anyway, it was inevitable that Liza's days were numbered. I mean, how does she keep working there when she rejected the world's most egotistical man? And how does she keep working there when he's stewing about her, and he has to go home to a wife? I saw some of the emails. Boy, they were saying nasty things about Liza after Paris. It was shameful."

"Did any of the emails discuss what happened in Paris?"

"No, just juvenile, boys-will-be-boys bravado. Nothing specific."

"What did they brag about?"

"How well endowed they are." Bonnie leaned towards me and grinned. "Trust me, Nick and Jerry are not." She sat back. "They wrote about how Liza craves them, can't get enough of them. Juvenile, delusional shit."

I ordered another round of drinks and got Bonnie talking about her tennis and workout routine. She was getting more and more comfortable with me. She kept folding her arms across her waist and leaning across the table, giving me a lovely view of her healthy cleavage. She liked talking about herself, and I wasn't going to stop her.

Finally, as she was finishing her third glass of wine, I drew myself into the conversation. I told her that I loved to work out, too, and tried to make time whenever I could.

"You look like you find a lot of time for that," she said, leaning towards me. "A sexy lawyer. You don't see that very often."

I blushed. "You're right. If you see that

somewhere, let me know."

She laughed and put her hand on mine.

"Hey listen, Bonnie. I don't know how you'd feel about this, but Liza really needs some help. She needs to know that her friends are there for her. Would it be ok if I wrote up what you said about how Liza changed after Paris?"

Bonnie yanked her hand back and sat upright. "What do you mean, 'wrote up?'"

"Well, I know you want to stay out of this. But if I could just write down what you told me, you know, about Liza acting differently, and Nick and Jerry's emails, that would mean a ton to Liza and be a big help to her."

"You want an affidavit, is that what you mean?"

"Well, yes."

"Do you know what they would do to me if I gave you an affidavit? There's no fucking way. I'll lose my job."

"I guess I'm just trying to figure out how to keep you out of this. I mean, there's depositions coming up, and I was thinking you wouldn't want to be deposed. And maybe it would be easier if you just gave a written statement. It wouldn't have to say that you believed Liza or anything like that, just that she was not her usual self like you said and that it was obvious that something disturbing happened in Paris."

"No way."

"Well, would you be ok if we deposed you?"

"Don't do that to me. Don't put me in that position."

"I don't want to, Bonnie. I'm trying to figure out how to help Liza without putting you in a bad spot."

"Just leave me out of it."

"I don't know if I can. We have to let the Judge know what happened."

"Listen, Ben." Bonnie leaned towards me and spoke quietly. Her glare was all daggers. Somehow the view didn't have the same suggestive appeal. "I won't risk my job. So don't fuck with me, ok?"

"Ok." I sat back and put my hands up. "I understand. I don't want to put you in a tough spot. I get it."

Damn. I had hoped to come back to the office and drop an affidavit on Rett's desk. I had this image of just leaving it there as I sat down at my desk and nonchalantly picking up a magazine or something. And Rett jumping out of her chair and shouting, "Holy shit! I can't believe you got this! You're amazing!" And her running over and giving me a hug and telling Joss what an incredible lawyer I was. And the two of them taking me out for drinks and telling me I didn't need to spend the night on the couch this time.

Instead I was going back to the office with nothing. As usual.

33

When I got to the office Wednesday morning, Rett was busy working on interrogatories and document requests. She was anxious to get Stanton and Greyson's emails, and particularly the one that upset Liza right before she was fired. And Rett wanted to know if other women had filed complaints against Stanton or Greyson. That could be really helpful in validating Liza's story. Luckily, Rett had forms from her firm, so she didn't think it would take long to get the papers off to Shaw.

I shared with Rett what Bonnie told me, and her refusal to give us an affidavit. Rett said it was not surprising, and we would just depose her. She said that it would give Bonnie more protection at work, because it would appear that she was there against her will, and not volunteering to help us. She sent a notice to Shaw, adding Bonnie's name to the deposition schedule on Wednesday.

Rett wanted to work through lunch, so at noon I wandered down to Joss's office. She usually had a break between patients then. It bothered me that I hadn't spent any time alone with her since our standoff in my office on Friday. And I guess to be honest, it bothered me that she didn't seem to care.

Joss was dictating in her office when I poked my head in. She waved me in. She dictated in perfect sentences for a few minutes about her last patient, some guy named Chris who had "malignant narcissistic traits" and "pathological tendencies" related to his reputation. He was a lawyer, of course.

She finished, finally, and looked at me. "How's

it going, Ben?"

"Ok. I just felt like dropping by, if you have a few minutes free."

She looked at her watch. "I have an hour. Come on, want to go for a walk?"

It was a beautiful July day, about 80 with no humidity, and we wandered outside. There was chatter all around from people sitting at tables having lunch. We walked around the corner and wandered through the tree-lined streets.

I had known Joss for almost a month now, and she still took my breath away. She was so fit and graceful and athletic. But mainly it was those big deep, soulful brown eyes that mesmerized me. When she smiled, I couldn't believe how bright and alive her face was, how perfect and white her teeth were, how her face just lit up like all the good in the world was bursting out of her. And still, there was sadness in her eyes.

We walked without talking, and after a bit she slid her arm through mine and held my arm against her side. It was so comfortable, so easy. So arousing. As we walked, I could feel her ribs and the side of her breast against my arm.

And then I started to get annoyed. I mean, come on, what was this? What was she trying to convey? What about Westy?

She pulled my arm tighter against her. "Just enjoy this, Benny. It's a perfect day."

This woman was scary. She could read my thoughts. The sun was warm and comforting. I felt full when I was with Joss, like she was the missing piece to my puzzling pathetic self. She was right. I'd be crazy not to enjoy this. I relaxed and leaned into her.

We wandered toward a ball field behind

Roxboro Middle School. Joss sat down in the outfield grass. I stood next to her. She patted the grass.

"Sit with me, Benny."

I sat down across from Joss. She crisscrossed her legs. She pulled out a long blade of grass and played it with her slender fingers.

"Man, it feels good to be out of that office," she said. She leaned back on her hands and dropped her head back, letting the sun warm her face. She was wearing jeans and a V-neck shirt that slid up and revealed her muscular stomach.

She sat up and caught me staring at her remarkable body. She grinned at me. "What are you thinking about, Benny boy?"

I blushed. "It wouldn't be gentlemanly to say."

"Life is short, Ben. Too short to ignore what moves us."

She smiled at me. This sounded very much like an invitation. But of course, I was paralyzed, so worried about offending her.

"The sun is on us," she said. "The grass is soft and freshly cut, my favorite smell in the world. What could be better than this?"

"I could think of a few things."

"Yeah, like what?" she asked with a mischievous grin.

What the hell. "Well, like kissing you."

"You want to kiss me?"

"I do."

"So kiss me."

Hallelujah! I leaned towards her, slowly. She smiled. I leaned closer, and kissed those full lips, gently. Slowly. She put her hand on my shoulder and pulled me towards her. She held her mouth against mine and licked my upper lip lightly. Then my bottom lip. I put my hand behind her head against her silky hair. She rested her face against mine. I could feel her breath on my cheek. My ear. She stood and pulled me up. She stepped up to me and held me, resting her head against my chest. Then she looked up and kissed me softly, holding her lips lightly against mine. We held each other, our lips touching, breathing together. I closed my eyes and felt only those soft, full lips, felt Joss's chest rising and falling against me, felt Joss breathing with me and never in my life did I feel so connected. I wrapped my arms around her and held her tightly against me.

She took a deep breath and looked up at me. There was concern in her eyes.

She forced a smile and turned. "C'mon, Ben. I need to get back. I have a patient at one."

We walked back to the office in silence. She didn't put her arm through mine.

34

The depositions were upon us in no time. Rett got the document requests and interrogatories out to Shaw on Thursday. They had 30 days to respond, so we wouldn't have their responses in time for the depositions. But even with the short window the Judge had given us to respond to their Motion, we thought we would be ok if the depositions went well.

Rett and I spent Friday and the weekend prepping for the depositions. We went over our goals for each witness and Rett's questions to achieve those goals. By 4 o'clock on Sunday, Rett was feeling pretty good about the week ahead. Rett insisted that Liza be with us for every deposition. We made plans to have dinner with Liza at The Fairmount at 7 to talk about the week.

I hadn't seen Joss since we got back from our lunchtime stroll on Wednesday. I had no idea what to make of that woman. I stopped by her office a couple times Thursday and Friday, but even though her light was on, she didn't respond when I knocked. Maybe she had patients in there, but I didn't hear any. What I felt when I was with her made my head spin. Time disappeared. She made me laugh. Made me think. Made me lust. Everything was spontaneous when I was with Joss. In those moments when I let me guard down and she gave herself over to me, I felt vibrant. Riveted. But then she was withdrawn and I wondered if it had all been a mirage. Like waking from a dream and suddenly what was so full and real was haze and gone.

By Sunday afternoon, Rett's prep for the depos

was driving me crazy. She had put together a separately colored notebook for each person she was deposing. Each notebook was filled with tabs. The first tab was an overview of Rett's goals for the witness. There was a separate tab for each specific goal, and a page of questions for each goal to obtain the answers Rett needed to accomplish the goal. She was absurdly well organized. We really had nothing in common.

I decided to walk outside for a break while Rett kept crunching away. When I got near the Starbucks, Joss walked out, holding a cup of coffee. Yes! Damn, she looked good, in jeans and a white t-shirt that couldn't hide her remarkable body. Maybe another walk to the ball field? I'd love to continue where we left off. I started to hustle down the hill to catch her when she turned back towards the door. She held the door open, and Westy walked out. He said something, and Joss burst out laughing.

Shit! I stepped between two parked cars so they wouldn't see me. My god, Westy was massive. He was only a few inches taller than me, but he was shockingly thick and wide. Next to tiny Joss, he looked like another species altogether.

Joss said something and flashed Westy a big smile. She put her hand on his shoulder and he laughed and hugged her. They turned and started walking down the street, away from me. When they were half a block away, I stepped back onto the sidewalk and walked slowly behind them.

Joss kept laughing whenever Westy said something. She slipped her arm through his while they walked. I stopped and stood on the sidewalk and watched. I couldn't believe it. She looked so damn happy.

I slowly walked down the hill, about two

blocks behind them. I was crushed. I had felt so special when Joss slipped her arm through mine. Just her touch made me aroused. But more than that, when Joss leaned into me and whispered in that mesmerizing voice, I felt so connected to her, so special, like what was between us was unique in all the world, a bridge between us that vanquished the loneliness that had been at the center of my life for as long as I could remember.

I watched them laugh and touch each other. I stopped on the sidewalk. I was such a fucking fool. I was utterly, utterly alone, just like I'd always been. How could I have let myself think anything else? I didn't know that woman. Nothing had changed, not ever, not for one minute since my dad died. I was small and wanted by no one. She was happy as could be with Westy and I was utterly alone.

They turned a corner and were out of sight. Were they headed to the ball field at the middle school? Part of me wanted to follow and see. But why? He was probably going to do to her what she started and stopped with me. Why would she want me when she could have a guy like that? Any guy, really. I was such an idiot for thinking she would want me.

I wandered back up the street to our office. Rett didn't need my help. I had nothing to offer her either. Might as well let her wrap up and just crash in my apartment. I was exhausted.

I went in the office. Rett hadn't even noticed that I was gone. I sighed and collapsed on the couch. Rett was going through one of the notebooks with a highlighter. Time to get out of here.

"Hey, Rett?"

"Hang on, Ben. Let me get through this."

"I'm going to head up to my apartment."

"No, wait. Hang on a minute."

Ugh. There were about 20 nerf balls lying around the office. I pushed myself up from the couch and started shooting baskets. Rett was oblivious. This was ridiculous. She'd been through her notes at least 50 times. She couldn't possibly be getting anything new out of it.

"Rett?" I couldn't get her attention.

I started shooting from behind her chair. She kept working, trying to ignore me. I started dribbling on her desk. She didn't acknowledge me. So I started dribbling on her notes before launching shots.

"Oh, sorry," I said, bouncing the ball off her head a few times. She ignored me.

I came around the front of her desk, and shot a fade away, falling back onto her desk and knocking the pen out of her hand.

"Oh, sorry," I said.

Rett sat back and folded her arms across her chest. I got up and stood next to her chair and leaned into her, shooting as I fell across her chair.

"Oh, sorry," I said as I lay across her lap.

"You're such a fucking child." Rett jumped up and I slid off her lap and onto the floor. She grabbed a bunch of nerf balls and began shooting. She had a soft touch and a perfect release, the balls coming off her fingers with backspin, her wrist folding toward the hoop.

I got up and jumped at her and blocked her shot.

"Foul!" she yelled. "Flagrant foul!"

"That was clean."

"Bullshit!" she said. "Two free throws. No, three, that was a 3-pointer!"

Man, I needed a diversion. We began running around the office, scooping up balls and shooting jumpers, dunking, blocking each other's shots. I scooped up a ball in front of the couch and turned to shoot. Rett lowered her shoulder and dove into me, knocking me back onto the couch. She fell on top of me, laughing, but made no effort to get off. My god, she was firm and full in all the right places.

"Nice defense," I said.

"You should see me when I've stretched." She grinned at me. "Want to go stretch?"

Well, this was a pleasant surprise. I thought about Joss. Off with Westy. Not tethered to me in any way.

"Sure," I said. "My apartment?"

She grabbed my hand and pulled me off the couch. "Let's go."

We walked into the hall and down to the elevator. Rett was so damn hot, in that determined, efficient kind of way. But part of me felt uneasy. I loved Rett as a friend, and was thrilled to be working with her. I didn't want to jeopardize that. I really wasn't interested in her romantically. I knew she wasn't interested in me that way either. And absurd as it was, I felt unfaithful to Joss, despite her being off doing who knows what with Westy.

Those thoughts swirled somewhere in my consciousness as we rode the elevator up and I unlocked my apartment door. I thought about saying something, but it was obvious that Rett needed a break from the tension. I didn't want to disappoint her. And truth be told, I craved connection with someone.

Somehow I managed to push my trepidation aside when Rett started peeling off her clothes. She folded them carefully and laid them over a chair. She was lean and strong.

"Get those clothes off, Ben, I'm not here to model for you."

I stripped down. She turned and faced me with her hands on her hips.

"Nice!" she said, looking me up and down. I blushed.

She was looking enticing as well. "Is that the bedroom?" she asked, nodding towards a closed door.

"It is."

"Let's go."

She turned and walked into the bedroom. Quite the sight from behind. I followed her in and forgot my misgivings. Until we were done, anyway.

35

Rett and I lay in bed, but not for long. Rett's cell phone kept buzzing, and she was scrolling through messages. No cuddling here. A workout in the sack, and then move right along. It was really impersonal, but I kind of liked it. If suddenly she needed all sorts of gushy affection, I don't know what I would have done. It would have complicated our friendship, and the work situation, that's for sure. But she acted like this was nothing more than a coffee break. I really love coffee.

"What the fuck is this?" Rett said. She sat up in bed, staring at her phone. "That fucker. Goddamn it. I should have known. That son of a bitch."

She got out of bed and began pacing around the room. She still wasn't wearing any clothes, and she looked like a tiger ready to pounce, muscles rippling, jiggling in all the right places.

"Goddamn it!" she said.

I was going to ask her what happened, but I was enjoying the view too much. She glanced at me. "Get dressed. We have to get back to the office."

I climbed out of bed reluctantly. I was aroused from watching her.

"Hmmm," I said, grinning. "What's up?"

She looked at me and scowled. "Stick it in your pants, Ben. Shaw just sent us an email. He said that they're not available for depos until the end of September. That's more than two months. He's such a cocksucker. He's trying to make sure we have no evidence for our brief. Of course he waited until the last minute so we can't reach the Judge. What a prick."

She stormed into the living room and dressed while she ranted. I threw my clothes on. We took the elevator back to the office. Rett didn't stop talking. She sat at her desk and I plopped down on the couch. Men and women are so different. Rett was completely fired up, and I was doing all I could to stay awake.

I forced myself to focus. "Why don't we just tell him that we've scheduled the depositions and we're going forward?"

"Because he'll tell us that his clients won't be there. And then what do we do? We could show up, and put on the record with the court reporter that they failed to show, but that only helps if we have a judge who cares. We're fucked."

"So what do we do?"

"We call the Judge and demand a meeting immediately. We have to find a way to make this the Judge's problem, too."

Rett picked up the phone and called the Judge's law clerk. "Anthony? This is Loretta Anderson. I'm calling about the RTG matter, Case CV-16-325748. We have an urgent issue that needs to be addressed. Can you call me first thing Monday morning? My number is 216-291-7541."

She looked at her watch. In was nearly 7:00. "Ben, go meet Liza. I'll be there in a few minutes. I'm sending Shaw an email objecting and telling him we're scheduling a meeting with the Judge."

Rett was already pecking away at her computer, completely oblivious to me. I left to meet Liza.

Joss's office was dark when I walked by.

36

I walked to The Fairmount. I was ten minutes late, but there was no sign of Liza. I stopped at the bar and asked Hal for a brew.

Ten minutes later Rett came in. She was agitated. She sat next to me at the bar. I asked Hal to get her a beer as well.

"Where's Liza?"

"I haven't seen her," I said.

She looked at her watch. She pulled out her phone and called Liza. There was no answer.

"We'll give her ten more minutes," Rett said. "Then I'm out of here. How about some respect? We're working for free at this point."

Rett had no patience when she was mad. Or ever, really. I guess I didn't blame her, though. It was hard to believe that just a few minutes ago she was naked in my bed.

Liza finally walked in as we were finishing our beers. She had her sunglasses on. "Is this where we're meeting?" she asked.

"Well, nice to see you, too, Liza," Rett said. "You could show us the courtesy of being on time."

Liza didn't respond. She turned to Hal. "I'll have a bourbon. Blanton's. Neat."

No one talked while Hal prepared her drink. When Hal handed it to her, I said, "Would you like to sit, Liza?"

"We're going to talk here?"

"Come on," I said. "Let's go back to our booth."

Liza sighed like we were troubling her. I

thought Rett was going to strangle her, so I took Rett by the elbow and led her back to our booth. Liza followed.

Rett and I started to sit on the far side of the booth, with our back to the back of the restaurant.

"I'd like to sit there," Liza said.

"Sure," Rett said. "Whatever you want."

Liza sat down and slid in. Rett sat opposite her. I was going to sit next to Rett, but didn't want Liza to feel like it was us against her. I sat down next to Liza. She immediately tensed up.

"I need to be on the end," she said.

"Pardon me?"

"I need the aisle."

Rett shook her head, but there was something desperate in Liza. She had that supercilious tone, but it was tinged with anxiety. I felt sorry for her. I slid out.

"No problem," I said. "I like to be in the corner. It keeps me from falling over if I drink too much."

We switched places. Rett was still fuming, so I took the lead.

"So listen, Liza. We just wanted to sit with you for a few minutes and talk about where things stand. You know we scheduled depositions for this week, but now there's some question about whether they'll go forward."

Liza was staring at her Bourbon and didn't say anything.

"Shaw just sent an email saying they're not available this week. They're playing games. We're going to raise it with the Judge and try to force them to appear."

"Why do they get to call the shots?"

"They don't call the shots," Rett said. "We set these depositions and now they're scrambling."

"I had to show up for my deposition just because they announced it. Why don't they have to show up?"

"They're just being dicks," Rett said.

I could tell Rett was taking the wrong tack. "Listen, Liza. This happens in every case. Shaw knows we need to depose his people, so he's trying to make it difficult. We'll go to the Judge to force him to appear. We'll get what we need."

"I don't understand why I need to be there. I don't want to see Nick or Jerry."

"You won't have to say a word. They can't ask you anything. But think about it. When Bonnie's testifying, I think she's going to be scared. It's going to be hard for her to tell the truth. But if you're sitting there at the table, she'll be loyal to you because you're her friend. She's not going to lie with you there. And when Nick and Jerry and Howard Morley testify, you can tell us if they're lying. You can help us ask things we might not know to ask ourselves."

"Why don't you know what to ask?"

"It's not that simple," Rett said. "Suppose Morley testifies that there's never been anyone who failed to help on an SEC filing. Just as an example. And you know that once one of the secretaries wouldn't help, but she wasn't fired. Ben and I can't know as much as you. If you're there, you can tell us that so and so had an issue. And then we can ask follow up questions. It's a huge help."

Liza stared at her drink. "This is so hard."

Rett had no patience for this. I thought she was going to say something nasty to Liza, so I said that Rett had to get going. I looked at her and she glared at me, but got my message.

"Yeah, I've got to run. We're going to talk to the Judge tomorrow and we'll call you and let you know about the schedule."

Liza didn't respond. She just kept studying her drink. Rett got up and shot me a death stare, and then left. I could feel Liza relax next to me.

"Sorry about Rett," I said. "She's a bulldog, and just goes right at things. I know that can be a pain. But it's also what makes her so great."

"Great."

Liza sipped her drink.

I leaned toward her and whispered, "Are you ok, Liza?"

Liza turned and stared at me. She took off her sunglasses. Her eyes filled with tears. She looked back at her drink. "No," she whispered.

I wanted to put my arm around her, but worried how she would react. I figured I'd just let her take the lead.

I waited. Finally she said, "I keep hoping it'll get easier."

"Have you seen anyone to help you through this?"

She shook her head.

"Maybe talking with someone would help."

"I don't want to talk about it."

"I can understand that."

"Every time I start to have a good day, something stupid just swallows me up. I get panicky over stupid things, like not being able to slide out of a booth. And I'm leaning on this bourbon way too much. I keep turning to it for comfort. Not comfort. But to distract me. To numb me."

"That doesn't sound healthy."

She nodded.

"You know what I keep thinking, Liza? I mean, those bastards did something really horrible to you. But as bad as that was, there's something that seems even worse."

"What could be worse?"

"It's that in a way, they're still doing it to you. Because they keep taking your days from you. You know what I mean? Instead of waking up in the morning and making this day what you want it to be, you're hounded by what they did to you, and spend your day struggling to get through. You're still forfeiting time because of them."

Liza nodded. Tears were running down her face. I resisted the urge to wipe them away.

"So, Liza," I whispered. "We're trying to get them with this lawsuit. But let's do something to get you out of their grasp."

"What?"

"You should see a counselor. You've been waiting a long time to feel better, and it's not working. So let's do something different."

"The idea of talking about it is horrible."

"I know a guy. He's the best there is. He's worked with hundreds of women who've been through what you've been through. And I'll bet you every single woman that he helped started out dreading talking to him. But isn't it worth a shot? You're smart and beautiful and funny, and you've got your whole life ahead of you. That should be something you're thrilled about. Maybe if you give it a shot, when you wake up tomorrow, you'll feel better. Maybe just a little bit, but still better."

"Where is this guy?"

"His office is right down the hall from mine."

"Is he there now?"

I looked at my watch. It was Sunday night. "I'll check."

I pulled out my phone. I thought it was important to do this in front of Liza. I found David's number and called his home. He answered after three rings.

"Yes?"

"Hi David, this is Ben Billings. Listen, I'm sitting with my client. I was wondering if I might bring her over to talk."

David was a smart guy. He knew how to put two and two together.

"Ok. Are you in your office?"

"No, we're across the street."

"I can be in my office in 15 minutes. I'll see you there." Now that was a professional.

I looked at Liza. She was staring at her drink. I waited.

"He's there this late?"

"No, but he's coming in to see you. The guy has no personal life at all. All he does is work. But he's really good at what he does."

"I don't want to talk about what happened."

"He knows that."

"What will I have to do?"

"I don't really know. But he's there to help you. My guess is that he won't do anything at all unless it's to help you feel better."

Liza nodded. She took another swig. "Will you come with me?"

"Sure."

Her glass was empty. She sighed and slid out of the booth. I put a 20 on the table and slid out after her. I stood next to her. I didn't think I should lead the way – it felt too much like I was dragging her.

Liza reached down and took my hand. We walked across the street together.

37

I walked Liza to David's office. He was waiting in the hallway and I introduced them. Liza gave me a woe-is-me look as they went into his office. I felt guilty, like I was leaving a puppy at the kennel or something, but I trusted David and knew this could only be good for her. And who knows, if things worked out, maybe David could help us with the case.

I saw a cone of light in the hall coming from Joss's office. I walked by her door without looking in.

"Hey, Ben!" she called out. I stopped and stood in her doorway. She was in her running gear, on the floor stretching. "What are you doing here on a Sunday night? I'm just here to pick up my Dictaphone."

She looked up and smiled. She pointed her legs straight out and flush to the ground. She bent forward and rested her head on the ground between her legs. Holy cow.

"Show off," I said.

She looked up and patted the floor in front of her. I reluctantly sat down across from her and crisscrossed my legs. She kept stretching, laying her head on one knee, pulling her toes back, and then laying it on her other knee. She leaned back on her hands and gave me a huge grin. I refused to be swayed.

"How are you, Counselor?" she asked.

"Just muddling through, same as always."

"I like the way you muddle."

"Yeah, sure," I said.

"I know," Joss said. "You've never heard it

called 'muddling' before."

I was not going to play with her. I mean, I wanted to, because it was fun. But wanting to made me mad.

"What are you doing tonight, Joss?"

"Man, I had a great run. Ever have one of those when you don't even realize you're running? Your mind is occupied and you're just floating over the ground? And the air smells rich and full and the colors are vibrant and you feel your muscles working? You get into that rhythm and just feel like you can go forever. You ever feel that?"

"No."

She looked at me. "What's going on, Ben?"

"Ah, you don't want to know." There was no way I was going to tell her that I couldn't stand seeing her as happy with another guy as she was with me. Couldn't stand that she could replace me with another and never miss a beat, that I was someone to pass time with and nothing more. That she scared the hell out of me, like I was stepping over a well blindfolded because she was the only person I had ever met who seemed infinite to me, such a disorienting mix of intelligence and insight and warmth that I could fall in and never find my way out.

Joss reached forward and held my hands. She pulled me towards her. I thought she was just stretching, but she kept leaning in and whispered in my ear, "You're wonderful, Ben." She put her hand on my cheek and held my face against hers. I closed my eyes and savored her earthy smell. She turned my face towards her and kissed me softly, just holding her lips against mine. I pulled away.

"What's the matter, Ben?"

"I don't know what you want from me. With me."

"What do you mean?"

"I'm tired of the games, Joss. You make me feel like I'm the most special person in the world. And I know that's not true."

"Tell me what you want, Ben."

"Come spend the night with me."

"That's it? Then you'll be happy?"

"It's a start. I don't know."

"You want to cook dinner together, right? You want to drink some wine with me, and curl up in bed together and wrap ourselves around each other and sleep through the night, safe and warm?"

Now I was mad. "So what if I do? What's wrong with that? That's not ridiculous, is it?"

"I'm a realist, Ben."

"What do you want, Joss?"

I could tell that my anger made her uncomfortable. But I wasn't going to let go. "It's not so easy to answer, is it Joss?"

She looked at her watch and stood up.

"Sorry, Ben, but I have to go. I told Westy I'd meet him at nine."

38

I didn't go down to the office until 9:30 on Monday. Rett had been there since 7, but I was having trouble facing the stressful week. And Joss's humiliating rejection didn't help.

It wasn't just the coming confrontation with Shaw that worried me, or the mocking looks from him and his cronies. It was the fear that I would let Liza down. The more time I spent with her, the more I felt responsible for her. I had asked her to trust me, and if we got tossed by Judge Williams, I'd be just another guy who failed her. I couldn't live with that.

"It's about time," Rett said as I walked into the office. "Where's your damn suit?"

Shit. I completely forgot. "Did we get a time with the Judge?"

"No, the fucker won't call me back. We're in limbo. But if he doesn't call by 11, we're going to go see him."

Rett was wearing a tight black dress with a healthy scoop neck. Standing above her, I had a lovely view of her ample cleavage.

"I know, I know," Rett said, looking at me. "I'm shameless. But this dress is our ticket to see Williams."

"You're kidding," I said.

"Hey, facts, fairness, the rules of procedure, and legal precedent don't matter with him. He's not going to call us back, so we're going to head over there. He'll see this ridiculous outfit, and then he'll listen to me. And hopefully do the right thing."

"I'm shocked! The ultimate feminist resorting

to showing cleavage to win the day? Isn't that two very full and round steps back for the women's movement?"

"Oh fuck off. I'm here to win. And I'm going to be the consummate professional. We're in the right and Shaw is fucking with us. My job is to get Williams to focus on what's going on and do the right thing. And that's what I'm going to do. Now go upstairs and put on a fucking suit."

"Well, he's going to focus on something, that's for sure." I chuckled and went upstairs and changed. When I came down, Rett was pacing in the office. It was 10 o'clock.

"Let's go see the Judge now," she said. "I'm not waiting any longer."

"Can we really do this? I mean, we're not allowed to have a conversation with him without including Shaw."

"It'll be fine. Let's go."

We drove to the courthouse. Once again I had to go through the security line with the general public and all the criminal defendants. When I finally got through, we went up to Williams' chambers. Rett walked up to Anthony.

"Hi, Anthony. We need a conference with the Judge on the RTG matter right away."

Anthony looked confused. "You're not scheduled for today. The Judge doesn't see anyone on Mondays."

"I know. I left you a message. We've got an urgent scheduling issue and need the Judge."

"There's no way the Judge is going to see you. Especially on a scheduling issue. But I can let him know you were here."

"Anthony. Please, this is urgent," Rett said.

Anthony just grinned.

"He's never going to see us, is he?" I asked.

Anthony sat back. "Very doubtful."

Just then the Judge walked out of his office in the middle of a big yawn. He was wearing a golf shirt and those plaid pants.

"Good morning, Judge," Rett said.

Anthony jumped up. "They just walked in, your Honor. Nothing's scheduled."

The Judge scowled and looked at Rett. Then he smiled at her. It was the first time I'd seen him smile.

"I'm so sorry to bother you, your Honor," Rett said. "I'm Loretta Anderson. I know we had nothing scheduled, but I was hoping I could spend a few minutes with you."

The Judge grinned at her lasciviously. Oh brother.

"Sure," the Judge said. "I've got a few minutes. C'mon in." He turned and walked back to his office.

I stood and waited. Rett walked behind him. She looked over her shoulder at me and waved frantically. I followed her into his office. The Judge started to shut the door behind Rett and was startled to see me.

"Good to see you again, Judge," I said.

He scowled and didn't say anything. Rett stood waiting, and I stood next to her.

He looked at Rett and back at me. He mumbled something that I couldn't make out and sat behind his desk. Rett sat in a chair across his desk, and I sat next to her.

"I can't tell you how much I appreciate you seeing us, Judge," Rett said in a sweet voice I had never heard. "There's something I need to share with you, and I hope you can help me."

The Judge stared at her, so she went on.

"We're representing the plaintiff in the RTG

case. I know you have a massive caseload, so you probably don't remember us." She pulled a copy of our deposition notice out of her briefcase and stood and laid it on the desk in front of him. Williams' eyes went right to her cleavage.

"I should mention, your Honor. I sent a message to opposing counsel that we were going to try to talk to you. He didn't give me the courtesy of a response. Do you want me to reach out to him?"

Williams responded to Rett's breasts: "Why don't you tell me what's going on, and then we'll decide."

"Sure, Your Honor. As you know, the defendants filed a motion to dismiss, before they've even filed an answer to our complaint. So we have to respond to it. And of course pursuant to Rules 12 and 56 we have a right to take depositions before we respond. So we scheduled depositions for this week just to be sure we wouldn't have to bother you with asking for more time."

He nodded at Rett's hips.

"The depositions were supposed to start this morning, but RTG's lawyer waited until last night, if you can believe that. Sunday night? He waited until last night to send me an email saying they wouldn't attend this morning. And he refused to give me any substitute dates. It's completely improper and an obvious attempt to hamper our ability to respond to their motion."

"So what do you want from me?" Williams asked.

Rett continued to stand in front of Williams' desk. "I guess if you could just order the depositions to go forward as scheduled, that would be wonderful."

Williams kept looking at Rett's chest. "That's fine, if that's all you want." Williams glanced at me and turned back to Rett. "Who's lead on this case."

"I am, Your Honor," Rett said.

"Good," Williams replied. "How long have you been a lawyer?"

"This is my second year."

"How old are you?"

"I'm 27," she said.

The Judge stroked his chin. "Well, you should do well, Ms.... What was it?"

"Thank you, Judge. Loretta Anderson. I typed up an order here, if you'd like to sign it. I thought it might save you some trouble."

Rett turned and reached into her briefcase for the order. She turned back to the Judge and put the order on his desk.

"Who's the lawyer on the other side?" he asked.

"Alexander Shaw," Rett said.

Williams sighed. "Well, I'd rather not sign anything. Just tell Shaw that I want the depositions to go forward."

Rett waited until he looked her in the eye. It took uncomfortably long. "I'm afraid that won't work with him," she said.

The Judge looked at Rett. "Ok." He pressed a button on his phone and Anthony answered.

"Get in here," the Judge barked.

Anthony walked up to the desk.

"We're going to issue this order," the Judge said.

Anthony read it. "Uh, I'm sorry, Judge. But should we do this without defense counsel?"

"We've covered that issue," Rett said in her sweet voice. "Judge Williams has handled it."

The Judge glanced at me and then focused back on Rett. "I'll tell you what. How many depositions have you scheduled?"

"Seven, Your Honor."

The Judge wrote "3 Depos" on the order. He signed it and handed it to Anthony without taking his eyes off of Rett. "File a short motion when you get back to your office. Just one page. Ask for seven depositions. When Anthony gets it, he'll release my order. I'll give you three depositions. Then Shaw can't complain."

Rett started to object, but thought better of it. "Thank you, Judge." She reached out and shook Williams' hand. "I can't tell you how much I appreciate this."

He shook her hand and watched her. "Ok. Well, I guess that's it, huh?" He kept holding her hand.

Rett let go of his hand. "Yes, I think so."

She packed up her briefcase and turned back to the judge. "Thank you so much, Your Honor. I really look forward to working with you."

We left his office. Rett strode to the elevator and pressed the button.

"Hang on," I said. "I need to stop in the bathroom and puke."

"I was completely professional. If he's a pervert, that's his problem, not mine."

"Uh huh," I said.

"Whatever works, Ben. Whatever works."

39

Rett and I went back to the office at noon. We climbed up the steps to the second floor and took the right turn down the hall to our office. The hall was dark and Rett was laughing about how angry Shaw was going to be when he got the Judge's order. Suddenly Joss flung open her door and stepped into the hall, the overhead light from her office shining on her, a huge grin on her face, high kicking her right leg again and again like a can-can dancer.

"Right this way, Counselors!" she said. She was wearing white shorts and a blue tank top, about to leave for a run. She kept kicking and grinning. "There are dragons to slay, widows to comfort, orphans to save, and damsels in distress waiting for their lawyers in shining armor!"

She finally stopped kicking and stood there grinning at us. She held up her right hand as we walked by. "High five, Benny boy! Go get 'em, Loretta! Woo woo!"

Rett gave her a high five. I didn't want to, but I did the same as I walked by.

"You're so funny, Joss," Rett said, grinning.

Yeah, so funny. Ha ha ha.

We walked to our office. Despite being annoyed, I was kind of hoping she would follow. I unlocked our door and looked back. She was gone.

I went into our office and sat at my desk, the image of that bundle of energy high kicking through my mind again and again.

Rett drafted our Motion for the depositions and filed it electronically, and emailed it to Anthony and

Judge Williams, with a copy to Shaw. An hour later, Anthony emailed the order granting our Motion, but limiting us to three depositions. Rett had put in the Order that the depositions would go forward "this week," so Rett emailed Shaw and told him that we would depose Bonnie on Wednesday, Greyson on Thursday, and Stanton on Friday. The other depositions were less important, and we'd depose them some other time if we could keep the case going.

Not surprisingly, Shaw was incensed. He called our office phone, and we let it go to voicemail. We listened to him ranting that we better not have had "ex parte" communications – conversations with the Judge without him – and that he was going to get to the bottom of this. Rett and I sat there grinning at each other, knowing we had won this small battle.

We spent Tuesday reviewing Rett's deposition questions. She asked me to leave her alone the last hour so she could make sure she wasn't missing anything. She sat at her desk in a short summer dress looking enticing, oblivious to me. I scrolled around on my computer and shot nerf hoops. As usual, I felt superfluous. Probably because I was.

Rett slammed her notebook closed at 6 o'clock. We were finally facing depositions starting tomorrow. I was a nervous wreck. Rett didn't get nervous. She got more fired up.

"Hey, Ben," she said. "I'm as prepared as I'll ever be. I'm never going to sleep tonight unless I burn off this energy. I could go to the gym and work out, but it would be more fun to work it off with you. Want some company tonight?"

As nice as that sounded, rather than fretting all night about the depositions, the truth was, I was leery. Even though Rett wanted to be with me, it was not really me that she wanted. Rett needed me to distract her from something else, and I was tired of being a steppingstone. I was good in that role, but at the end of the day, where did it leave me? Just someone who'd been walked on. And I couldn't shake that image of Joss high kicking in the hallway, her face full of life. That soft, tender kiss in her office. I know I'm a complete fool, but despite Joss casting me aside for Westy, jumping in the sack with Rett still felt disloyal somehow.

Rett stood there with her hands on her sexy hips, looking at me with her head tilted to the side.

"So, Rett, I gotta tell you. That sounds like maybe the best way ever to prepare for depositions. But, um, I'm just wondering if it would be a mistake."

"It depends where you put it."

"Ha. No, I mean, I'm really flattered that you want to be with me, but I'm just wondering if, you know, it's really smart to spend the night together just to avoid the stress."

Rett stared at me. Then she sat in the couch and crossed her legs and grinned.

"You're an idiot," she said.

"I know that."

"It's only sex. I know you too well to get involved with you. You don't need to worry."

"I'm not worried. Ok, I am. I don't know, Rett. It's just, I'm everybody's point guard. You're doing these depos, and all I can do is be your cheerleader. Liza is going through who knows what, and all I can do is get you and David involved. I'm greasing everyone's skids to go somewhere else."

"I like how you grease my skids."

"You've got nice skids."

I sat next to Rett.

"You really are stupid, Ben."

"Thanks."

"No, you're missing it, Ben. You and I have a bond. We have from day one, right? We'll be friends for life. It doesn't matter if we have sex or not. Or never see each other. When we're 75 and gimpy, it'll be great every time I get to talk to you. How can you not know that? You're smart and loveable, and you don't see it."

I looked at a picture on the wall across from us. A railroad cut through a clearing, narrowing in the distance before disappearing in the autumn fog. I imagined Rett and Joss, David and Katrina, walking down those tracks, chatting and laughing. I was just the guy who hung the picture.

I leaned into Rett. "Sorry for being selfish."

She laughed. "You have no clue how fucked up you are. You think not having sex with me is selfish? Don't worry about it. It's no big deal. I'll manage just fine on my own. I've got lots of practice."

She stood in front of me and pulled her dress at her hips to straighten it.

"You're not mad at me?" I asked.

"No! Your judgment is for shit, but it wasn't a marriage proposal. Just a fun way to pass the night."

I hated to disappoint her. And we were partners. It was my job to help her any way I could.

"Is it too late to change my mind?" I asked.

She laughed and took my hand and pulled me up. I flicked off the light and pulled the door shut as we went out.

Joss's light beckoned behind her closed door. We walked by her office, Rett leading me by the hand, and I looked down as we went by the door. Ridiculous as it was, I hoped Joss didn't see us.

40

Rett and I went to the office at eight on Wednesday. It had been a rousing evening. Repeatedly. When we finished, Rett was out like a light and slept until morning. I was up all night.

Bonnie's deposition was set to start at nine. I was a bundle of nerves. I kept wishing there was a way to jump forward. Just to the weekend, when we'd be done with these miserable depositions. Time is such a fiend, so scornfully obstinate with no regard for me.

I went down to the conference room and filled the water pitchers and made sure there were glasses for everyone. I remembered that Shaw had coffee when Liza was deposed, so I ran down to Starbucks and got one of those big box containers. I stuffed my pockets with sweetener and cream and napkins. If I worked at it, I could create the impression of a professional operation.

Liza showed up at 8:45. She had that stony look, with deep circles under her eyes. Her sunglasses were on top of her head.

"Are you ready for this?" I asked.

"I'll get through it." She slid the sunglasses on.

Rett gave her a yellow pad and a pen. "Come on," she said, "let's go down to the conference room." Rett went first, and Liza followed. I walked behind them.

As we walked down the hall, Joss came up the steps and walked towards us. "Hi, guys! Good luck today!"

She was so damn cheerful. She walked towards

us and passed Rett and Liza. She winked at me after passing them, and reached back and whacked me on the butt as she went by. Not funny at all.

We went into the conference room and Rett took charge. "Come over here." She wanted to face the door. "Liza, the court reporter will sit here, at the head of the table. I'll sit next to her. Ben will sit next to me. You sit next to Ben. Pay attention. If you think of anything I should know, anything at all, I want you to write me a note and give it to Ben. He'll pass it on to me if he thinks he should. Don't be offended if I don't respond. I have to use my judgment about what to ask and when. But keep passing notes – it can only help."

"Where will the others be sitting?"

Rett walked around to the other side of the table and stood at the seat opposite hers. "Bonnie will be here. Shaw will be next to her. The company is allowed to have a representative here. That could be Morley, Callahan, or anyone they pick. On top of that, since Stanton and Greyson are defendants, they're entitled to be here as well. And Shaw can bring as many lawyers as he wants who are working on the case."

Liza got that frozen look on her face. "Don't forget, Liza," I said, "you don't have to talk to them. If they ask you anything or say anything, just ignore them. You're not on the hot seat and won't be again. Today should be easy. Bonnie will repeat what she told me, and then we'll be done. That will be a huge help, because it will obliterate their claim that there was no sign of wrongdoing until they fired you."

Liza didn't respond.

The court reporter came in and set up her gear. Liza sat in her chair, staring straight ahead. I looked at my watch. It was a few minutes before nine. My heart was pounding. I couldn't wait to get through this.

Finally, at 9:15, Shaw and the others arrived. Fifteen minutes late, without an apology. Shaw walked into the room wearing an expensive gray Italian suit with a thin black tie. Bonnie was behind him. She had her haughty work face on. She didn't acknowledge me, and wouldn't look at Liza. Shaw patted the seat next to the court reporter, and Bonnie sat down. Callahan came in a few minutes later. He didn't acknowledge us. Regardless, I walked up to him and said hello and put out my hand. He shook it reluctantly. I introduced him to Rett. He nodded at her. She nodded back. Callahan refused to look at Liza.

"In what capacity is Mr. Callahan here?" Rett asked.

"He's the company's attorney," Shaw said.

"Is he the company's representative?"

"No, we haven't decided on that yet."

"He's also a witness," Rett said. "I'd like him to step out during Ms. Flannery's testimony. Separation of witnesses."

We had a right to keep witnesses from listening to each other's testimony so it wouldn't influence what they had to say. But Rett was wrong here. There was an exception for the company's lawyers. She knew the rules inside and out, so she had to be testing to see if she could get away with it.

Shaw just snorted. He sat down next to Bonnie, and Callahan sat next to him.

"No one else coming?" Rett asked.

"No. They have more important things to do," Shaw said. Nice.

Rett asked the court reporter to swear in the witness. Rett then went through a litany of background questions, ensuring that Bonnie knew she was testifying under oath, that there was nothing preventing her from answering Rett's questions honestly, where she lived. It worried me that Bonnie still hadn't looked at Liza.

Rett opened her notebook to the first tab. She had my notes from my meeting with Bonnie, with key points highlighted in yellow. Rett asked Bonnie to describe her work and education history before coming to RTG. She had gone to high school, and then was hired by RTG. Same as Liza. She'd worked there the last 22 years. The CEO before Stanton hired her when he was the head of one of the company's subsidiaries. He moved her to the Pool when he was promoted to Chief Operating Officer, and kept her on board when he became CEO. When he retired, Stanton was named CEO, and Stanton kept Bonnie in the Pool.

I couldn't help but wonder why Bonnie and Liza got their jobs. Their bosses were hot shots at one of the world's biggest companies, and they hired 18-year-old girls straight out of high school? What were these young women expected to do to stay in management's good graces all those years?

"How long have you known Liza?" Rett asked.

"Since she got promoted to the executive Pool," Bonnie said. "That was about ten years ago or so."

"Would you consider her a friend?"

"A friend? Oh, I don't know. We worked together every day. We talked about work. We went out for drinks like co-workers sometimes do. So I guess you could call her a friend."

"Have you talked to her since she was fired?"

"No."

"You mentioned that you and Liza worked in the Pool. Were your work stations near each other?"

"Yes. We had desks. Not work stations."

"Ok. Could you two talk to each other from your desks?"

"Yes. They were five feet apart."

"Ok. Did you talk to Liza at work when she came back from her trip to Paris?

"Objection!" Shaw barked. "Foundation."

Rett gave Shaw a dirty look.

"Are you aware that Liza took a trip for work to Paris in last year?"

"Yes."

"Were you both still employees of RTG at the time?"

"Yes."

"And you both sat near each other at work at that time?"

"Yes."

Rett looked at Stanton and scowled. She turned back to Bonnie.

"Did Liza talk to you after she came back from her trip to Paris?

"Objection!" Shaw said. "Ambiguous."

Rett looked at Shaw and went back to her questions.

"You understand that Liza traveled to Paris last year for work, correct?"

"Objection! Asked and answered."

"Ms. Flannery, you understand that, correct?"

"Yes."

"After Liza returned from that trip, did she have a conversation with you about her trip?"

Bonnie hesitated. Then she looked at Rett and said, "Liza told me it was a nice trip. She said she loves Paris, that it's her favorite city in the world."

I couldn't believe she was lying. Rett picked up my notes and read them.

"What else did Liza say about her trip to Paris?"

Rett asked.

"I don't remember."

"You don't remember if she talked to you about the trip?"

"I don't remember."

"Are you saying that you don't remember if you talked to Liza about the trip, or that you talked to Liza about the trip, but you don't remember what else she said to you?"

Bonnie squirmed in her seat. "I'm saying I don't remember anything else about Liza's trip."

Liza folded her arms across her chest. She glared at Bonnie. Bonnie kept her focus on Rett.

"After Liza returned from that trip, was her demeanor different in any way?"

"Objection. Foundation." Shaw said.

Rett glared at Shaw. "Mr. Shaw, I would ask you to stop interfering with my deposition."

"If you would ask a proper question, dear, I would gladly keep quiet."

Rett jumped up. "Listen to me, Shaw! You have an ethical obligation to behave professionally. Don't you dare call me 'dear' again. My name is Ms. Anderson and I expect you to show me the courtesy of using it."

"OK, Ms. Anderson," Shaw said, smiling. "I'll be sure to use your formal name as we go forward."

Rett sat back down. Shaw was ruffling Rett's feathers.

Rett leaned over to me. "Where was I?" she whispered.

"You asked about a change in Liza's demeanor after the trip. She never answered the question."

"Did you notice a change in Liza's demeanor after the trip, Ms. Flannery?" Rett asked.

"Objection, Ms. Anderson," Shaw said

sarcastically. "Foundation."

Rett dropped her pen and folded her arms. I thought she was going to dive across the table and strangle Shaw. Callahan was grinning like a third grade fool.

"Fine," Rett said. "Ms. Flannery, you worked within five feet of Liza for eight years at RTG, correct?"

"Yes."

"And during that time, you talked to her, correct?"

"Yes."

"And during that time, you had occasion to observe her at work, correct?"

"Yes."

"And during that time, you had an opportunity to observe her usual demeanor at work, correct."

"I guess so."

"After Liza came back from her trip to Paris, did you notice a change in her demeanor??

Bonnie looked at Shaw for a second. Then she said, "No."

"No? You didn't see the change in her demeanor?"

"Objection!" Shaw said.

"Please answer the question, Ms. Flannery," Rett said.

"I didn't see any change in her demeanor. She was the same as she always was."

Liza stood and glared at Bonnie. Bonnie refused to look at her.

"Ms. Anderson," Shaw said. "Kindly control your client. Let the record reflect that Ms. Allen is standing and threatening the witness. Sit down right now, Liza!"

Liza glared at Shaw and then stormed out of the

room. She slammed the door behind her.

Rett jumped to her feet and leaned across the table. "Don't you dare talk to my client!"

I stood up. "Ok, ok. How about we take a little break here? Let's start again in 15 minutes."

I took Rett by the elbow and walked her out of the room. Liza was standing down the hall by our office door. We walked over and I unlocked the door. We went in. Liza stood by the window and Rett started pacing.

Liza spun and glared at us. "You said he couldn't talk to me!"

"Oh, chill out," Rett said.

Liza turned her back to Rett and stared out the window. This was going well.

I walked up to Liza. "You ok?"

"I can't believe she's lying."

"Why is she lying?" I asked.

"She's scared for her job. I thought our friendship meant something to her."

"We'll figure it out."

I walked to Rett. "You ok?"

"I'm so fucking pissed at Shaw. What a fucker."

I sighed. "So, Rett? We have to figure out where to go from here. Bonnie's going to deny everything she told me."

"Yeah, no more kid gloves. I was going to try to protect her. That changes right now. If she's going to try to screw us, then she's going to pay a price."

"Liza," Rett said, "do you have any problem if I lay it on the line with Bonnie? Let them know she met with Ben? Even if it puts her job in jeopardy?"

"She's no friend of mine, apparently. Do what you have to."

Rett stood up and clapped her hands. "Ok, let's

go, I'm going to nail that bitch."

We walked back down the hall. Joss's light was on but her door was closed.

We sat in the conference room. Rett turned to the court reporter. "Back on the record."

The court reporter nodded.

"Ms. Flannery, you understand you're still under oath?"

"Yes."

"This is my partner and co-counsel, Ben Billings, sitting next to me. I understand that you've met him before?"

Bonnie looked uncomfortable.

"Yes."

"When did you meet him?"

"I don't know. A couple of months ago, about a week after Liza was fired."

"And you met with him at the Cedar Creek Grille more recently?"

"No."

"No?"

"No. I met him at company headquarters when he came to see Mr. Callahan."

"You talked to him at headquarters?"

"Yes. He had a meeting with Mr. Callahan, and when he arrived I brought him to Mr. Callahan's office."

"But you met with him another time, right?"

"No."

"You've never talked with him other than when he came to visit Callahan?"

"Well, he called me. He said he wanted to get together. But I refused."

"In fact, you met him just last week at the Cedar Creek Grille and had drinks with him, correct?"

"That's a lie!" Bonnie said angrily.

"You talked to Ben about playing tennis, right?"

"No."

"Do you recall telling him that after Liza's trip to Paris, she was frequently crying in the bathroom at work?"

"No, that never happened."

"If witnesses testified that they saw you at the Cedar Creek Grille with Ben last week, would they be lying?"

"Objection," Shaw said. "Speculative."

"Please answer my question," Rett said.

"Yes, they'd be lying."

"What's your understanding of the reason that Liza was fired?"

"She refused to work on the 10-Q. She left us in a bind and Mr. Stanton was furious," Bonnie said.

"You understand that Liza complained the day before she was fired about the way she was being treated by Nick Stanton?"

"No."

"In fact, you saw emails between Nick Stanton and Jerry Greyson in which they said horrible things about Liza?

"That's not true."

"What's your understanding?"

"I don't know anything about emails. I know that Liza was unhappy because she wanted to be with Nick. You know, romantically. But he put a stop to it. And she was always trying to figure out a way to be with him. She was constantly texting him and pestering him. I warned her that she needed to stop, but she just wouldn't."

Rett glanced at Liza and then back at her notes. "In fact, what actually happened is that Liza called it off with Stanton, right? She ended the relationship."

"That's not my understanding."

"All these texts that you say Liza was sending to Stanton. When was that?"

"Right up until the time she was fired. Like ten a day for months. Liza was furious with Nick because he wouldn't see her anymore, and Liza couldn't handle it. She kept saying that she couldn't believe he wouldn't talk to her. He tried to avoid giving her work, just to minimize his interaction with her. But he had no choice with the 10-Q filing, and she flipped out."

"How do you know that Liza was texting Stanton all that time?"

"Because I watched her, and she told me she was texting him. And Nick showed me some of the texts. He asked me if I knew how to get her to stop. It was sad, really."

"Objection!" Rett yelled. She jumped up. "I need to put on the record that we've requested all relevant documents, emails, and texts, and the defendants haven't produced any. Not one. The witness is now testifying about alleged documents that we haven't had a chance to review."

"Well, for the record, Ms. Anderson," Shaw said, emphasizing her name, "your document request was served just last week. Our responses are not due for another 3 weeks. And the only reason that Ms. Flannery testified about these texts is that you asked about them."

Rett was incensed. "Off the record!" She got up and stormed out of the room.

I leaned over to Liza and whispered, "C'mon, let's go."

We walked into the hallway. Rett was pacing back and forth. "Let's go to the office," I said.

We went to our office. Rett was furious. "Liza, were you texting Nick?"

Liza didn't respond.

"Liza, there's no time for bullshit here. This is important. If Bonnie is making up these texts, we'll prove it. But I find it hard to believe Shaw would let her talk about these texts unless he's seen them."

Liza sat on the couch. She stared at the floor.

"Yeah, I texted him. I couldn't believe what they did to me. I still can't believe it. He left me alone in a hotel room in Paris, naked and bleeding on the floor. My life was falling apart. I reached out to him, I don't know why. But I needed to understand what happened. I needed to know it really wasn't that bad."

"How many texts did you send him?" Rett asked.

"I don't know. A lot. He wouldn't respond to me. He wouldn't talk to me. We went out for eight years. And then after acting like I don't exist for nine months, he dumps work on me like I'm some lowly piece of shit and nothing happened between us. I lost it."

"Rett," I said, "slow down. This is great. Those texts are our proof about what happened."

"Do you have the texts?" Rett asked. "Can we see your phone?"

"It was my work phone. They took it when they fired me."

"Great, just great," Rett said. "In these texts, did you mention the rape?"

"No."

"What?" I asked. "Not one word? Did you talk about Paris?"

Liza looked at me fiercely. "Maybe you can't understand it, but I wanted to protect him. I was worried about him getting in trouble and losing his job. I know how important his job and reputation are to him. I was thinking that he could lose everything. I know that sounds crazy. But I needed his support. I didn't want to disrupt things. So I didn't say anything until he gave me that damn assignment. And that's when they fired me."

"Didn't you think this was important for us to know?" Rett asked. "Why would you keep this from us?"

"I don't know."

"Ok," Rett said. "I get it." She stood up. "Ben, we need to talk." She walked out of the office and left the door open.

I looked at Liza. "We'll be back in a minute." I walked out and shut the door behind me.

Rett was pacing in the hallway. "Do you know how much trouble we're in, Ben? She's been lying to us from the beginning. Can you believe this? She was texting Stanton for nine months? Her supposed rapist? And no mention of anything? They're going to prove that everything we've claimed is bullshit. We're going to get sanctioned. We're going to lose our law licenses. I can't believe she did this to us."

I didn't know what to say. Had Liza lied about everything?

"Listen, Rett. We haven't seen those texts."

"You heard Liza. She just told you she sent them. And not one word about rape? It's bullshit, Ben, and you know it. We're fucked."

"Let's not try to solve this now. We've got a deposition going on. What do you think we should do?"

"Every time I ask a question we're more and more fucked. We should just end the goddamn deposition and then figure out how to get out of this lawsuit."

I didn't like that, but I didn't know what else to do. "Ok."

Rett walked down the hall to the conference room. She had no interest in bringing Liza with us. I stepped into our office.

"Listen, Liza. We're going to end the deposition and figure out where to go from here. You can come with us if you want, but if you've had enough, you can just wait here for us."

Liza nodded and sat back on the couch. I pulled the door shut and walked down to the conference room.

Rett went back on the record and said she had no more questions. Shaw stood up and packed his briefcase. He, Bonnie, and Callahan walked out without a word. The court reporter packed her things, and I thanked her for her time.

Rett and I walked back down the hall to our office. "We've got to get to the bottom of this," Rett said. "This case is over. We have to figure out how to limit the damage."

We opened our door and walked in. Liza was gone.

41

For the first time since I met her five years ago, Rett had all the steam taken out of her. We had depositions scheduled the next two days with the Chief Financial Officer and the Chief Executive Officer of one of the biggest corporations in the world. And Rett had no interest in spending another minute on the case. I couldn't blame her.

It was 1 o'clock, and we walked over to Starbucks. We got our drinks and sat at a table in the back. The place was buzzing with college students who looked a whole lot happier than us.

Rett sipped her drink. "Where do we go from here, Ben?"

"You've lost faith in Liza?"

She snorted at me. "C'mon. These guys raped her? And then she's texting him over and over? And trying to protect her rapists? No, I don't believe her. If some guy raped me, I'd kill him. I sure as hell wouldn't be protecting him.

"But that's not the half of it. She keeps lying to us. How the hell can we represent her if she won't be straight with us? How can I conduct an effective deposition if I don't know what happened? Why are we spending our time on this case? We have to pay for the court reporter. It's costing us money. And all that's going to happen is we're going to lose, and Shaw's going to ask Judge Williams to sanction us. Why would we pursue this?"

"But Judge Williams is your buddy," I said, trying to humor Rett. "He'll do anything you want, as long as you're wearing the right dress."

Rett ignored me. "The task now is getting out of this case with the least amount of damage. Maybe we call Shaw and offer to drop the case if they won't make any claims against us. We could agree to a public statement that gives them the exoneration they want, and allows us to say that going forward is no longer in Liza's best interests."

"Do you know what that will do to Liza? She'll feel like we abandoned her like everyone else."

"So what? She's been lying to us and hasn't been doing anything to help us, has she? And come on, do you really think she was raped? He dumped her, and they fired her and it pissed her off."

"That just can't be. Remember Bonnie told me that Liza changed. Something must have happened in Paris."

"Yeah, well maybe Nick dumped Liza in Paris and she didn't like it. Maybe she thought Nick was going to leave his wife and he told Liza he wouldn't do it. Maybe that's how Liza works. You walk away from her, and she tries to hurt you. Regardless, we can't prove she was raped. How are we going to do that? She slept with this guy for a decade. And she's been texting him non-stop since he supposedly attacked her without mentioning it? It doesn't fly."

I looked at Rett and sighed. She was such an inferno. Liza crossed the line with her, and now Rett was hitting back. I couldn't blame Rett, but something wasn't right. I couldn't put my finger on it. I guess my mind just works more slowly than Rett's. Maybe I just wanted to believe Liza. I wanted to help Liza and I wanted her to appreciate me.

Rett finished her coffee, crumbled her cup in one hand and tossed it in the trashcan two tables away. "C'mon, Ben. We've got to get out of this case. Let's go call Shaw."

She got up and walked out of Starbucks. I followed her.

"Listen, Rett. How can we call Shaw and talk about resolving this unless Liza gives us permission? We have no authority."

"No, but we can find out what our options are and put them to Liza. We can tell her we're done representing her and get her out of the case if she wants to pursue it."

Rett was walking 100 miles an hour. I had to jog to keep up.

"Hang on. Just hang on," I said. "You're going too fast."

"I thought you were an athlete."

"No. I mean about Liza. Why don't we finish the depositions and then figure out where we stand?"

Rett stopped and turned and faced me. She folded her arms across her chest. I knew how competitive she was and this was torture for her.

"Listen," I said. "This isn't about Shaw getting the better of us. The facts are what they are, right? We'll dig in and get to the bottom of this and then do what makes the most sense."

"You're killing me, Ben. You're too nice a guy. This is a fist fight and we're losing."

"One more day, Rett. Take Greyson's depo tomorrow and then we'll see where we stand. I promise, if it goes poorly, I won't ask you to spend another minute on this."

"You just don't want to disappoint Liza even though she screwed us."

"You're right. But let's see where we stand tomorrow. If it's still looking like we're screwed, we'll get out."

"I'm going to hold you to that."

I knew she would.

42

I stopped by Joss's office later in the afternoon. I'm not sure why, since I was still mad at her. It wasn't that I expected her to be devoted to me or any of that. I couldn't say she was jerking me around, since she was being completely straight with me. It just sucked. Simple as that. I wanted to be with her and she wanted to be with someone else. Maybe I was being immature, but I didn't really care.

In any event, after Rett left Wednesday afternoon, I didn't know what to do about Liza. And Joss always seemed to know the right thing to do. Her door was open and her light was on, so I leaned in and knocked on the doorframe.

"Hey, Joss. Got a minute?"

"Counselor! Nice to see you. C'mon in."

I sat on the couch, and she sat in the chair next to it. She was wearing black yoga pants. I could see the muscles in her legs and just how firm and fit she was. She wore a loose-fitting Northwestern t-shirt, looking relaxed and enticing at the same time.

"How's the case going, Benny?"

"Ugh, don't ask. Not well."

She frowned. "Anything I can do to help?"

"I don't think so. As my granddad used to say, if it weren't for people, this would be a hellofa world."

"He sounds like a smart guy."

"Yeah, you would have liked him. Smart and kind and funny."

"He sounds like his grandson."

"I don't have a brother."

Joss laughed. She jumped up and grabbed a

plum out of her minifridge under her desk. Man, she filled out those yoga pants just right.

She took a bite of her plum. "Want a bite?"

"No thanks."

"Too bad. How 'bout the plum?"

She chuckled and licked the juice that trickled down her hand. I looked away.

"The case is getting to you, isn't it?"

"It is. I really want to help Liza. But I don't think it's possible."

"Why not?"

"Well, I'm not sure she's entitled to legal relief. And even if she is, the cards are so stacked against us, I think it's an impossible battle to win. And even if the battle isn't impossible, I don't think I'm the guy who can win the fight."

"Yeah, but other than that?"

"You're right," I said. "What am I worried about?"

"You're missing it, Ben."

"No, I'm not. Missing what?"

Joss grinned at me. We were sitting facing each other. I looked at that mischievous smile of hers and got irritated. I was tired of people telling me that I didn't understand what was going on. Especially when they were right.

She kept looking at me, and I didn't know what she was waiting for. I stood up. "Well, nice chatting with you. I've got to go."

I turned to walk out. Joss jumped up and scooted between the door and me.

"Whoa. Wait."

I stopped but wouldn't look at her. She stepped up to me and put her hand on my chest. I kept my arms at my side.

"If I needed a lawyer, there's no one I'd rather

have than you," she said.

"What are you doing tonight, Joss?"

She stepped back and looked at me. She folded her arms across her chest. "I've got plans."

"Westy?"

"Does it matter?"

"You know what? No. It doesn't. Not one bit. Have fun."

I stepped by her and walked out.

43

Rett took Greyson's deposition on Thursday. Callahan and Shaw were there again, and Stanton was not, which I thought was a mistake. Why wouldn't he want to hear Greyson's testimony? Then again, he probably knew exactly what Greyson was going to say. The only surprise was that Liza showed up. She wore her movie star sunglasses the entire time, and didn't speak to Rett or me.

Greyson was 60-years-old, about five-six and fat. His hair was curly and dyed black. He coughed throughout his testimony, and kept dabbing his hair around his collar with a handkerchief. I think he overdid it with the hair dye, and was trying to keep it from running onto his white dress shirt.

Despite his farcical appearance, Greyson was professional and precise. He denied that he or Stanton had any sexual involvement with Liza in Paris. He said that they were at the Board dinner and Liza had too much to drink. He said Liza was "all over Nick," and it was "an embarrassment." He said Liza was so drunk by the end of the evening that Nick felt compelled to call a cab to get her back to the hotel, even though it was just two short blocks away. Nick insisted that Greyson ride in the cab with them, because Nick didn't want to be alone with Liza.

Greyson testified that they had to help Liza into the hotel elevator. Greyson fished Liza's key out of her purse, and they walked her to her room. Greyson unlocked the door, and they helped her into the room and sat her on the couch by the entryway. The idea that they stayed or had any sexual contact with Liza was "preposterous." Greyson and Nick then left Liza's room and took the elevator up to their rooms for the night.

Near the end of Greyson's testimony, Liza passed a note to Rett. The note said that Greyson had an affair with Bonnie, and Bonnie ended it because Greyson was rough with her. Liza wrote that Greyson's wife heard about the affair, and divorced Greyson because of it.

Rett read the note and gave me a dirty look. I knew she was unhappy hearing this now for the first time. As in, it would have been nice to know this before Bonnie's deposition. She asked Greyson why he had gotten divorced. Shaw objected and instructed Greyson not to answer on the grounds that it was "harassing." Rett then asked if Greyson had ever been accused of being physically abusive towards a woman. Shaw again objected, but permitted Greyson to answer the question. Greyson was indignant and denied it.

Rett then asked, "In fact, Mr. Greyson, the reason you were divorced is because you had an affair with Bonnie Flannery. Ms. Flannery ended the affair because you were physically abusive to her during sex, correct?"

"Objection," Shaw said.

"That's the most ludicrous thing I've ever heard," Greyson said.

"You are divorced, correct?"

"Objection."

"Yes," Greyson said. "Divorced and remarried."

"In fact, your first wife divorced you because of your affair with Bonnie Flannery, correct?"

Greyson glared at Rett. "No."

Liza sat at the conference table with her sunglasses on without flinching. When Rett ended the deposition, Liza got up and left without a word.

After Liza left, Shaw asked if he could have a word with us. We left Callahan and Greyson in the conference room, and walked down to our office.

I let Shaw into our office and he looked around. He walked to the window and looked at the intersection below. "Wow, this is a nice place. I love the floor-to-ceiling windows. It reminds me of my dad's law office. It was right across the street from here in the old Professional Building."

Rett sat down at her desk. I pulled two chairs over and Shaw and I sat down.

"I want you to cancel Nick's deposition tomorrow," Shaw said. "He's the CEO of a Fortune 50 company. He has better things to do than waste a day here. I think we all know that your client's story doesn't hold water. There's no evidence to support her claim. Her behavior belies any claim that she was mistreated."

"Why won't you show us the texts, if that's true?" I asked.

Shaw grinned. "Ben, this is not a game. This is a fight to the death. Maybe you'll see the texts someday, but only if Judge Williams orders me to give them to you. Between September, when Nick got back from Paris, and June, when Liza was fired, she sent 497 texts to Nick. And not one of them says a word about rape. Not one. Not one word about inappropriate conduct by Nick or Jerry."

"If that's true, then why not share them?" I asked.

"Because every shred of information that I have that you don't helps me. That's the game, Ben, like it or not. Loretta knows that. She's represented companies before."

Rett didn't respond.

"So what's going to happen, if you don't end this," Shaw said, "is that Nick is going to testify tomorrow. He's going to share some humiliating details about your client, who is a sadly troubled woman. And then Judge Williams is going to grant our Motion and dismiss your case. And then he'll grant our Motion for costs and attorney's fees because you filed a frivolous lawsuit. My fees to date are over $200,000. We're going to rake you and Liza over the coals in the press. And my clients are going to insist that I seek sanctions against you and Loretta. I'm sorry to go after two fellow lawyers like that. I, more than anyone, am a believer in the brotherhood of lawyers. But my clients will insist that I go after you."

"So what do you want?" Rett asked.

"We will never pay Liza a dime. Never. Cancel tomorrow's deposition. Dismiss the case with prejudice. If you do that, so we know we will never hear from Liza again, I will convince my clients not to seek costs or sanctions. We will make a public statement that my clients were wrongfully accused. We will say that your client has received no payments, and never will. Liza will agree to non-disparagement and non-disclosure clauses. Do that, and you have my promise that your client will never hear from mine again.

"But here's the thing. I need your answer by 7 o'clock tonight. Not a minute later. If you don't accept this offer by seven, there's no deal and we're coming after you."

Shaw stood up and buttoned his suit coat. "You know how to reach me." He nodded at us and left.

44

It was 5:30 and we had 90 minutes to meet Shaw's deadline.

"What do you think," I asked Rett.

She leaned back in her chair and put her feet up on her desk. Then she jumped up and began pacing. "You know what I think? He's a fucker to dictate terms to us. Not even the courtesy of a dialogue. It makes me want to kick the shit out of him. That's what I think."

Rett kept pacing. She picked up a nerf ball and took a half-hearted shot. She sat on the couch.

"You know what, Ben? We have to be smart here. Shaw's offered exactly what I said we should do to get out of the case. We can't let pride get in the way. He's offering us the chance to get out without any more bleeding. Without any more time on a losing battle. It's the only way to avoid getting sanctioned, unless I'm willing to do a lot more than wear a tight dress for the judge."

I looked at Rett and raised my eyebrows.

"Don't even think about it, you perv," she said. "There's no question here. Let's take Shaw's offer and move on."

I sat behind my desk. I felt like crying.

"Ben, look, I know what you're thinking. Of course I'm wondering whether I made a mistake leaving Warner Levitt and coming here. Nothing against you. I can't think of anything I'd rather do than make a living with you. But we have no cases other than this disaster and no prospects. You can't blame me for worrying."

I nodded and looked out the window.

Rett looked at her watch. She stood up. "Look, Ben, I have an idea." She walked over to my desk and sat on the edge, facing me. "Why don't we drive over to Liza's and tell her it's over. She'll do whatever we recommend. Then we'll send Shaw an email confirming that we have a deal. And then we can get a bottle of wine and spend the night working off our frustration. We can sleep in tomorrow and get lunch. And then we'll figure out what makes sense for the future."

I was so depressed. Two weeks in, and my partnership with Rett was ending.

Rett stood and pulled me out of my chair. She hugged me. She was wearing a business suit with a tight blue skirt and a white blouse, and I could feel every curve.

She stepped back. "Come on, let's get this done."

We walked down to Rett's car. She pulled out her phone and sent a text to Liza that we were coming by to talk. A second later, Rett showed me Liza's response. All it said was, "K."

We drove to Liza's in silence. I felt like a kid being dragged to the dentist. Rett parked in front of Liza's house and stopped the car.

Rett looked at me. "You ready?"

I looked away from Rett. On the sidewalk, a mother stood with a baby strapped to her chest in a wrap. The baby slept, innocent and trusting and safe. The mom held a golden retriever on a leash. Mom was cooing softly to her baby while the retriever wagged his tail. Mom saw me looking at her and smiled.

"You know, Rett? This doesn't feel right."

"What doesn't feel right?"

"The whole thing. Telling Liza that we're done

with her. Dropping her case. Walking away."

I turned and looked at Rett. She folded her arms across her chest.

"We had a deal," Rett said, "that if we got nothing from Greyson, you wouldn't ask me to do more."

"I know."

"I meant it. Why would we pursue this case? We'll get fucked."

I looked up again. Mom and baby and dog were gone. "I don't know, Rett. I feel like I can't abandon Liza. I know there are a million reasons to walk away from the case. But it's not just about winning. I feel like she needs us to stand by her. She needs us to fight for her."

"That's very noble, Ben. But it's the wrong reason to stay in the case. That's how you run a law practice into the ground. That's how you get sanctioned by the Judge. We don't know if there's a shred of truth to her claims. We have no evidence and no way of winning. You're only hurting Liza by dragging on a losing case. If you want to help her, the best thing we can do is be straight with her and convince her to minimize the damage and move on."

I nodded. It made perfect sense. I could never win an argument with Rett. "I know," I said. "You're right. " I sighed. "Hey, Rett? I think I should talk to Liza alone."

Rett looked at me. "Ok, I get it. You bonded with her and I butted heads with her. Just don't lose your nerve, ok? Go do the right thing."

I nodded. "Why don't you head home? I'll walk back when I'm done."

45

I walked to Liza's door and took a deep breath. I dreaded this. I was going to abandon Liza. I knocked. A minute later Liza opened the door. She was wearing her baggy gray sweats. I came in and shut the door behind me. Liza walked to her living room without a word and sat on the couch. She had a fire going. She pulled a blanket over her. I sat down on the opposite end of the couch.

"How are you, Liza?"

"I'm sure you can imagine."

I nodded. She looked like she'd been crying.

"I'm sorry," she said. "I'm not much of a host. Would you like anything?"

"No, thanks. I'm fine."

"The case isn't going well. I know that."

"I'm really sorry, Liza."

"It's not your fault."

"I wish we could do more."

"Don't beat yourself up, Ben. I'm not surprised. Nick doesn't lose. At anything. I was a fool to think something good would come of this. I should have accepted what happened and just gotten away from him."

"You did the right thing, Liza. It's important that you stood up to him."

Liza stared at the fire. "I'm so tired. All the time," she said. She pulled her legs up under the blanket and rested her cheek on her knees. The blanket was wool and soft and worn. There was something familiar about it.

We watched the logs glow. I wanted to slide

over and pull Liza to me, the two of us under the blanket, fading to sleep in the fire's warmth. I took a deep breath and sighed.

"So, Liza, we've had a settlement offer. It's not fair to call it that, really. Basically, Shaw said that if we drop the suit today, by 7 o'clock, they won't pursue any claims against us. As they see it, we can't win the lawsuit. The Judge will throw out the case. And then we may have to pay their legal costs, which Shaw said are over $200,000. So the offer is if we drop the case, they'll make a public statement that the case is dismissed because our claims are without merit, and then you're done with them forever."

Liza sat in silence. I glanced at my watch. It was 6:30. We were running out of time, but I wasn't going to rush her.

"I can't believe Bonnie lied," she said. "She was my friend."

"She must have been scared for her job. That doesn't justify it, but that's got to be what's going on."

"I'm sure they made her scared for her job."

We sat in silence. "What about me?" Liza asked.

"I'm sorry?"

"What about me and a job? Who's going to hire me? With the publicity that's out there, and whatever awful things they're going to say about me, nobody's going to hire me. I should have taken their severance offer. Do you think we could still get it?"

"No, I don't think so. Shaw said this is a take-it or leave-it offer. No money."

We sat in silence. Liza slid over and pulled the blanket over my legs. She leaned her head against my shoulder.

"You make me feel safe, Ben. Thank you for that."

"I wish I could do more."

"Feeling safe is worth more than you can imagine."

We sat and I could feel Liza relax. After a time she said, "Well, I guess we have no choice, huh? Just take it and be done?"

I liked Liza leaning on me. It was the first time she let her guard down with me. We were warm and comfortable. "You know, Liza? It doesn't feel right to me. It feels like they're getting away with it. I just don't know what other choice we have."

Liza hugged her knees under the blanket.

"Have you been seeing David?" I asked.

"Twice. I'm supposed to call him to make another appointment, but I dread it."

We sat there under the blanket, Liza leaning against my shoulder. She drifted to sleep. For the first time since I met her, she seemed at ease. I thought of the baby wrapped safely against her mom's chest, the retriever wagging his tail and dancing happily around them, the mom cooing in her daughter's ear. Someday that little girl might grow up to be Liza. Someday I might have a daughter.

It was warm under the blanket with Liza. Her sweats were soft and comforting. Gently, I dropped my arm over her shoulder. I glanced at my watch. It was 6:55. Rett had told me to do the right thing. I let Liza sleep.

46

I got home after 9 o'clock and saw that I had missed seven calls from Rett. I couldn't imagine why she was calling.

I had a rising level of panic about the next 24 hours. I would have to take Stanton's deposition. It was my first deposition, and I was fucked. It was bad enough that Stanton was probably a hundred times smarter than me. Shaw would be shooting objections at me that I would have no clue how to handle. Rett would be furious with me for missing the chance to get out of the case. Liza would be devastated for putting herself in the hands of such a putz. Rett and I would get sanctioned. And Joss would scorn me for failing Liza. Other than that, things were good.

I decided not to call Rett. I had enough stress already. I sat at my table in my apartment with a pen and paper. I was determined to find a way to go after Stanton. After sitting for 15 minutes with nothing coming to mind, I decided to go for a run.

I took the elevator down and walked outside. It was a beautiful summer night. Cool, the sky full of stars. I ran up Fairmount Boulevard and got angry. I was so tired of flailing away and getting nowhere. Tired of being inept and unable to help Liza. Tired of wanting to help Rett and never being able to do it. And suddenly just furious with Joss. She read me so easily and knew exactly how to make me feel better. I felt like a puppy hoping for her to come pet me. This dance was bullshit. Juggling guys, leaving me wondering every time I reached out whether she'd take my hand or turn away. Suddenly it hit me. I hadn't been disloyal to her when I was with Lynn, or when I was with Rett. I was disloyal to myself. I was doing whatever it was everyone wanted. Always dancing to make everyone happy and getting myself nowhere. I wanted more.

I was running hard, pounding my way into Shaker Heights and around a lake. The woods thickened. It felt good to run on dirt. I was running under moonlight and I pushed to a sprint, fueled by a lifetime of longing for some vague thing that was always beyond me. I'd had enough. I'd fucking had enough.

I reached the far side of the lake and weaved my way through the woods. I slowed and walked toward the water. A few feet before the lake was a huge square boulder, nearly eight feet high. I climbed on top and lay on my back.

The sky darkened as clouds slid in front of the moon. I watched them drift by and the moon looked down on me. I was 26-years-old. I was woefully lonely. For so long. But of course I was. An orphan pinballing through time desperately trying to be unscathed. Of course I was alone.

I'd spent a lifetime getting by. It was time to get to work. I might as well play my cards. I couldn't be any worse off than I was now. It was time to get to work.

I climbed off the rock and ran home.

I went into my building and took the steps two at a time to the fourth floor. As I turned down the hall, I saw Joss sitting on the floor, leaning against my apartment door. She jumped up when she saw me. She was wearing blue jeans and a gray t-shirt. She raised her hands above her head and started dancing like Rocky after he ran up the Philadelphia Art Museum steps.

"Hoo Hoo! There he is! Usain Bolt! Running champ of the world!"

"What are you doing here, Joss?"

"I had dinner with Westy. He's entertaining, but I couldn't stop thinking of you. So here I am."

I was wearing shorts and a t-shirt, and was drenched in sweat. Joss stepped up to me and put her hand on my chest. She looked at me and grinned, that enticing, mischievous smile. "Man, you really went at it tonight," she said. "Maybe a shower's in order. Need to wash away your worries? What do you say, Counselor?"

"You know what, Joss?" I pushed her hand off my chest. "No."

I put my key in the door and opened it. I went in, shut the door, and locked it.

47

I didn't sleep all night. I kept trying to envision the deposition, and me taking control and turning the tide in the case. But I just had no clue what to do. I had no prayer of out-lawyering Shaw, since I knew nothing about lawyering. I churned and churned all night, clammy, my stomach gurgling. I was freaking out, to be honest. I kept looking at the time. It crawled, prolonging my torture, but bringing me closer, minute-by-minute, to what I dreaded.

I went down to the office at eight. The deposition was scheduled for 9. Rett was waiting for me.

"I'm going to fucking kill you, Ben. Why didn't you pick up your damn phone?"

"I talked with Liza. She needs us to fight for her. So I'm going to fight."

"Don't you think you should have called me? If we get sanctioned, it hits me, too."

"You know what, Rett? When you came on board, you were fired up for this case. We shouldn't jump ship at the first sign of trouble."

Rett frowned at me. "But there's no way to win this fight. Stanton's going to deny everything, and the Judge will throw out the case. Why fight a losing battle?"

"Because we owe it to Liza to fight for her. Win or lose. It's the right thing to do. And while we're at it Rett, I gotta tell you, I'll probably hate myself for this later, but I'm not having sex with you anymore. Please don't take that the wrong way. You're spectacular. You're gorgeous and unbelievably sexy.

But it doesn't feel right to me. You're my best friend in the world, but that's not the relationship we have."

"Ok," Rett said, "one thing at a time. Let's talk about us. You're not using me. I'm the one who dragged you into the sack. And we've both been perfectly clear that it's just fun. So I haven't thought for a minute that you've been using me. It's just plain fun. Nothing more, nothing less."

I nodded.

"But as long as it's fun," Rett said, "why not? You got anything better to do tonight?"

"I've got nothing better to do. I can't even imagine something better."

"Well, life is short. Why not have some fun tonight?"

"I don't know, Rett. I'm a moron. Everyone knows that. But it doesn't feel right and I'm not going to do it anymore if it doesn't feel right."

Rett looked at me and smiled. "Wow. Hello, Ben."

I looked back at Rett. "So we're cool?"

"No worries, Ben. I agree you're a moron, but we're cool. We always will be. Except for this goddamn case."

"Good. I need some quiet time, Rett. I'm taking today's deposition. We can talk about the case and our firm later."

I walked behind my desk and pulled out my pad of paper. "Hey, Rett? Do you mind? It's your turn to get the coffee."

I sat and stared at my yellow pad. I had no clue. Nothing. I kept taking deep breaths, trying to calm myself. It wasn't working. I was sweating. I started pacing around the office. I had no idea what the rules were. I felt like I was shoved on stage to act in a play and the whole audience was staring at me and I'd never seen the script. I thought I was going to puke.

Liza knocked on our door at 9. She had the shades on. I walked up to her and leaned in and whispered in her ear. "Hi, Liza. Thanks for coming. Leave the sunglasses on my desk, ok?"

She nodded.

Rett, Liza, and I walked down to the conference room a few minutes after nine. My heart was pounding. What was I thinking? I can't do this! They're going to laugh their asses off at me.

I was on the verge of begging Rett to take the depo for me, when Shaw walked around the corner. He stormed up to Rett and leaned down in her face. "Why didn't you get back to me?" he demanded.

He was glaring at her with an angry scowl, threatening. Without thinking, I jumped between them and shouldered him away from Rett. I looked him in the eye. "We didn't get back to you because we're not interested in your offer. Is your client here?"

Shaw looked at me and took a step back. I opened the conference room door. The court reporter was waiting for us. We went into the room.

Callahan and Nick Stanton were standing and talking on the far side of the table. Stanton was a good-looking guy, about six-two and thin, with neatly cropped dark brown hair that was starting to gray at his sideburns, which made him look even more distinguished.

"Go ahead in, Mr. Shaw," I said. "We'll be a minute."

Shaw walked in the conference room. I pulled the door shut and turned to Rett. My hands were shaking.

I was about to ask Rett if she would take the depo. I looked at Liza. She looked like she was going to be sick.

"It's going to be fine, Liza," I said.

She looked frantic. I walked closer to her, and said quietly, "It's ok, Liza. When we go in there, you don't have to talk to him. You don't have to shake his hand. If he says something to you, you don't have to respond. Ok?"

Liza nodded.

"Come on," I said. "Really, it's going to be ok." If only I believed that. I couldn't ask Rett now. Rett would kill me.

We walked in and I sat down next to the court reporter. I tried to force myself to breathe normally. Rett sat next to me, and Liza next to Rett. I pulled out my yellow pad. I had no notes. The audience was watching and I had no script.

Stanton sat across from me, and Shaw next to him. Callahan sat next to Shaw. Stanton looked at me calmly, like he was sizing me up. There was a forced nonchalance about him, like he was determined to show how unflappable he was.

Shit! What was I doing? These were grown men! They were sophisticated businessmen who ran businesses and traveled the world and worked with bankers and congressmen. I hoped they couldn't see me sweating. Come on, Ben! Come on! Nick Stanton wasn't my dad. He's just another guy. I'd lost my dad. This was nothing.

I went through the introductory questions that I remembered Shaw and Rett had asked about his home address, whether he had plans to move, and his obligation to tell the truth. Nick spoke carefully, polished and precise. Now what? I was blank. We were five minutes in. Too soon for a break.

I stood and walked to the credenza and shakily poured myself a glass of water. I asked if anyone else wanted one. There was no response. I poured one for the court reporter and handed it to her.

She was surprised and looked at me and smiled. "Thanks!" she said. "That's so nice of you!"

She liked me. Man, did that feel good. I looked at Nick, sitting there smugly. I wasn't sure how to dig in with him, but maybe I could just have a conversation. I was good at talking with people. I could do that.

"So Nick – hey, I'm sorry. Is it ok if I call you Nick?

"Yes."

"And you should feel free to call me Ben. Sound good?

"Sure."

"So Nick, tell me about your background. Let's start with schools."

"I grew up in Westchester, New York, and went to Choate Boarding School. I was valedictorian, and then went to Bates College in Lewiston, Maine. I was valedictorian in college as well. After that..."

"Excuse me for interrupting. Did you go straight from high school to college?"

"Yes."

"Ok, thanks. So what did you do after college?"

"After Bates I went to the Wharton School of Business in Philadelphia. That's where I received my MBA."

"Wow, lots of degrees. Very impressive. Were you valedictorian at Wharton, too?"

"No, I was not. My spouse, Brock, was."

"Brock? Are you married to a guy?"

Nick stared at me and turned beet red. He stood and put both hands on the table. He leaned towards me and seethed, "You stupid fucking moron. Her name is 'Brook.' What the fuck is the matter with you?"

"Whoa!" I said. I put my hands up. "I'm sorry! Why would I care if you're married to a guy? I thought you said 'Brock.'"

Nick sat back down. He smoothed out the sleeves to his suit coat. "I'm married to a very attractive woman. Her name is 'Brook'."

"Ok, got it. I'm sorry, I thought you said 'Brock.' I was just asking, I didn't mean anything by it. Are you ok? Do you want to take a break?"

"I'm just fine," he said. He glared at me.

Wow. What a homophobe!

"Ok," I said. "Really, no hard feelings. I just didn't hear you. So anyway, did you start working then after Wharton?"

"Yes."

"Tell me about it," I said.

Stanton took a deep breath and let it out slowly. "I took a job with RTG in strategic planning here in Cleveland."

"Really? So you've been with RTG your whole career? All the way through today?"

"Yes, I have."

"That's amazing. You don't meet many people who spend their whole career in one place."

"If it's the right company, and the right fit, and there's appropriate room for advancement, no one should ever leave."

"Makes sense," I said. "So tell me about your career at RTG."

"I spent three years in strategic planning here at headquarters, first for the Transportation division. Eventually they moved me to strategic planning for corporate. After three years in corporate, I was moved into operations."

I could tell that Stanton was starting to calm

down. I wanted it to feel like we were just chatting in a bar. Even though my stomach was fluttering, I sat back and put my hands behind my head. And clearly, he liked talking about himself. I figured the more he talked, the better for me.

"I started as the number two operations guy for the Energy division. Within two years, I was promoted to the head of operations for Energy "

"Was that here in Cleveland?"

"No. Energy is run out of Mesa, Arizona. I spent seven years in Mesa. I lived in Scottsdale."

"Ah, I've been to Scottsdale. Just last year for a buddy's wedding. It's a great place."

"Well, it is these days. Back when I was there, it was largely for old folks – retirement communities. But every year the people there get younger and younger."

"I wish I could learn that trick."

"Yes. You could make a pretty penny if you could."

I could see how Liza had been drawn to Stanton. He had charisma. A real charmer, despite that explosive temper.

"So seven years in Mesa, then what?"

"After that, they asked me to move into the finance department. This was about 12 years ago, and they were starting to groom me for the CEO position. They wanted me to get more experience with the company's financial and S.E.C. reporting."

"So you were back in Cleveland then?"

"Yes, at headquarters. After two years, I was made Chief Financial Officer, and then they made me CEO."

"That's amazing. How old were you then? Forty-two?"

"Forty-one. I've been CEO for nine years now."

"I should have asked earlier. Are you still married? Do you have kids?"

"Yes, of course I'm still married. No kids."

"Ok, thanks. So let's talk about Liza for a bit. Liza was one of the secretaries for the top management at RTG?"

"Yes, she was for ten years or so. There's a pool of secretaries for the Executive team, and she's was in the pool for quite some time before she was terminated."

"So I'm sorry to ask you this, but I understand you were involved romantically with Liza?"

"Yes. We dated for much of the time she was in the Pool."

He said it like he was commenting on the weather. I felt sorry for his wife.

"Ok, so tell me about this pool of secretaries. What was their role?"

"It's an arrangement that started long before I was CEO. I'm not sure who started it. But the management team at RTG consists of six people. There are six secretaries, and they're all available to each of us as we need them. We try to promote a sense of teamwork throughout the company, and that's reflected in the shared responsibilities of the Pool girls."

"Ok. And sometimes the Pool secretaries traveled with you?"

"Occasionally. The Chiefs often have working meetings around the world, with RTG operations, customers, suppliers, regulators, lobbyists. We bring whatever resources we need to those meetings. Sometimes we need administrative support, and when we do, the Pool girls travel with us at the Chiefs' discretion."

"Do they typically come to Board meetings?"

"We have several Board meetings each year, and at least one Pool girl comes to those meetings. RTG has 11 Board members, including me. We meet in different spots around the world, typically near one of our international operations. The Board members are high-achievers. So when we have a Board meeting, we usually bring one or two Pool girls. They're the best we have, and they take care of us."

"And you brought Liza to the Board meeting in Paris in last fall?"

"Yes."

"Were any of the other secretaries from the Pool at that Board meeting?"

"No. Just Liza."

"And the last night of the meeting, I understand that Liza was invited to the Board dinner?"

"Yes, she was. The last night of the annual meeting is always a celebration. We've just concluded three grueling days, working through difficult strategic issues that are accompanied by fierce debate. Being a Board member at RTG is not like so many other companies with figurehead positions, sipping wine and collecting a check simply for offering your name. It's one of the reasons RTG is so successful. We don't work on cruise control. We break glass. That's our goal. Shatter glass. We forge new ways. We push ourselves, and then hammer out a consensus. And by the end of the Board meeting, we have reason to celebrate a difficult but productive process."

"I'd like to take a hygiene break," Shaw said. "Off the record."

Liza, Rett, and I walked down to our office. Rett pulled the door shut.

"Ben!" she said. "You're a natural! You're so comfortable in there."

"This doesn't count. We're just talking."

310

"No, you're great. But stay on your toes. Shaw took that break to make sure Stanton doesn't relax with you. He wanted to remind him to avoid being conversational and to only answer your questions. Stanton's been talking and talking and Shaw's got to hate that. Your style is really effective. "

I sat down on the couch. My heart was racing. I had no idea where to go next. I just had to keep him talking and hope he opened a door somewhere.

We went back to the conference room and went back on the record with the court reporter.

"Ok, Nick, we're back on the record. I'm sure you know that you're still under oath."

"Of course."

"Ok. So we were talking about the dinner after the Board meeting in Paris. Tell me about the celebration that night. Where was the dinner?"

"Objection!" Shaw barked.

I had no idea what to do. I sat in silence and started to sweat. Rett leaned over and whispered, "Just tell him to answer your question."

"Go ahead and answer," I said.

"We were at Le Tastevin restaurant."

It worked! "Where is that restaurant," I asked.

"On L'ile de St. Louis."

"In Missouri?"

Stanton smiled condescendingly at me. I grinned back. "Just kidding," I said. "That's in Paris?"

Stanton laughed. "Yes. It's the original section of Paris. A tiny island on the Seine just across from Notre Dame."

"Not the place in South Bend, I assume?"

Stanton smiled. "Correct."

"I'm guessing it's quite a nice restaurant?"

"Objection. Vague," Shaw said.

"You can answer," I said. It worked last time, I figured why not try again.

"It's lovely," Stanton said. "It's a small, family owned and run restaurant, just one room with a small bar. The food is exceptional. We reserved the place for ourselves."

"Did you book the place for the entire night?"

"Objection." Shaw said.

"You can answer," I said.

"Of course," Stanton said.

"Sorry if I'm slow, but is that normal?"

"It is in Paris. Dining in France is quite unlike here. The restaurant owner would be offended if anyone came in, ate quickly, and left. That's a crass American habit. In France, they expect dinner to be your entire evening."

"Tell me about the evening," I said.

"Objection."

Nick continued without waiting for direction. We were both starting to ignore Shaw.

"We finished our meetings and got to the restaurant at 7. It was just two blocks from our hotel. A short walk. We had drinks and hors' doerves. There were toasts and speeches. The owner of the restaurant is the chef, and his wife is the waitress and bartender. Charming, wonderful people. They helped make the evening, joining us in conversation, sharing their experiences. They both have a sensational sense of humor, notwithstanding that English is not their primary language. We talked with them at length throughout the evening."

"Who was at the dinner?"

"Everyone is invited to the final dinner celebration. All of the Board members and Chiefs. We include the support staff to show our appreciation. So Liza was there as well."

"Was there a dance floor?"

"No. With the Chiefs and the Board and Liza, there were 17 of us. We were packed into the restaurant. There was enough room to wander from table to table – I think there were three tables – and to the bar, but that's about it."

"So tell me about the rest of the evening at the restaurant."

"Objection," Shaw said.

"It was quite pleasant. Sensational food. No one ordered anything. They kept bringing out huge pans of different dishes, one after another after another. If you liked what was there, you indulged. If not, another dish soon followed. Everyone ate far too much. But the food was wonderful, and the Board was quite happy with the choice."

"Did everyone take cabs back to the hotel?"

"Objection!" Shaw said.

"You can answer, Nick."

"To my knowledge, just about everyone walked to the hotel. It was only two blocks. We were staying at the Hotel du Jeu de Paume, a charming place just a few minutes away. It was a chilly fall night, but not too cold. Everyone wanted to get some fresh air and stretch their legs."

"Well, not everyone," I said. "Liza took a cab?"

"Yes, she did. Like I said, it was an open bar, and Liza had too much to drink."

"Did you sit with Liza at dinner?"

"No. There were three tables, so five or six people per table. Liza was at a different table. But like I said, it was a small room, and people wandered and talked all evening"

"Were you and Liza still seeing each other then?"

"Objection!"

"No," Nick said. "I had ended things a few weeks before."

"Did you end them or did she?"

"Well, let's be diplomatic and say it was mutual."

"Ok. Sorry to be personal, but you and Liza were staying at the same hotel during the Board meeting in Paris?"

"Yes."

"Ok. I guess what I was wondering, was, before the night of the Board dinner while you were in Paris, did you spend personal time together? Did you go see her in her hotel room? Or did she come to your room?"

"No. Not at all. Like I said, I had ended our relationship some time before that. And I was working every night. I probably made seven presentations to the Board during those three days of meetings, in addition having to stay on top of day-to-day issues at the company. The hotel provided us with a suite for office tasks. Liza worked with the Chiefs and me during the evenings to get ready for the next day's meetings. But that was it. I didn't even know which room she was in."

"Ok. So Liza had to take a cab back to the hotel?"

"Yes. We were at the restaurant until after midnight. Liza had a lot to drink. Far too much. I worried about her. She was all over me after the meal, and it was an embarrassment in front of the Board members. She certainly wasn't capable of walking back to the hotel. It was late, and she was wearing a revealing, suggestive dress. Inappropriate, really, for a Board function, although there were no complaints, as you can imagine. Nothing good would have happened if she wandered out into the street like that.

I asked the restaurant owner to call a cab, and asked our CFO to help me get Liza back to the hotel."

"The CFO is Jerry Greyson?"

"Yes."

"How did everyone get along in the cab?"

"Get along?"

"Yeah, you know, was it pleasant? Tension because you and Liza broke up?"

"No. It was nothing like that. By the time we got in the cab, Liza was really feeling the booze. I worried she might get sick. I propped her up between Jerry and me. I don't even think she was awake at that point."

"So what happened when you got back to the hotel?"

"We managed to get her out of the cab. Jerry had to hold her up while I paid the fare. The two of us had to practically carry her into the hotel. It was embarrassing."

"And then did she tell you she wanted to go to her room?"

"You have to understand. She was not coherent. We helped her up to her room. Jerry had to support her while I unlocked the door. They had one of those old fashioned keys, a big one that you actually insert into the door, not the swipe cards they have here. Jerry and I got her into the room, which was not a simple task. There was a sitting area in her room with a couch. We got her onto the couch and made sure she was ok. Then Jerry and I left."

"Did you take the key with you?"

"The key? No. Why would we?"

"Did you get her coffee to help get the alcohol out of her system?"

"Coffee? No. She wouldn't have been able to drink hot coffee in that state."

"Ok, makes sense. How did you know which room was hers?"

"What?"

"I'm just wondering, if she was passed out, and you hadn't been to her room before, how did you know which room was hers?"

Stanton glared at me. Then he gave me a condescending smirk.

"I can tell you've never been to Europe. Is that right, Ben?"

I raised my hands, palms up. "What can I say? Nope, never. I've barely been out of Cleveland. How did you know?"

"The finer hotels in Europe still have large, old, hand-made keys for the locks. They're very expensive. To make sure that no one walks off with them, the hotels attach bulky, heavy adornments to the key. It's very effective. It would be impractical to lug around such an unwieldy object. The custom is to leave your key with the hotel clerk. Give the key to the clerk when you leave, and get it back when you return to the hotel. The clerk handed us Liza's key, along with mine and Jerry's, and told us Liza's room number."

"Ok," I said. "I got it. Sorry for my ignorance. It gets in the way of everything I do."

"Yes. I'm sure."

Nice guy. I kept going. "So you didn't fish the key out of Liza's purse when you got to the hotel, right?"

"Objection!" Shaw said. "Where are you going with this?"

"You can go ahead and answer," I said.

Nick glanced at Shaw.

"No. The clerk gave it to me."

"You talked with the clerk when you got back to the hotel?"

"Yes. Briefly. You walk in the hotel and the clerk's desk is right next to the door. It's not like a hotel chain here. These are intimate places. There's just a desk, a very old, ornate desk next to the door, with a clerk sitting there. The lobby is half the size of this conference room. The hotel is only six floors high, with four rooms on each floor, starting on the second floor. We had most of the rooms. The clerk knows everyone staying there. He could see Liza's condition. I asked for her room key, and he gave it to me and told me which room she was in."

"Ok, makes sense. Got it. So Jerry's testimony that you were in the elevator and fished the key out of Liza's purse would be false?"

"Objection! Mischaracterization!" Shaw said.

"I, uh, I would not call it false," Stanton said. "He may be misremembering."

"Misremembering?" I asked. "Ok, I understand. So the clerk saw Liza's condition and gave you her room key and told you which room she was in?"

"Objection," Shaw said. "Asked and answered."

"Yes," Stanton said.

"Do you remember his name?"

"Whose name?"

"The desk clerk."

"The desk clerk at the hotel in Paris last year? No. Of course not."

"He knocked on the door, right? While you were in Liza's room with Liza and Jerry?"

Stanton looked at Shaw. Shaw started writing on his pad.

"I don't remember any knocking."

"Does the name Pierre sound familiar? Pierre Fullmiere?"

"'Pierre what?"

"I'm not sure I'm pronouncing it right. I can't speak French. As you can tell, I can barely speak English."

I pulled an envelope from my coat pocket and turned the front towards Nick and Shaw. In bright blue fancy print, on the upper left of the envelope, it said "Hotel du Jeu de Paume." I pulled a piece of paper out and unfolded it.

"I'm not sure how to pronounce this, Nick. It's spelled F-U-L-L-M-I-E-R-E. Pierre Full –me -ay, or something like that. Was it Pierre Fullmiere, the desk clerk, who was knocking on Liza's door?"

"Objection!" Shaw said. "Foundation!"

"Was Pierre Fullmiere the name of the desk clerk who gave you Liza's key?"

"Objection! Asked and answered."

"It might have been. I'm not sure."

I put the letter back in the envelope. "Ok. Regardless of his name, was it that person, the desk clerk, who was knocking on Liza's door when you were in there with Jerry?"

"I don't remember any knocking."

"Did you hear Pierre when he came to the hall outside of Liza's room?"

"Objection!" Shaw barked.

Stanton's jaw was clenched. He looked at Shaw and then glared at me.

"What I'm just trying to get at, Nick, is when Pierre was outside Liza's room after you and Jerry went up, did you hear him or talk to him?"

"Objection," Shaw said.

I stared at Stanton and waited. He stared back at me.

"Nick, I'm just trying to make sure you understand my question. I apologize if I'm not being clear. Pierre Fullmiere, the clerk at the Hotel. That's the one I'm referring to. Ok?"

"I know who you mean."

"I'm just asking if you talked to Mr. Fullmiere when he was in the hall outside Liza's room that night."

"Objection," Shaw said.

"No, I did not."

"Did you talk to him after he went back down to his desk?"

"No, I did not."

"So the only time you talked to him was when you and Jerry helped Liza to the elevator when you first got to the hotel?"

"That's right."

"I guess I have to ask. You know that Jerry Greyson testified yesterday, right?"

"Yes."

"Did you talk to him about his testimony?"

Nick looked at Shaw again. "Not really. Just about where your office was, how long it took to get here. How long the deposition lasted."

"Did you talk to him about the substance of his testimony?"

He looked at Shaw. "No."

I pulled the letter back out of the hotel envelope. I slowly read the letter, silently, from top to bottom. When I finished, I said, "In fact, Nick, you were told that a number of hotel guests called Mr. Fullmiere and expressed concern about the noise they heard in Liza's room, correct?"

"Objection!" Shaw said. "If you've got a document, I would like to see it. We requested all documents at Liza's deposition, and you said there were none. This is misconduct."

I hesitated. Rett said, "There were no

responsive documents at that time, Mr. Shaw. If and when you make an additional request, Ben and I will respond as required by the rules. Ben has not offered an affidavit as a deposition exhibit, and has no obligation to show you one at this time."

Shaw glowered at Rett but didn't respond. Ok, I love this woman.

"Nick," I asked, "did you talk to Pierre about the complaints he received about people having sex, well, I should say, the noises in Liza's room when you and Jerry brought her there?"

"Objection."

Stanton didn't respond. He looked at Shaw. Shaw said, "We'd like to take a break here."

"Not now," Rett said. "As the rules provide, you can have a break when Mr. Billings finishes this line of questioning, but not until then." I really love this woman.

"Please answer my question, Nick."

Shaw scowled at Rett. He pulled out his cell phone and dialed. "Fine, just keep going," he said. "Don't let me interrupt."

Shaw said quietly into his phone, "Alicia, I need you to connect me immediately to the Hotel du Jeu de Paume in Paris. Right now."

"What was your question?" Nick asked.

"Did Pierre, the desk clerk, have a conversation with you about the complaints he received from guests about noise from sex, and about his concerns about what was happening in Liza's room?"

"He did not."

"So are you saying that he is 'misremembering' as well?"

"Objection," Shaw said, while holding his phone to his ear.

"Mr. Shaw," Rett said, "you are disrupting the

deposition. Let the record reflect that Mr. Shaw is making a phone call and talking on his phone while we are in the middle of questioning."

"You just go right ahead with your questions, Ben," Shaw said. "There's no disruption, dear."

"Please answer my question, Nick."

"I'm telling you we did not have a conversation."

"Ok. Were you still in Liza's room when Pierre opened her door with his key to check on her?"

"Objection."

"What? No, I didn't see that."

"He may have opened the door to check on her but you were not aware of it, correct?"

"Hello?" Shaw said into his phone. "Bon jour. Parlez vous Englais?"

"Mr. Shaw!" Rett said.

"Yes," Shaw said into his phone. "Is there a Mr. Pierre Fullmiere working there?"

There was a pause. Then Shaw said, looking at me with a triumphant grin, "He does not work there? Are you saying there is no such person?"

Suddenly Shaw's face fell. "Do you know when he'll be in?"

Shaw hung up his phone and whispered something to Nick.

"Objection," Rett said. "Let the record reflect that Mr. Shaw is coaching the witness."

"There is no coaching here," Shaw said. "Who's taking this deposition? You should not be speaking, Ms. Anderson."

"Please answer my question, Nick," I said.

"What was your question?"

"I asked if it's possible that you simply did not see Mr. Fullmiere when he opened the door to Liza's room when you and Jerry were in there."

"Yes." Nick folded his arms across his chest. "Yes, of course that's possible."

I pulled out the Hotel envelope again and opened the paper in it. I leaned over to Rett and pointed to a line in it. I looked at her and she nodded at me.

"Nick, when you got Liza's key from Pierre Fullmiere, was he drinking?"

"Drinking? No."

"Did he appear drunk to you?"

"No."

"Ok, so you have no reason to doubt his observations?"

"I wouldn't know."

"Did he do or say anything that made you think there was something wrong with him?"

"No."

"If he said that he observed a sex crime in progress, would you have any reason to disagree with him?"

"Objection!" Shaw barked. "Don't answer that."

I waited, but Nick didn't respond.

"Nick," I said, "you and Jerry Greyson were the only ones in Liza's room with her after the Board dinner?"

"Yes, to my knowledge."

"So if Mr. Fullmiere is right, that there was a sex crime in progress in Liza's room when he checked on things after receiving complaints, the only ones who could be committing those crimes were you and Jerry. Is that right?"

"Objection!"

"You can answer."

"No! That's not right!" Nick leaned towards me with a fierce look on his face.

I sat back and looked defeated. "Are you saying that there was no crime?"

"That's right. That's exactly right," Nick said.

"Nick, I gotta ask. You were in there with Liza and Jerry. Are you gay? Or bisexual?"

"What the fuck?"

"Objection! Nick, don't answer that question. This is outrageous."

"I'll be more specific, Nick. Did you and Jerry have sex with each other in Liza's room that night in Paris?"

Nick turned red again. "No! What the fuck is the matter with you? Jesus Christ."

"Have you ever had sex with another man, Nick?"

"Objection!" Shaw said. "Keep this up and I'm calling the Judge."

Stanton folded his arms and smirked at me. "Trust me," he said, "I am completely heterosexual. You can confirm that in spades with Liza."

"Do you find this funny?" I asked.

"Not at all."

"We're talking about serious crimes here, Nick."

"There's nothing illegal about sex, Ben."

"Well, there's nothing illegal about consensual sex, right?"

"Yes, I stand corrected," Stanton said.

"And you're saying that what Pierre Fullmiere observed was consensual sex?"

"Objection."

"You can answer."

"There was no rape. That's an outrageous claim."

"Nick," I said, "Are you saying that there was consensual sex between you and Liza? And Jerry and

Liza? But there was no sex between you and Jerry?"

"Yes. Of course. Jesus Christ. I've never had sex with a man. What's the fuck is the matter with you?"

"I wish I knew the answer to that question, Nick. I really do. But anyway, listen, can you tell me why you think the sex was consensual?"

Stanton looked at me with a steely glare. After a minute, he said, "She urged us on."

"Both of you?"

"Yes. This woman is no saint. Far from it. To be perfectly candid with you, she was always trying to bring others into our bed. She likes to experiment."

"Had you ever done that with Liza before?"

"Done what?"

"Had a threesome with Liza?"

"No, I refused."

"More than three?"

Nick snorted. "No."

"But the three of you were having sex that night in Paris?"

"I never touched Jerry. Never. You know, it happened more or less before I knew what was going on. Liza encouraged us. She was dressed provocatively. She was all over me in the restaurant. She made clear what she wanted. I think Jerry was shocked. But Liza has a way of getting what she wants."

"So you're saying that she consented to the sex you and Jerry had with her, but you and Jerry did not have sex?"

"Objection."

"How many times do I have to tell you?" Nick said angrily. "What we did was with Liza. And only Liza. It's what she wanted. I shouldn't have let it happen, to be honest, because our relationship was not good by then, and it could only complicate things. The wise thing was just to stay away from each other. But make no mistake about it – this woman loves sex, and it's what she wanted and she made that clear."

"So is that why you didn't talk to her after you got back to Cleveland? That's why you didn't respond to her texts?"

"That's exactly right. She wanted to resume our relationship, and I thought it was unhealthy. It's so easy to keep falling back into bad habits, to keep falling back into a bad relationship. We had a wild night in Paris, and I think Liza took it to mean we could resume our relationship. And I wanted to make it as clear as day that it was over. So I chose not to engage with her any longer."

"Those relationships are tough," I said. "The ones where you break up and get back together over and over again."

"Exactly! They're like a drug. They're too easy to fall back into and too hard to extract yourself from. I was determined to be strong and not let that happen. We slipped in Paris. I decided, look, we had said we were done, and we shouldn't let one crazy night upend things. So I chose not to respond to her texts for her sake and mine."

"I assume you read her texts. How could you not?"

"Yes, I read them, at least at first, and it was difficult for me. But it was also crucial to be strong for both of us if we were going to move on from a relationship that was not healthy."

"Do you still have those texts?"

"Have them?"

"Yes. Do you have your cell phone with you?"

"Objection!" Shaw said.

"Why are you objecting, Mr. Shaw? I'm just

asking if he has his cell phone with him."

"You can answer," Shaw said.

"Yes, but it's turned off."

"Do you know how to turn it on?"

Stanton gave me an angry look. "Of course."

"Why don't you turn it on and show me the texts you have from Liza?"

"Objection. You've made no request that Mr. Stanton bring any documents today. There was no request attached to the deposition notice. He has no obligation to produce any documents. Nick, put your phone away."

I glanced at Rett. She had prepared the deposition notice. She quickly wrote on her pad and slid it to me. "Shit! Sorry!!!!!!"

"Ok. So Liza kept texting you after the Paris trip, and you didn't respond to her?"

"Right."

"We've got a document request out to see those texts, but generally, what were they about?"

"Objection," Shaw said.

"There were hundreds of them. She wanted to talk. She couldn't understand why I wouldn't meet with her. She said she was confused. But listen, it was all very simple. It wasn't smart for us to keep rehashing old issues, keep getting back together and breaking up. We'd already done enough of that. So I didn't respond."

"Would you say that Liza was discreet?"

"What do you mean?"

"Well, she was texting you on your phone, right? She wasn't confronting you in the office. Or the cafeteria. She wasn't sending you personal messages on the company's email system where any IT technician or secretary could look at them?"

"That's right. We had an agreement. Never

bring our personal relationship into the workplace."

"So even after Paris, Liza tried to respect your wishes? Protect you in some way, and not let what was happening between you become a spectacle at the office?"

"Only for a time. When I gave her an important assignment, she made a scene in front of everyone, and then she tried to blackmail me on my personal email with a video she had made surreptitiously. That was very upsetting. It was extortion."

"You're talking about right before she was fired?"

"Yes."

"Did you show that email with the video to anyone?"

"Of course not."

"You didn't show it to your wife?"

Nick snorted. "Are you stupid? Why the hell would I do that?"

"So no one has seen it?"

"Only my lawyers."

"But while Liza was at work, when she was upset about how you gave her an assignment, she complained about how you treated her, right?"

"Yes. We were in a real bind with the 10-Q filing. I asked her to edit a document so we could get it filed, and she refused and made a scene."

"And that's when she accused you of raping her, right?"

"Absolutely not! She said she was outraged that after our relationship ended, I wouldn't talk to her, and that I had nerve giving her work like that. It was bizarre. She was incensed because I asked her to do her job."

"By 'relationship,' do you mean the intimate, sexual relationship that you and Liza had once had?"

"Well, yes. That's what we once had, but it was over."

"You routinely scolded Liza at work, right? That's how you treat the women employees?"

"Objection!"

"What? Never. That's ridiculous. I never scolded anyone. That is not how I treat women."

"Never?"

"No! You may want to make me into some kind of monster, but I do not treat women that way."

"You never scolded Liza at work?"

"Never! The only time was that last day when we had a crisis and she refused to do the work that was needed."

"There were five other women in the Pool at the time Liza was fired?"

"What? Yes. Five."

"Bonnie was at work that day?"

"I have no idea."

"Well, I'll tell you. Bonnie was here two days ago and testified that she was at work that day. Do you have any reason to think she's misremembering?"

"No."

"So that day, Bonnie and four other secretaries from the Pool, in addition to Liza, were there to help?"

"I would think so."

"And after not asking Liza to do any work for you for nine months, you turned to her that day for help? Why?"

"Because we were in a bind. We had a mandatory government filing due and it was crucial that it got done."

"So you turned to Liza to do it and not the others because the work was crucial and she was the one you wanted handling it?"

"Yes. No! All of the Pool girls are excellent.

They don't get in the Pool unless they're excellent."

"Including Liza? Or was there some other reason you brought Liza into the Pool?"

"Of course not. She got that job because she was outstanding at what she did. I can't possibly recall what the other secretaries were doing at the time. I gave the task to Liza because it needed to get done and for no other reason."

"And that day, when you were under the gun and turned to Liza to get this crucial task done, you scolded her after she complained about how you had treated her, right?"

"Yes. I gave her a vital assignment and instead of doing the work she bitched at me."

"So you gave Liza an assignment, and she raised your relationship with you, and then for the first time ever, you scolded her, and then she was fired?"

"I just said that."

"What time did she raise your relationship with you?"

"I don't know. It was probably around four, because our filing was due at 4:30."

"What time do you get to work in the morning?"

"What? It varies. I work out every day before work."

"Every day? That's impressive."

"Every day. Without fail. I swim. At least 50 laps."

"So what time do you typically get to the office after working out?"

"Usually around nine, if I don't have morning meetings."

"Mr. Callahan fired Liza at 8 o'clock the next morning. Was she fired and gone the next day by the time you got to work?"

"Objection."

"Yes. She was gone. Someone from HR was packing up her desk when I came to work."

"So you told Callahan to fire Liza the night before? It was not in the morning she was fired because you were not at work yet?"

"I don't know."

"Well did you tell Callahan to fire her while you were swimming the next morning? Does that phone of yours work in the swimming pool?"

"Of course not."

"So you told Callahan to fire Liza the day before?"

"Probably."

"So let me make sure we're on the same page from a timing standpoint. For the first time in nine months, you gave Liza an assignment. It was a crucial assignment and you turned to her to handle it, and not other employees. Then she raised your intimate, sexual relationship with her. You responded by yelling at her for the first and only time at work. Liza got upset, and you instructed Callahan to fire Liza. Is that right from a timing standpoint?"

"Objection."

"Yes," Nick said, "but I fired her because she wouldn't work."

"Thank you. Let's take a two minute break and then I think we're done."

Nick and Shaw walked into the hallway. Rett shut the door and turned and looked at me. "This is fucking unbelievable, Ben."

"Quick," I said. "Can you think of anything else?"

"No! End this right now! Don't give him a chance to change anything."

Something was nagging at the back of my mind, but I couldn't quite place it. Nick and Shaw came back in and sat down. Nick had a haughty, arrogant look. He stared at Liza and smirked. Something occurred to me.

"You're still under oath, Nick, you know that?"

"Of course I know that."

Rett put her hand on my thigh and squeezed. She wrote frantically and shoved her yellow pad to me. It said, "End this now!"

"Ok, Nick, I have no more questions."

"Mr. Shaw," Rett said, "do you have any questions?"

"No," Shaw mumbled.

"Then the deposition is concluded," Rett said. "We're off the record."

Shaw, Stanton and Callahan walked out without a word.

48

I picked up my blank yellow pad and the envelope from the Hotel du Jeu de Paume. I leaned over to Rett and Liza and said, "Not one word. Let's go."

We walked down the hall. Joss's door was open and the cone of light illuminated the hall. We walked past it to our office.

We went in our office and Liza turned and wrapped her arms around me. She buried her face against my shoulder. She stepped back and said, "Thank you, Ben. No matter how this comes out, thank you for standing up to that prick. No one ever challenges him. But you have to believe me, it was not consensual. That was bullshit, and that talk of me wanting a threesome? That's all bullshit."

Liza walked to the couch and sat down. She buried her face in her hands and wept. Rett walked up to her and stood in front of her. She put her hand on Liza's shoulder. "Liza, are you ok?"

Liza looked at Rett and wiped her tears. "I never consented. You have to believe me."

Rett started pacing. "I think our boy Ben here just won the case! Our boy is a stud! I can't believe it!"

"What do you mean?" Liza asked.

"He nailed them. He just nailed those assholes. It's easy now. Greyson testifies that there was no sex. And Stanton, that fucking, arrogant jackass, testifies that there was sex, but it was consensual. So now we've got them lying. One of them is lying.

"And even better, that smug prick Stanton

testified that you were so drunk, you were incapacitated. Yet at the same time, he says there was sex and it's because you wanted it. You cannot consent to sex if you're incapacitated. That, my dear, is the definition of rape. Stanton can't have it both ways. He's got this huge fucking ego, and he's trying to present himself as the hero, taking this passed out woman back to her room. But if you're passed out, there's no way you can consent.

"And on top of that, Ben nailed them on our retaliation claim. He got Stanton to say that you complained about how he treated you in your relationship, and then he fired you. That will get our retaliation claim to a jury. This case is going to a jury and Stanton and Greyson are in huge fucking trouble."

Liza stood up, and the three of us stood there grinning at each other. "Hey," Liza said, "when did you get an affidavit from the desk clerk? I didn't know."

I pulled out the envelope and handed it to Liza. She opened it and pulled out the paper. It was the hotel invoice she had given me earlier, with the hotel manager's name, Pierre Fullmiere, stamped on the bottom with red ink.

Liza looked at me. "This isn't an affidavit."

"Nope," I said. "There isn't one."

"That was all a bluff?"

Rett gave me a high five. "That was a brilliant move, partner," she said.

"Thanks for helping," I said.

"We make a great team."

I couldn't stop smiling.

49

Rett, Liza, and I walked to Nighttown. The women were ebullient. We sat at a window at the front of the restaurant. I ordered a round of drinks.

"I loved that!" Liza said. "Nick's such an arrogant prick. He sat there, thinking he's god's gift to mankind, so worried that someone might think he's gay that he just screwed himself. Did you see Shaw squirming? Did you see how miserable he was when we finished? That was great. And did you see Callahan? The poor bastard was sitting there watching his career go down the drain. He's tethered himself to Nick for so long, sucking up to him all these years, and now they're caught in their lies."

Liza was beaming. She was beautiful when the darkness lifted.

"My god, Ben," Rett said. "You're a natural. Just talking and chatting, and getting Stanton to stumble into everything we needed. My boy has talent!"

"I didn't do anything," I said. "I just let his ego take over. He couldn't help himself. He made it easy."

"The funny thing is that he probably thinks he's a hero and just saved the day," Liza said. "When Shaw tells him that they're in big trouble, Nick's ego won't know how to process it. So what happens next?"

"Pretty simple," Rett said. "Now we have ammunition to oppose their motion to dismiss. We've got them contradicting themselves, so the Judge will know one of them is lying. We've got evidence of rape, and close to an admission that they retaliated when you complained about Nick's behavior. So there's no way the Judge can throw out the case. Even if he does, the appellate court will force a trial. That means we'll get a trial eventually.

"We still have lots of work to do. Assuming the Judge won't dismiss the case, we'll fight about getting their emails and texts. We'll take a bunch more depositions. We'll depose Callahan and Howard Morley and try to find out the other employees Stanton and Greyson screwed around with. It may take another year, but we'll have a trial and tell a jury what they did to you. And hopefully the jury will hammer those bastards and give you a ton of money.

"You're kidding me," Liza said. "Another year of this?"

"Unfortunately, and it doesn't end there," Rett said. "If we win, they'll appeal. And the appeal typically takes another year. And it could be even worse. If we win, but the appellate court says something was done wrong at trial, it can order a re-trial. And then the whole process would start all over again.""

Liza looked at me. I could see the glaze forming in her eyes.

"It's not going to happen that way," I said.

Rett looked at me and raised her eyebrows.

"Look. There's no way RTG can let this go to trial. Do you know the public reaction if we prove they're rapists? It won't happen. We're going to get a call from Shaw, probably before we file our brief on Wednesday. He's going to try to settle before we can put evidence on the public record showing what scum they are."

"What do you think they'll offer?" Liza asked.

"I have no idea. No idea at all. But you need to

start thinking about what you want. You're finally going to have a choice. They're going to offer you something. And then you'll have to decide. Do you take what we can get from them and be done with this, or do you want to show the world what those assholes did? If we settle, they're going to insist on a non-disclosure agreement so you can't talk about what happened or what they paid you. And they'll want a non-disparagement clause, so you can't ever say anything bad about them."

Liza stared at me. She folded her arms across her chest. "I can't imagine living with this for years. It's torture. But if I settle, haven't they gotten away with it? What's to stop them from doing this to someone else? The women there are just prey for them."

"Don't be shortsighted here, Liza," Rett said. "We should hammer those fuckers. We should bury them so that they can never work again. If we have a trial..."

I put my hand on Rett's arm and stopped her. "Hey, we don't have to decide anything today. Let's wait and see what happens. And then we'll have time to think it through."

I looked at Liza. She was retreating into herself.

"Listen, Liza. Here's the really good thing. You're in control now. I know it probably still feels like you're getting dragged along. But no matter what they offer, it's completely up to you to decide what you want. Fight for a better settlement? Tell them to piss off because we want the world to hear what happened? It's your choice. So for now, you should just relax and enjoy yourself. You're in control, and we'll do whatever you want when the time comes."

Liza looked at me and smiled. "You know what? Let's have lunch and not even talk about it.

Let's have fun. It's a beautiful day. When we're done, I'm going for a nice long walk and I'm going to enjoy this."

It was the best thing I'd heard in a long time.

50

I went back to the office with Rett. I was exhausted. My adrenaline had been racing all morning. Now I just felt like crashing.

Rett wanted to get started on the brief opposing Shaw's motion. I climbed on the couch.

I was really out. Just a deep, heavy sleep. I had no idea how long I slept. I floated up to the edge of consciousness, and saw that the office was dark. The lights were off, the sun was down and the street was quiet. Slowly I realized that behind me, nestled between me and the back of the couch, was a warm, firm body, breathing deeply.

Joss's left arm was draped over my shoulder, her hand resting against my chest. I lay there and listened to her breathe. Felt her chest rise and fall against my back. My breathing matched hers. I leaned back into her, fit snugly against her. The world faded. I felt only Joss.

I fought drifting back to sleep. I turned and faced her. She looked so innocent. I reached down and brushed her hair off her face. She smiled. Eyes closed, she pulled me against her, nestled her head into my chest. She drifted back to sleep, content.

Was it because of me, or would any warm body do?

I slid out from under her arm and sat on the floor, my back against the couch. Joss lay there for a minute, and then sat up, crisscrossing her legs on the couch behind me.

"Where are you going, Ben?" she asked, rubbing her eyes.

I sat for a long time. It was quiet. Friday evening and Rett and the shrinks were long gone. Just us. I was lonely.

Joss slid off the couch and sat next to me on the floor. She waited.

"You know what, Joss? I keep thinking about my grandfather. Just a memory that came to me. He was such a gentle man. He loved baseball. He and my grandmother lived in a small apartment not far from here. We'd go over when I was little and he'd take me out back and we'd play catch with a tennis ball. We'd be out there for hours. Just the two of us, laughing goofing. Talking about everything, nothing. Time just evaporated. My grandmother would yell at us for being out so long. We'd go up to their apartment, and I'd climb in his lap. He always needed a shave, and when he'd hug me, I'd feel the scratch of his whiskers against my cheek, soothing and familiar. He always wore this old, gray wool sweater. It was soft and worn. And every time we went there I'd sit there with him. Safe. There was nowhere I'd rather be. He'd be talking with my parents and I could feel the vibration of his voice in his chest. More than any other place, that felt like home for me."

"He sounds like you."

"I miss that."

Joss leaned against me and put her head on my shoulder.

"You know what, Joss? As dull as it is, that's what I want. That's what I'm looking for. That person who makes me feel I'm home and I'm safe. "

Joss sat up. "There is no safe place, Ben. That's not the world we live in."

"I won't accept that. But I'll tell you this: I could never have felt that with my granddad if I worried that at any moment he might shove me off his lap for some other boy."

Joss stood and folded her arms across her chest and looked down at me.

"You want something that doesn't exist."

"Why not, Joss? We just need to try."

Joss turned and walked to the window and stood with her back to me. I walked up behind her.

"People aren't built the way you imagine, Ben," she whispered. "You're wanting a fairy tale."

I didn't respond. She turned and put her hand on my chest. I reminded myself that my days of settling were over. I took a step back.

"So I should go?"

"I guess so."

"Life isn't simple, Ben. There's more to this than you know."

I looked at her.

Joss walked out and pulled the door shut behind her. I sat back on the floor in the dark office, leaning against the couch. I was there a long time. Alone.

I became conscious of a soft yellow flashing light on the office phone. I walked over and picked it up and pressed the button for voice mail. There was a message from Shaw. He wanted me to call at my earliest opportunity.

51

I got to the office at eight on Monday. I was dying to call Shaw to see what he wanted, but wanted to wait for Rett. I sent her a text that I'd be waiting at Starbucks, and wandered over and got coffees. She texted back: "c u in 5."

I watched the crowd hurrying through the coffee shop. Mostly college kids. A guy and a girl sat at the table next to me with their books. First year law students struggling with contract law.

Rett came in a few minutes later and sat down. I slid her coffee over to her.

"Thanks, buddy," she said. "You didn't put any shit in it, did you?"

"Nope, jet black. The way us tough hombres like it."

She rolled her eyes at me. I tilted my head toward the table next to us and grinned.

"Poor saps," I said.

"First year law - - hell on Earth!"

The two looked up at us.

"First year, summer term?" Rett asked.

"Yes," the girl said.

"We feel for you, " I said. "We've been there."

"Who's your contract prof?" Rett asked.

"Jacobson," the guy said. "Does it get better?"

"Jacobson? Oh, you poor soul," Rett said. "It started being fun in the second year."

"Not for me," I said. "Never."

"How long have you been out?"

"A year and a half," I said. "I'm just starting to find my way out of the misery. Hopefully."

"He's a slow learner," Rett said. "You'll be having fun after first year, trust me. Don't use him as your gauge. He's short every time."

"Funny woman," I said. "Nothing's long enough for her."

The students looked at each other and grinned and went back to their books.

"We gotta go," I said and stood up.

"What's the hurry?"

"Shaw called Friday and left a message. He wants us to call him."

"You're just telling me now?"

"Yup. We needed a break this weekend. And I thought it would send the wrong signal if we called back too quickly."

Rett grabbed her things. We walked out to the street. She hurried to keep up with me as we walked up the hill back to the office.

"Did he say what he wanted?"

"Nope."

"Shit. Do you think it's an offer? What if it is?"

"It probably is, Rett. Here's what we do: no matter what we think of it, even if it's the greatest offer in the history of offers, we tell him we're really disappointed with it. That we would have hoped he'd make a serious attempt to get this case resolved."

"Don't you dare chase him away, Ben. This might be a really good development, and we have to keep that conversation going. In case you've forgotten, money is an issue. As in, we have none and no hope of any."

I kept walking. I saw a dim light behind Joss's closed door. We walked past her office and into ours.

It was almost 9 o'clock. I told Rett that I wanted to wait until ten before we called Shaw so we didn't seem anxious. She rolled her eyes at me and dug around in her briefcase.

"I'm working on our brief," she said. "It's due Wednesday, in case you've forgotten. And you're a royal pain in the ass."

We called Shaw at ten. He was "occupied," but took our call after a minute on hold. He was all charm and pleasantries. I put him on the speakerphone.

"Rett and Ben, R&B!" he said. "How was your weekend?"

Rett looked at me and rolled her eyes.

"Just fine, Mr. Shaw," I said. "How was yours?"

"Ah, it was wonderful. Plenty of work, of course. But a lovely weekend for a hike in the Metroparks. "

"That sounds nice," I said. "We're returning your call from Friday. How can we help you?"

"Well, I've had some conversation with my clients. They're finding this lawsuit to be a distraction from running the business. Despite my suggestion to the contrary, Nick and Jerry have instructed me to have a conversation with you about the possibility of resolving this matter. So I'm calling to see if your client has any interest.

"By the way," Shaw said, "this is a conversation under Evidence Rule 408. Can we agree to that?"

I looked at Rett and raised my hands.

"Yes," Rett said. "This is a settlement discussion under Rule 408, and cannot be presented as evidence." Oh.

"Well," Shaw said, "my suggestion is that if your client has an interest, you let me know what she's looking for to wrap this matter up, and I'll take it back to my clients to see what their reaction is."

Rett started waving at me and pointing to the phone. "One second, Mr. Shaw," I said. I put the phone on mute.

"This is great," she said. "What should we ask for? We can't go overboard."

"No. No. He called us. He needs to put something on the table."

Rett snarled at me. She was way too impatient.

I took the phone off mute. "Sorry about that. Mr. Shaw, you're calling us. I can't tell you if Liza is interested in settling. But if you have an offer, we'll take it to her and discuss it."

"No. I'm not going to make an offer without some indication from you that your client wants to resolve this. The custom is for the plaintiff to make the initial demand. We can't do anything until we see if your client is willing to be reasonable."

"You know what, Mr. Shaw?" I said. "In the time that I've known her, Liza has always been reasonable. And I have to tell you, we're very happy about where we stand on this case. Your clients have a huge problem after last week's testimony, and I think you know that. So if your clients have a proposal, let's hear it. If not, we'll go back to working on our brief that we'll be filing Wednesday."

There was a long silence. Rett moved up to the phone and started to say something, but I put my hand on her arm and shook my head. We waited.

Finally, Shaw said, "Well, Nick and Jerry continue to believe that your claims are nothing more than extortion, a naked attempt by a fired employee to coerce a payment. But Nick and Jerry have said that to resolve this matter, they are willing to reinstate the severance offer that we initially made to Ms. Allen. As I indicated before, they will also require the right to make a public statement that they have resolved this matter only to avoid the time and expense of litigation."

"Mr. Shaw," I said, "I can tell you now that your offer is rejected. This is nothing new. It's the same old joke you put on the table before. If you'd like to have a serious settlement discussion, call us back with a serious number. We have at least one of your clients committing perjury, and probably both. We all know that you've got a big problem on your hands."

"That testimony can be explained by the fact that sophisticated businessmen were trying to be diplomatic about a sensitive, personal matter."

"Nice try." Rett said. "We're going to impeach your witnesses, at least one of whom committed perjury. They've admitted to having sex with a woman who was incapable of giving consent. The jury will see your clients for what they are: liars and rapists. So if that's the way you want to go forward, bring it on."

There was another long silence. "I will have a conversation with Nick and Jerry and I will call you back. But I suggest that you make a demand. I'm not going to bargain against myself. Make a demand and I'll take it to my clients."

"No," I said. "You haven't made a meaningful offer. Come to us with something real, and then we'll see if there's anything to talk about. Meanwhile, we'll keep working on our brief."

"Let's talk about that," Shaw said. "If we have a chance to get this matter resolved, I'd hate to see you put in needless work on the brief. We'd be willing to contact the Judge and let him know that settlement talks are underway, and stipulate to a stay of the briefing schedule while we see if this matter can be resolved."

Rett looked at me and gave me a thumbs up. She was under the gun to get our brief done.

I shook my head at Rett. "Sorry, Mr. Shaw.

We're not interested. It's important to Liza to correct the nonsense that your clients have said about her publicly. We're going to file our brief no later than Wednesday. Maybe sooner if we can get the transcript from the court reporter today. So it's full speed ahead for us. Meanwhile, if your clients have something serious to discuss, let us know."

There was another long pause. Finally, Shaw said, "I'll be in touch." The line clicked dead.

I sat on the couch. Rett walked up to me and crossed her arms.

"You know I'm going to fucking kill you," she said.

"Why? That was perfect."

"You're playing this so fucking cool. Now we may never find out what they're willing to pay. What if Callahan and Stanton tell us to fuck off? We should have made a counter offer to see where this goes. Now I've got to keep writing that fucking brief."

"Listen, Rett. He wouldn't have called us unless they want to get this resolved. He's bullshitting us. This is a 97 billion dollar company. It's not like they can afford to settle for one year of pay, but not for two. The fact that he wanted to postpone the briefing schedule tells us a ton. They don't want the public to hear what came out last week. They're scrambling. So let's just chill out. He'll call back."

Rett sat next to me on the couch. "You'd better be right."

"Anyway," I said, "let's not get ahead of ourselves. Liza's torn about settling. It might be therapeutic for her to have a trial. So let's just keep plugging away and see what plays out."

Rett went to her desk and dug into the brief. I called the court reporter to see when we could get

Stanton's and Greyson's transcripts. She said she hoped to have them to us by the end of the day. When I hung up, the phone rang. It was Shaw. That was quick.

Shaw said that his client was willing to double the offer. They would give Liza two years pay, as well as the value of her benefits for two years. "All combined," Shaw said, "that's a $150,000 offer. That's a lot of money for a secretary, Ben."

He also said the company would still require a "comprehensive non-disclosure and non-disparagement agreement," meaning that Liza could not discuss the case or the settlement, and could not say anything bad about RTG or Nick or Jerry. And RTG would have the right to make a public statement that they denied any wrongdoing, and were only settling to avoid the inconvenience of litigation.

"Now listen to me, Ben. You talk you your client. This is a generous offer and she would be foolish to walk away from it. But this is important. If you file that brief on Wednesday, there will be no settlement. Our offer will be withdrawn and we'll have no more discussions. So I strongly advise you to extend the briefing schedule. If you file that brief, Liza will not get a dime unless a jury awards it, and two appellate courts agree with the jury. So either take our offer or postpone your filing. Do you understand?"

I told Shaw that I understood, but there was no chance we would postpone filing our brief. I said that I was disappointed he was not making a more serious effort to resolve the case, but that I would take the offer to Liza and be back in touch.

Rett was ecstatic. We called Liza, and arranged to meet her at 5 o'clock at The Fairmount. Things were starting to get interesting.

52

Rett and I left to meet Liza. As we walked down the hall, Joss walked out of the bathroom and turned towards us. We said hello, and Joss nodded and walked into her office. She shut the door behind her. Ouch. But what else could I expect?

We got to The Fairmount and Liza was waiting for us at a table by the window in front. She put her sunglasses in her purse as we walked in. Her hair was pulled back in a ponytail, which made her look ten years younger. It also gave a clear view of her face, which was beautiful. Thin, angular. Firm jaw line. Her smile was striking.

She gave us each a hug. "How was your weekend?" she asked.

Rett and I sat down next to each other, across from Liza. "It was great," Rett said. "I had a date!"

I looked at Rett. "Really? You didn't tell me."

"I'm a woman of mystery, Ben. There's so much you don't know. I went out with Zach Wilkens. He's a lawyer at Patch Simons."

"Oh my god!" Liza said. "Is everyone a lawyer?"

"Just about. But you should see this guy. He's gorgeous. He's a real estate lawyer, so he's not crazy like us litigators."

"Ok, ok," I said. "You two can gossip later. Listen, Liza. We had a call from Shaw today. They made a settlement offer."

I explained to Liza what had happened, and what was on the table. Liza looked back and forth at us. "What do you think I should do?"

"It's a good offer," Rett said. "Two years of pay and benefits is a nice chunk of change. If we win at trial, I think you'd do better. But there's always a risk of losing at trial. And the Judge is a wild card. He could still throw out the case, even though he shouldn't. And even if he doesn't, he's so lazy, it's possible he'll never set the case for trial. Some of his cases have sat for nearly a decade. So you have to think about how you feel about the ordeal of trial and risk and delay, on the one hand, versus being guaranteed money in your pocket now on the other."

Liza sat back and folded her arms across her chest. She looked out the window.

"What are you thinking?" I asked.

"I'm so confused. I don't know. I want to be fair to you two. You've been great. But there's just so much. So Nick keeps thinking he's God's gift to the world? Who knows how many times he and Jerry have done this. They get to keep hiring 18 year-old girls and coercing them into abusive relationships? And just like that, I'm erased from RTG like I never existed. I worked there for 20 years and I'm done and unemployed and those bastards never miss a beat? I can't think through this. It makes me sick.

"And on top of all that, where do I go from here? I mean, not to belittle your work, but what does $150,000 get me? You get a third, right? So that leaves me $100,000. And I probably owe taxes on that, right? So I'll take home maybe 60 grand? That's a lot of money, but I can't retire on it. And who's going to hire me?"

I stood up. "I'm going to get drinks. You guys want the usual?"

I came back with drinks and sat down. "So I'm just wondering, Liza. I know it's an impossible question. But let's assume that you live with this case

349

for a couple of years, and we have a trial and it comes out well. Let's put the money aside for a minute. Do you have any sense of how you'll feel at the end of that ordeal, having received public vindication from a jury?"

Liza looked out the window for a long time. Rett and I waited. "Do you know that Scream painting?" Liza asked. "I feel like that's me. You know, nothing but terror and anguish. I don't know how to get rid of it. I don't think a trial will make it go away. I don't know how to make it go away. It would be nice for the world to know what criminals they are. But..."

Liza started crying. People watched us, but she didn't seem to care. I got up and sat next to her.

Liza pulled Kleenex out of her purse. She blew her nose. I put my hand on her back. She didn't pull away.

"I'm so tired," she said. "I have no idea where to go with this."

"What if we could get a lot more money out of RTG?" I asked. "I don't know if we can, but if we could get a much better settlement, would it be easier to decide what to do?"

Liza shook her head. "I don't know. There isn't a number. It's really not about the money. I know that sounds like bullshit, but I don't have a clue how to process this."

"There's got to be a number out there that makes it worth being done with them," Rett said. "We have to identify it."

We sat in silence for a time. "There's a time component to this," I said. "Shaw said that if we're going to resolve this, it has to be before we file our brief on Wednesday. They don't want the public to hear what they did. If the public hears it, they're going to fight."

"Goddamn it!" Liza pushed her chair away from the table. "I'm so sick of them telling me what I have to do. Fuck it. I'm not doing it. Tell Shaw he can go fuck himself."

"I know it feels they're pushing us," I said. "That was my first reaction, too. But then I realized that it's really the opposite. They're scared of what we're going to file on Wednesday. And that's a good thing. It gives us leverage. We can get more out of them with the threat of our brief hanging over their heads. Shaw wanted us to agree that we wouldn't file it. We refused. So the pressure's on them to do what we want, or we'll file the brief and give the public proof of what really happened. So it's just the opposite, Liza. This is us turning the screws on them."

Liza watched me like a hawk.

"Seriously, Liza, we're making them dance. This is something to feel good about. But if we're going to pursue settlement, now's the time to do it."

Liza slid back up to the table and held her drink. She swirled it around and then put her glass back down. "I have no idea. No idea. Isn't it wrong to keep silent about what they did to me? I'm a mess. I don't know."

We sat for a while longer. "When do you see David next?" I asked.

"I still have to call him."

"Do you think talking with him would help?"

"Help answer what to do in the case? I don't know."

"Would you be ok if Rett and I talked to David with you?"

"Why?"

"I don't know, to be honest. The most important thing is that you get your life back. That you get healthy and have hope and friends and relationships and all of those things that make life worth living. This lawsuit doesn't really get at any of that. So I was wondering if we should include David in the conversation and have his help figuring what we should do.

"Of course, you could just talk to David and get back to us about what you want. But time is short. I was thinking it might be more productive if we all talked. It's really now or never."

Liza looked at me and then at Rett. "Sure," she said. "Let's talk to David. I trust you."

53

Rett and I stayed at Nighttown and had drinks after Liza left. We called David and arranged to meet him at eight the next morning. The bar filled up, and at nine a singer came in. An Italian guy with a guitar named Youri sitting by himself on a chair in the corner. He was sensational, playing old, familiar covers. Rett and I danced, moving to the soft, rhythmic tones.

We walked back to our table when Youri took a break. Rett hugged me before we sat down. "We make a good team, Ben."

"R&B. We could name our firm that."

"Rhythm & Blues," Rett said. "You're definitely the Blues. We know I've got the Rhythm."

"That's bullshit. I've got the rhythm. Maybe 'R&B' is 'Rhythm & Boobs.' I'll bet that's what Shaw was thinking. Then I'm definitely the Rhythm."

"No, you're a boob," Rett said. "Ok, I've got a question for you."

"Let's have it."

"No bullshit?"

"Of course not. We're partners."

"Ok. So we know that Jerry and Stanton had sex with Liza. Right?"

I nodded.

"Come on!" she said. "You have to be thinking this, too."

"What?"

"What if Stanton's telling the truth? How do we know it wasn't consensual?"

"You heard Stanton. He said Liza was drunk.

So how could she have consented? And look at that poor woman. She's a wreck. Her whole life has unraveled. Even you can't doubt that."

"Hey, I know she's devastated. But who's to say why? Maybe she thought Nick was going to marry her, and then he dumped her and she fell apart. Maybe she's the biggest flake who ever lived. Maybe if we found her high school friends, they'd tell us that she pulled a stunt like this every time she wasn't invited to a party.

"I'm not saying I don't believe her," Rett said. "But it's possible she wasn't incapacitated once they were in the hotel room. Why in the world would she be texting him for months if they raped her? Why would she be bending over backwards not to embarrass him at work? If someone did that to me, I'd destroy him. I'd be in front of the Board the next day. I sure as hell wouldn't be trying to protect him and his career.

"And screwing Morley like that? Going to his condo when his wife was away? Maybe she was trying to make Nick jealous. It sounds like she was stalking the executives. We know what Shaw will do with that at trial."

I shook my head. "So then why is RTG offering her two years' pay to go away? If Stanton's telling the truth, why wouldn't they fight this to the bitter end to prove that this is nothing more than a crazy woman out for revenge?"

"Because they'll look awful to the public. Because even if it was consensual, they have to admit that their married CFO and married CEO took turns having sex with a secretary they brought on a business trip. Maybe Jerry is petrified that his new wife would find out he screwed Liza, and that's why he denied it. Just because they weren't forthcoming doesn't mean it was rape."

"I don't know, Rett. I trust Liza."

"You trust everyone."

Rett polished off her beer and stood to get another. "Ok," she said. "One last question. Here's our best argument: Liza was unconscious. She wasn't capable of consenting. So it was rape when they had sex with her. But answer me this: if she was unconscious, then how do we prove she was raped? Pierre Fullmiere saw nothing. Liza says she was bleeding and bruised, but there's no evidence. No bloody sheets. No doctors' exams. No police reports. No selfies. She told no one. There's nothing. How do we win at trial?"

Rett stood and looked at me. She raised one eyebrow and tilted her head. Then she clapped me on the shoulder. "I'll get you another one, too." She walked off to the bar. Out the window, under the streetlight, I watched the rain bounce off the sidewalk.

54

Rett and I met at Starbucks at 7:30 for our morning caffeine injection. We didn't have an agenda with David, other than to see if he could help Liza decide what to do.

We walked to David's office. Liza was waiting for us in the hallway looking worn and nervous. We knocked on the frosted glass door.

"It's open," he called.

We pushed the door open and walked in. Holy cow! I assumed his office would be modest like mine and Joss's and Katrina's. But his was on the opposite side of the hall, on the inside of the building, and it was huge. We walked into a full kitchen, with a granite counter in the middle. There was a sink and a convection oven and a refrigerator with a glass door with dozens of foreign brews chilling inside. The floors were parquet, beautiful checkered polished wood. The kitchen dropped down two steps to David's office, which looked more like a showcase living room. He had couches and lounge chairs and a desk at the end. There were bookshelves on the sidewalls, and four large windows spanning the back of his office overlooking the courtyard behind our building. The place reeked of culture and sophistication. Maybe David wasn't the nerd I'd pinned him for.

"This is amazing!" I said. "You could live in this place. It's spectacular."

"Thank you," David said. He was wearing brown loafers and dark slacks, a white dress shirt, and a light grey sport coat. "Can I get you some coffee?"

Sanctioned

"No thanks," I said. "We just had some."

"I'll have a cup," Rett said. She looked at me and shook her head. "And I thought you knew me."

David walked into the kitchen. He had one of those French press coffee makers.

"Let's sit here and talk," David said, sitting on a bar stool at the kitchen counter. Rett and I sat facing him, with our back to the door, looking out into that amazing office. Liza sat down next to David.

"So how can I help?" David asked.

"Well, as I mentioned," I said, "Liza's got to make a decision about whether to settle the case. And she's torn about what to do."

"Do you know what you want, Liza?" David asked.

"No. I don't want them to get away with it. I don't want them doing this to anyone else. But I can't imagine living with this and lawyers for years." She looked at me. "No offense."

"None taken," I said. "It's how most women feel about me."

I heard David's door swing open behind me. I turned as Joss walked in.

"Sorry," I said. "We're having a work meeting. Can you come back?"

"I asked her to join us," David said. "Liza's ok with it. We can talk openly about this."

"I don't understand," I said, looking at Joss. "I thought you don't work in this area?"

"I don't."

Joss walked around the kitchen island and stood next to Liza. She looked at me.

David said, "Joss knows Liza. I thought it would be helpful if she joined us. She can offer the benefit of some personal experience."

Joss turned and walked down into the living

room. She went to the windows and looked outside, her arms folded across her chest.

I looked at David. "Personal experience?"

He nodded.

Shit! Shit shit shit shit! I was such a moron, thinking I knew this woman. When would I ever learn?

Joss came back slowly and stood next to Liza. My head was spinning.

"Ok," David said. "Let's talk."

"Well," Rett said, stepping in for me, "as we were saying, the question is whether or not to settle. If we're going to settle, we have to do it now. Today, before our brief is due tomorrow. We can get something pretty good for Liza now, but not enough to tide her over more than a year or so, and she's worried about whether anyone would hire her after what's gone on.

"Or, we can just push forward to trial. But that would be a yearlong process, at best. We may never get a trial. If we win, then we have appeals, but she'll likely get more money. Of course we can't know if we'll win. And we don't know how she'll hold up through that process. We could be at it for years."

"Liza," Joss said, "are you feeling lost?"

Liza crossed her arms. She looked down at the counter and began rocking back and forth. Joss put her arm around Liza. Liza leaned into Joss. Joss started whispering to Liza. I couldn't make it out. Liza kept nodding her head while Joss whispered, and then Liza laughed out loud. How did Joss do that?

"Give me a minute with these clowns," Joss said to Liza.

"I'll be in your office," Liza said to Rett and me. She walked out and pulled the door shut behind her.

Joss turned to Rett. "Why do you say you don't

know if you can win at trial?"

"Because no outcome at trial is certain. We don't even know if this slug of a judge will give us a trial. If he does, we still have to prove she was raped, and there are no witnesses. There's no physical evidence. All we have is Liza's testimony. It's a crapshoot.

"Don't bullshit me," Joss said. "Do you believe Liza?"

"It doesn't matter," Rett said. "The question is whether we can convince a jury."

"If you're not convinced," Joss said, "settle now. She's got enough to deal with. The last thing she needs is being doubted by her own lawyers. Trust me, she senses mistrust like a lion senses fear. Don't torture her. Just get out and leave the poor girl alone."

"We didn't say we don't believe her," Rett said. "But there are questions we can't help but wonder about. And if we have questions, then you know a jury will as well. The burden of proof is on us. Combine that with a lack of evidence, and we have an uphill battle."

"What questions?" Joss asked.

"She dated one of the rapists for years. And after the rape, she kept texting him. Hundreds of times, for months, and she never once mentioned rape. He tried to avoid her, and she kept texting him. She bent over backwards not to embarrass him at work. She says she wanted to protect him, even though he did this horrible thing to her. She never told anyone about the rape, not the cops or friends or anyone, until after she was fired nine months later. And during that time, she hooked up with at least one other executive while his wife was away. So Liza did some things that don't fit. You know how the company's lawyers will use that. She won't get sympathy from the jury."

Joss looked at me. "If you don't have faith in a girl, leave her alone."

This was just getting worse.

"Listen," David said. "What Liza's done - those are classic behaviors of a rape victim. Her behavior should evoke the deepest sympathy. I know it's counter-intuitive. Listen, please. You are not grasping the level of trauma here. You cannot pass judgment on behavior without understanding the ordeal rape victims have suffered.

"Most women who are raped are victimized by someone they know. The notion of a stranger jumping out of the bushes is a myth. It almost never happens. Virtually all rapes are acquaintance rapes. When it happens, no victim has the psychological ability to cope.

"Fewer than ten percent of rapes are reported to the police, for a host of reasons. First and foremost, the victim doesn't think anyone will believe her, and for good reason. Of the tiny portion of rapes that are reported, less than five percent of those are prosecuted. That's a sliver of a sliver."

"But Liza hasn't behaved like a rape victim," Rett said. "She's been pursuing Nick and other guys. A jury won't see her as a victim."

"No. No," David said, stroking his beard. "Her behavior makes perfect sense, but only if you understand the devastation that results from being brutalized by a trusted friend. You're judging her from the perspective of someone who has never been injured at a fundamental level. You have to suspend your judgment here, and observe from a perspective that's grounded in a different reality.

"Although the world around these victims seems unchanged, without thinking about it, their anxiety level skyrockets beyond a manageable level.

Liza used to be a runner, five, six times per week. She hasn't run once since the Paris incident. There's a subconscious, primordial fear that churns constantly. To try to manage that fear, most victims try to convince themselves that nothing happened, that nothing changed. So they try to copy their routines to calm themselves.

"Her texts to Nick are exactly what I would expect. She has a profound need to believe that everything is just as it was. From her perspective, if nothing has changed, then she should be safe, right? So despite everything, she craves pleasant, casual time with Nick. Nick's refusal to interact with her is particularly cruel. Liza desperately needs to connect with him, to convince herself, in her anxious way, that she is safe. So that twisted safeguard that Liza needs, to feel that things are as they always were, was taken from her on a daily basis.

"Rape victims often try to re-create the scenario that led to the trauma. If Liza is pursuing other executives, that's classic behavior. Without understanding it, she's trying to re-create the scene of the attack, but in a way that will permit her to manage it. It's the unconscious behavior of someone needing to feel that if this ever happens again, she can control it. She needs to prove to herself that she can protect herself from the horror. So she re-creates it. It's self destructive, of course. As is her drinking. Imagine a bug stuck on its back, twisting away, futilely trying to make things right. That's what rape victims do. They are overwhelmed with fear and anxiety and anguish and self-blame, and flail around, trying to give themselves relief from the anguish. But they have no ability to do it.

"They crave comfort and companionship, but they can't bear letting anyone get close. No one has the tools to endure a brutal attack, especially from one who was trusted. There's no way to digest it, and no simple way to trust anyone after it happens. So the victims try to find coping mechanisms, and those mechanisms are perfectly logical, even if they seem illogical to those who have not been through that trauma."

We sat there at the table. David looked back and forth through his coke bottle lenses, from Rett to me. I looked at Joss. She was standing across from me, her arms folded across her chest, watching me with an intensity that made me blush.

David looked at Joss and then at me. He stroked his beard. "Sometimes rape victims need to make everyone love them," he said. "It makes them feel safer. And yet they're afraid to let anyone get too close. Too much intimacy and desire makes them feel at risk. If you want something passionately it makes you vulnerable, it creates a fear of losing control, with no way out. So it's easier to keep things light and easy, even though it prevents you from having what you want most – something safe and meaningful."

Joss grabbed my wrist and turned me towards her. She tightened her grip with a strength that stunned me. I looked at her. She glared at me. My wrist ached.

Joss let go of my arm. She walked out.

I jumped off my stool. "Ben!" David said. "Sit."

I looked at him behind those thick glasses. He nodded at my chair. I looked at the door and sat back down.

"Whoa," Rett said.

We sat in silence for a minute.

"Ok, David," Rett said. "Let's keep at this. We still have no proof to give the jury. Their lawyers will argue that Liza's behavior is nothing but that of a jilted lover. How do we prove she's been traumatized?"

"I'm confident she has."

"Ok," Rett said, "if we go to trial, would you be willing to be a witness? You could be both an expert witness, testifying about how women react to rape, and a fact witness, having examined Liza, to explain that she fits exactly within the profile of someone who was raped by an acquaintance."

"No," David said flatly.

"No? Even if Liza agrees to it?"

"No. Liza might need a trial, but it will still be devastating to her. I've been through this many times. With the resources Nick and his company have, they will come after Liza. It will be brutal. They will brand her a slut, a liar. They will scrutinize every one of her relationships since high school. It would be devastating to her. The legal process will be another trauma for Liza. I won't be part of it because I can't be associated in her mind with something else that wounds her. I need to be her safe place where she finds refuge from that. So you'll have to find another psychotherapist for that role. But hopefully you can put a successful end to these proceedings, so Liza can find healthier ways to address her wounds than the legal system can provide."

"But she wants revenge," I said. "Isn't that part of healing? Making them pay for what they did to her? She's worried that if she doesn't fight, then Nick and Jerry will do it again. She can't live with the thought that another woman will be attacked because she took their money and kept silent."

"Revenge is an important urge. It's a healthy urge. But the reality is, from a psychosomatic standpoint, one can never really attain revenge. A public flogging of Nick sounds healthy, but will do nothing to cure Liza. It won't help her trust people. It won't help her feel safe. It won't restore her self-esteem."

"What will?" I asked.

"Maybe nothing. For most, this is a permanent wound. It takes a long time to build trust. With psychotherapy, she can get better at managing the wound. At recognizing when the trauma is affecting her judgment. With time, possibly she can limit the wound from interfering to some extent with the very things that she craves: intimacy and security."

"So we get out of the lawsuit?" Rett asked.

"It has to be Liza's decision," David said. "This can't be another thing that is forced on her. Personally, I hope you resolve the case so she can focus on making herself healthier. Many victims won't end the litigation because, without realizing it, the litigation helps distract from their deeper psychological issues. Instead of facing their wounds, they focus on lawyers and judges. The legal battle becomes a coping tool that helps them avoid the more difficult trauma.

"But at the end of the day, Liza needs to make the choice. If she gets out of the case because we say she should, this will be just an extension of the wound she suffered."

David looked at his watch. "I have a session," he said. "We can talk more later if need be."

55

Rett and I went back to our office. Joss's office was dark when we went past.

Liza was waiting for us. We asked if she had come to any conclusions.

Liza threw up her hands in exasperation. "No. This is getting me nowhere. You aren't helping at all."

We sat in silence. Finally, I suggested that we take another day to sit on it. We agreed to meet Wednesday in our office at 10 o'clock. Time was running out. Our brief was due Wednesday afternoon at 4:30.

Rett and I walked to Starbucks. We sat there sipping our coffee in silence.

"Boy, do I feel like an asshole," Rett said.

"You do? What about me?"

"Yeah, I know. So we have to get Liza out of this case, huh?"

"You heard David," I said. "She has to decide. But Rett?"

"Yeah?"

"If she wants to fight to the bitter end, then we're in it with her. Right?"

"Right. I'm on board, partner. I'm an ass. I thought I knew everything. I'm all in, and I'm sorry."

"Yeah, you're not the only one."

"Joss?"

"Yeah."

"That was scary," Rett said. "It's like that playful, cheerful patina was pulled back, and something raw and terrifying was hiding underneath."

I looked out the window. "I gotta go. You go

to the library and work on the brief?"

Rett watched me. "She's really got her claws in you, doesn't she?"

"I gotta go. I'll see you later."

I went back to the building and walked up to Joss's office, but her door was closed. It was 9:30. I would have to wait until lunchtime.

At noon, I walked down to Joss's office. Her light was on, but the door was still closed. I knocked, and waited. I could hear her moving in the office, but she didn't open the door. I started to knock again, but thought better of it. She would let me in if she wanted to see me.

I went back to my office, feeling foolish. I pulled out a pad of paper, thinking maybe I'd write her a note. But I had no idea what to say. I could try to help Rett with the brief, but she didn't really need it and I had no interest. I packed and left to go down to the gym. It had been awhile since I worked out.

On my way back to the office, I called Rett on her cell. She said she was making progress on the brief, and was going to stay at the library until she had a draft done. I told I'd see her at the meeting with Liza Wednesday morning.

I went back up to my apartment and suddenly felt exhausted. I set my watch for 4 o'clock and crashed on my bed.

I woke with a start when my alarm went off. I had been out like a log, but woke knowing I needed to see Joss. I hurried down the steps to the second floor and walked to Joss's office. Her light was off and the door was locked.

She was gone.

56

Liza came in Wednesday morning. She was wearing jeans and a t-shirt. It was nice to see her so casual.

Liza and Rett sat on the couch. I made us coffee and sat in a chair in front of them.

"Any new developments?" Liza asked.

"Nope," Rett said. "Shaw is waiting for us to get back to him."

"So what do you think I should do?"

Rett glanced at me. "David was a big help," I said. "The guy knows what he's doing."

Liza nodded.

"I keep coming back to something David told us," I said. "He said that wanting to pursue Nick and Jerry in this lawsuit and make them pay for what they did is a healthy thing. Pursuing your desire for revenge is a healthy thing. But he also said that it's just a lawsuit, and the reality is that it can only do so much. That the damage they did can't be fixed by litigation. That healing has to come from other things."

"So he thinks the lawsuit is a waste of time?"

"No," I said. "But it can only do so much. It can let the public know what Nick did. If we succeed, a jury might order them to pay you a lot of money. But at the end of the day, Liza, regardless, you're still going home to that house of yours. You're going to have to figure out how to feel safe. And how to trust people again. How to laugh and love and live. That's what's really important. This lawsuit can't touch that.

"But Liza, I can't stress this enough. You have

to decide now. Our brief is due in a few hours. We need your decision."

Liza stared at me. I thought she was going to disappear, but she stayed right there, looking at me like I was the biggest moron she'd ever met. I probably was.

Finally, she stood and said, "I want it all."

"I'm sorry?"

"I want it all. I want my fucking life back. I want to go out and not be scared. I don't want to walk in a room and have to scan it to see who's there. I want to wake up in the morning and be excited about my day. I want to dash out of my house for a run without worrying if someone will hurt me.

"And Ben? I want those fuckers to pay. I don't want to spend one more minute of my time thinking about how unfair it is that I lost my job and I have no prospects because of them. I want those fuckers to pay and suffer and I don't want to fret another day. I want it all. That's what I want. I don't want them getting out cheap and I don't want them telling people that they paid me a pittance to make me go away. I don't want to be scared about whether I can pay my bills while they keep working like nothing happened. I want my life back and I want them humiliated. And I want to be done with them forever.

"You're my lawyers. That's what I want. You figure it out."

57

Rett and I walked to Starbucks and sat in the back.

"Ok, old wise one," I said. "What do we do?"

"That's easy. We get her everything."

"Ok. Why don't you call Shaw and tell him to send it over?"

"No, you go ahead. I'll keep working on the brief."

We looked at each other and laughed.

"Seriously, Rett, what do we do?"

"No fucking clue."

"C'mon. Let's grind. What does 'getting her everything' mean?"

"There's no such thing. Let's just try the damn case and hope we win her a million bucks. Then at least she can sustain herself. And if we win at trial, the world will see that Nick and Jerry are rapists. That would go a long way, I would think."

"Yeah, but you heard David. The litigation will make her feel she's been raped all over again. And it'll take years. What's she going to do for a living in the mean time? And what if we lose? Can you imagine what that would do to her?"

"Nothing's easy," Rett said.

I sipped my coffee. I looked around the coffee shop. There were students with their heads buried in their phones. There were two old men playing chess. There was a foursome of elderly women knitting, laughing their heads off at something.

"You know what, Rett? Look around. Any of these people could wind up on our jury. People waiting at the checkout line at Wal-Mart could be on our jury. None of those people has an inkling of Liza or Stanton, and yet we're willing to put Liza's fate in their hands? Doesn't that seem foolish? Why would we take such a gamble?"

"Because that's the game, Ben. Every trial is a crapshoot. It's the risk you take to get the big payday."

Rett looked at her watch. "It's 10:30," she said. "We're out of time to get this settled. I'm going back to the library. You call Shaw. Figure out what seems right and go for it. I trust you. If it doesn't work, we'll file the brief and hope we get a trial."

"I have no clue how to do this," I said. "They didn't teach us this in law school. Not that I would have been listening if they did."

Rett leaned over and punched me in the shoulder. "C'mon, Ben. Pretend it's a basketball game. You're a stud. Go play ball."

Rett turned and walked out. I had to call Shaw. Fuck.

58

I was a nervous wreck. I had no idea what to say to Shaw, and we were running out of time. I wanted to talk with Joss. She had such a way of getting to the heart of things. A hug would be nice, too. I walked down the hall.

Her door was closed, but the light was on. I knocked. After a minute, Joss opened the door.

"Can we talk?" I asked.

She folded her arms. She was wearing jeans and a loose fitting sweatshirt. Her long brown hair was tucked behind her ears.

She walked into her office and sat on the front of her desk. I followed her in and stood in front of her. No hugs for me.

"Listen, Joss. I'm really sorry I misjudged, well, everything. I had no idea what you've been through. I have no idea what you're coping with. I'm so sorry."

"I don't blame you."

"You're mad at me."

"I'm not mad."

I looked at her. She watched me impassively. I wasn't sure where to go next.

"Any chance we could start over?"

"Why?"

"Because I want more with you."

"You haven't acted like it."

That pissed me off. "C'mon, Joss. What do you want? Are you blaming me for not knowing that you've had horrible things to deal with? I wish I'd been more aware, but how could I know? All I know is that you're brilliant and beautiful and intuitive and somehow at the same time the most comforting and exciting and distant woman I've ever met. But you've got to be fair. I'm wanting to be with you and it's not reciprocated. I'm enjoying your company, only to hear you're leaving to spend the night with Westy. We're having a great time, and it's, 'see you later, I have plans for the evening.' Of course I'm going to pull away."

"I reached out to you," Joss said. "I sent Westy home because I wanted to be with you. Why do you think I was sitting on the floor outside your apartment? You didn't even give me the courtesy of talking to me. You shut the door in my face.

"Here's the thing, Ben. I've got my scars. We all do. I may go overboard keeping space between others and me. I may work too hard to please people so they don't turn on me. I know I have little capacity for rejection, because it opens old wounds. But what you've seen is what I am. I don't lie about what I want and who I am. If what's below the surface sends you packing, then go. I'm not going to chase."

"But I'm here, Joss. I don't get it. I'm here telling you I want you. Wanting more with you. Wanting to dig below the surface. I know that all my relationships have been shallow. You scare the hell out of me, but if you'll have me, I'm all in. But every time I reach out, you brush me aside. I can't be there if you won't have me."

"I don't buy it," Joss said. "Let's be honest here. You've got a million buddies who want to hang out with you. You've got a client who adores you and a law partner who worships you. You walk into a bar and the women can't take their eyes off you. You go home with college girls who write love notes on your hand. That's fine, but I've got no one. You don't want what's lurking here. It's not light and fluffy. It's dark and ugly requires real work. You don't want to sign up for that.

"So don't blame me for getting by the only way people let me. I let them see what they want. They don't want to know more and we both know it. Let's stop pretending. It's one in five, Ben. One in five of us have been raped. I've got ugliness to manage. You want the happy dancing girl and not the baggage that makes her dance."

"I don't know who you're describing, Joss, but it's not me. I'm the guy people laugh at, the guy who finished last in his class. I'm the guy no one would hire. But I'm telling you that I want you, baggage and all. You're the one who keeps insisting that I have to be no different than all the rest."

"Give me a break, Ben. You don't want to stand out. Everything you do is to blend in and be one of the guys. You want me to put myself out there with you? Tell me how you're putting yourself out there? Where's that ledge you're willing to stand on and lean over for something special? And then jump to go get it? You'd go scurrying behind a rock at the first sight of me."

She looked at me with such fury. My head was spinning. I was lost. I couldn't get her to hear me.

"I've got work to do," she said. She walked behind her desk and picked up her Dictaphone. She sat in her chair, spun so her back was to me, and started talking into the recorder.

I kept standing there, but she wanted no part of me. I walked out and closed the door.

59

The day was going great. It was 11:20 and I had to call Shaw. But I was paralyzed. Joss was exactly right. I wanted to blend into the woodwork. Now was the time to show her I was something more.

I thought about what Rett said: "pretend it's a basketball game." It was an interesting idea. I'd played a thousand games against guys bigger, more athletic, and better than I was. And yet I didn't fret on the court like I did with Shaw. Not ever. It was fun. Why was I so comfortable playing hoops, and such a sputtering wimp here?

I couldn't really figure that one out. But I could think what I'd do if it were basketball. I'd turn his strengths into weaknesses. If I were going against a great shooter, I'd encourage him to shoot, but from spots that weren't his best. Maybe a few feet outside his range. Or maybe get him to dribble with his off hand so he couldn't get into his rhythm. Make him try to do too much until it came back to bite him.

The thing that made me nervous about Shaw was his arrogance. He was on a pedestal in the legal community and with RTG. His comfort with the legal process that was so foreign to me was so familiar to him. We were playing his game.

I realized that I was playing into Shaw's hands all along. I hadn't done anything to make him fear that his status as RTG's "trusted counsel" was in jeopardy. I had to find a way to push him to a weakness. Finally, I had an idea.

I took a deep breath, clapped my hands, and called Shaw. His secretary picked up the phone, as always. She asked me to hold. A minute later, Shaw barked into the phone, "Alexander Sebastian Shaw!"

"Benjamin Billings!" I said.

"Where do we stand, Ben?"

"Hello, Alex. I'm fine, thank you for asking. And how are you today?"

"I'm very busy, Ben. Have you had a chance to talk about our settlement offer?"

"I have, Alex. I won't bore you with my clients' reaction, other than to say that she took our advice and summarily rejected it."

There was a long pause. I waited.

"I find that surprising, Ben. We made her a generous offer."

"Come on, Alex. Let's cut the bullshit. I've got Stanton and Greyson contradicting each other. They're accusing each other of committing perjury. And I've got a witness to the rape. Think about that, Alex. We're talking rape. The jury is going to see in our opening statement that your clients are calling each other liars. And an all-expense paid trip to lovely Cleveland is mighty attractive to Fullmiere, and he's going to be the centerpiece of the trial.

"On top of that, I have Stanton testifying that Liza was unconscious, but that he had sex with her. So if we're to believe that version of his testimony, he's admitted that he and Jerry raped her. You've got a huge problem on your hands. So we have no interest in your offer."

"I think that's a big mistake, Ben. A big mistake. Your client's going to be out on the street with nothing."

"You know what, Alex? I don't think we should even be discussing settlement. You have an ethical problem."

"Pardon me?"

"You can't be representing all three defendants in this case. Stanton and Greyson contradicted each other in their testimony, so they have adverse interests and can't have the same attorney. On top of that, RTG needs to distance itself from Stanton and Greyson, unless the company sanctioned their admitted felonies. So RTG is required to have separate counsel from them.

"I'm calling you as a courtesy, Alex, to give you a chance to withdraw as counsel in this case. You never should have tried to represent all three defendants. If you won't withdraw, we'll be filing a motion with our brief today to have you removed from the case. If you won't step down, as you know, I also have an obligation to file a complaint against you with the Bar Association to have you sanctioned for unethical behavior."

"How dare you!" he shouted. "I don't know what you're suggesting, Mr. Billings, but I assure you I have no ethical issues. I've been practicing law for nearly 40 years, and representing RTG for a quarter century, and no one has ever accused me of violating the Rules of Professional Responsibility!"

"But Alex, have RTG's two most senior executives provided contradictory testimony about committing rape before?"

There was a long pause. I could hear Shaw breathing heavily.

"So what you're telling me, Ben, is that you have no interest in settling? You're going to file this brief today?"

"Are you kidding?" I said. "You won't get serious about this. We'll be filing our brief and pushing the Judge to set a trial date. We'll be filing a motion to have you removed from the case. When a jury gets their hands on this one, especially a jury here in Cleveland, your pretty rich boy clients are going to get fried."

"Well I have to tell you, I think you're making a substantial mistake. You haven't even made a settlement proposal."

"If you want to come back to me with something realistic, then I'll take it to my client," I said.

"You have an ethical obligation to share all settlement offers with your client!"

"Of course. And I have. But I'm just being straight with you, Alex. You haven't even made Liza think about it. We haven't had to have a serious conversation. You're offer is such a joke, there's nothing to discuss on our end. So we're going to file our brief at the end of the day, along with the ethics motion. If you want to make a meaningful offer before then, I'll take it to Liza."

"Now you wait a minute. You just wait a goddamned minute! I've made two offers in a row already. Two offers in a row! That's not proper form. You need to make a settlement demand if we're going to have further talks. You make a demand, and I'll take it to my clients."

"What's the point? We're a universe apart," I said.

"Listen, I'm telling you, sir, you need to be smart here. I'm asking you to tell us what you want. That's a signal, Mr. Billings. It's a signal. I shouldn't be telling you this, but I'm telling you that my clients would like to get this resolved. That there's value in resolving this before you file your brief today. Whatever that value is, you're going to lose it when you file. So be wise, and make a settlement demand here."

This was perfect. I had him pleading with me

to ask for money.

"I'll tell you what, Alex. I don't want to put Liza through an exercise that's going to needlessly upset her. I'll make a demand. But only if you make a professional commitment to me. I need your promise that you will call me with a good faith response to our demand. I told my client that I would not go down this path while you and your clients are playing games. So I'll make a settlement demand, but only if you promise me that you'll provide me with a good faith response to get this case settled.

"And let me be clear, Alex. I'll need your response by noon. That's in 20 minutes. If you can't make that promise to me, then let's stop wasting time and end these talks now."

Shaw paused again. "That's not realistic. I'm representing one of the largest companies in the world. William Callahan, Nick Stanton and Jerry Greyson are running a hundred billion dollar company. I don't even know if I can track them down, much less commit to our response."

"So why are we talking, Alex? Are you just running up your bill here? All this talk of getting something done today? You must have access to your clients. And if you don't, then let's end these discussions right now."

"Why don't we just extend your filing deadline for your brief so we have time to let the negotiations play out?" Shaw asked.

"No."

There was another long pause. Finally, Shaw said, "Ok. You have my commitment."

"Noon."

"Pardon me?"

"I'll make a settlement demand now, and then we'll talk at noon with your response. And you need to commit to me that your clients will be available for the rest of the day. And by 4:00, we'll either have a settlement, or I'll file by the 4:30 deadline."

"Fine," Shaw said. "What's your demand?"

"Here's the deal. Liza is 38 years old and unemployed. Because of the games your clients played, she's unlikely to find work again. So here's what we want:

"Liza was earning a base of $60,000 per year, and she would have worked another 25 years if your clients didn't abuse her. That's $1.5 million, not including benefits, raises, promotions and cost of living increases. So make it $2 million."

"That's outrageous!"

"I'm not done. I want a public statement that this case has been resolved to Liza's satisfaction. I want RTG to make a public statement that it's committed to treating women properly at work, and that it will never tolerate the abuse of women in any form. I want a glowing letter of reference written on Liza's behalf for her to show to any prospective employer, and an agreement that the defendants will not bad-mouth her."

"This is a joke! You need to get serious here, Mr. Billings."

"And last? Alex, I want an agreement that RTG will remove Stanton and Greyson from their positions."

"Are you kidding me? That's preposterous. You have no say in how this company is run. You want us to tell the public that your claims are true? That Nick and Jerry are rapists? That's what you're asking here. Why would we ever agree to that? We might as well try the case and see what a jury does. This is a joke."

"That's our demand. I'll talk to you at noon to

hear if we have a deal. In the meantime, we'll be polishing off our motion to remove you from the case."

I hung up without saying goodbye. I stood and raised my hands above my head. Yeah! I was such a hard-ass. I giggled.

60

Rett came into the office a few minutes later. "I can't spend another fucking minute on this brief," she said. "It's as good as it's going to get." She wanted to be with me when I talked with Shaw.

I gave her a quick rundown of my conversation with Shaw. She stood there staring at me.

"Are you serious?"

I shrugged.

"I can't believe it," she said. "I knew you had it in you! Holy shit!"

I just grinned.

"You know," she said, "I think you're right about the conflict. I can't believe I didn't think of that. Where'd you come up with that?"

"Beats me. I took your advice and was thinking of how we could get to Shaw. He thinks he's sitting pretty, having all these clowns dependent on him, and the reality is, he's sitting on a hornet's nest. If we go after them at trial, Stanton and Greyson and RTG will be at each other's throats trying to pass the blame. There's no way Shaw can represent them all."

Rett looked at her watch. It was nearly noon. "I can't wait for this call. What do we do if he tells us to fuck off?"

"Then we fight. But Rett?" I looked at her and waited.

"Oh, shit. You want me to write the ethics motion?"

"Yup. But I promise, next case, I'll do the writing. If you're willing to take that risk."

"You know what, Ben? I don't believe for a

minute that you're a shitty writer. It's all an act to dump the work on me."

"True. But next case, I promise."

"Actually, I think I can do the ethics motion easily. Just a few sentences saying that the three defendants have adverse interests. I can refer to our big brief," she said, picking up the monster she planned to file that afternoon, "for a description of the underlying facts. It's no big deal."

I gave her a hug. Damn I loved working with her. I'd be lost on my own.

The phone rang. I looked at Rett. "Ok, it's show time! Let me take the lead."

I put the phone on speaker. "Ben Billings," I barked.

Rett grinned and shook her head at me.

"Ben, this is Alexander Sebastian Shaw. I'm meeting my commitment to call you back."

"Hello, Alex. I have Ms. Anderson here with me. And to state the obvious, your commitment wasn't to call me back. It was to make a good faith response to our settlement demand."

"Despite your insulting comments about my ethical practices, I always keep my word."

"Where do we stand, Alex?"

"I've consulted with Nick and Jerry. As expected, they found your demands outrageous. They have no problem litigating this case. Lest you forget, RTG has an unlimited budget, Ben. If this case costs them 10 million dollars to litigate, they don't care. It's not even a drop in the bucket. So your threat to take this to a Cleveland jury doesn't faze them. Not in the least."

Rett jumped in. "You know what, Shaw? How about some decency here? You're clients are rapists, and you know it. So let's cut to the chase. Do you have an offer or not?"

I shook my head at Rett. I scribbled a note to her on my yellow pad: "Stop!!!!! Let him talk!!!!!!"

Rett rolled her eyes at me.

"I have to say, Alex," I said, "I'm surprised. I would think the Board of Directors has more important things to do than spend the next few years defending rape charges. Do they really want years of publicity about Nick and Jerry's sexual proclivities? All of Nick's affairs while his wife sat at home waiting for him?"

"Of course they have more important things to do," Shaw said. "And don't get me started about the Board. They're incensed about having to defend this lawsuit. And trust me, they're not happy to hear what you're asking to resolve this."

"Did you share with them the ethical issue that must be addressed?"

"Now you listen to me! What I talk about with my clients is none of your business. None at all. I will not concede that I have a conflict. I will not. You can't bring claims and then insist they need to hire different lawyers. You don't get to decide that!"

"It's not my decision. It's the decision of the Ohio Supreme Court about what lawyers can and cannot do. You have to play by the rules, Alex, just like everyone else."

Rett looked at me with wide eyes. I winked.

"Listen to me, Mr. Billings. Now you just listen to me. You are not, do you hear me, you are not going to tell me what I do. I decide what RTG does, not you. I decide. So don't you try to interfere with my relationship with my client. I spent a quarter century working on that relationship, and I'm a partner in everything they do. Don't you dare get in the way of that."

"Alex, I'm just doing my job. This isn't personal. We all have to play by the same rules. But I'm not pulling any punches. This is a fight to the death, as you said. Rett and I will insist that the rules are followed, whether you like it or not."

"Do you really, do you really think you can dictate to a Fortune 50 company that it has to fire its CEO? Do you think some punk rookie plaintiff's lawyer is going to tell the most sophisticated Board in America that it has to fire its CEO and CFO? You've got to wake up and smell the roses, son."

He was really mad. Rett was jumping up and down. I put my finger up to my mouth to keep her quiet.

"Alex, you can call me names but it doesn't change the fact that RTG has a substantial legal problem. Now tell me, what's your good faith response to our settlement demand?"

There was a long silence. Finally, Shaw said, "Our response is this. Nick and Jerry categorically reject your proposal. We will raise our offer to $200,000. That's a substantial jump. That's more than three years pay for a secretary. We still get to tell the public that we settled the case to avoid the nuisance of litigation. Liza cannot disparage us. And a strict non-disclosure provision for your client, along with liquidated damages if she breaches the clause. It's a generous offer, and your client should be giddy to take it."

I had no idea what liquidated damages were. I wrote a question mark on my pad of paper to Rett. She shook her head that it was not acceptable.

"Ok," I said, "it sounds like we're done talking here. I told you our number, and you've come back at ten percent of that. What's the right price for rape, Alex? If two men raped your wife, would you be giddy to get a couple years' pay? We're not just talking about lost wages here. We're talking about compensating her for a horrific assault. And I've got to tell you: Liza is very motivated that Stanton and Greyson have no opportunity to do this again to another young woman. You've offered nothing in that regard."

"So where do we go from here, Ben? The ball's in your court. We've made a generous offer. I think your client should take it."

"I will present it to her, but I can tell you she won't take it."

There was another long pause. Finally, Shaw said, "Then make another demand, Ben. I may be able to get a little more money out of my client if we can get this resolved. Talk to your client and call me back."

I looked at my watch. It was 12:30. "Let's talk again at 1:30," I said. I wanted to keep things moving, but not seem too anxious.

"Fine," he said.

We both hung up.

I looked at Rett. "Holy shit!" she said. "They're up to $200,000! I can't believe it. Just like that! You're tough!"

I started scooping up nerf balls and shooting baskets. "I'm one tough mother, that's me all right," I said, throwing up a hook shot from behind Rett's desk. I sat in her chair.

"Hey listen, Rett, sorry I stopped you there. But we want Shaw talking all we can. He shows his cards when he talks. I know we disagree with everything he says, but there's so much to learn when he talks. He just told us there may be more money available. So let him go, even if he's insulting us. There's nothing to be gained by talking over him."

"You're right," Rett said. "But he pisses me off.

He's an arrogant prick."

"I know, but don't miss the point. He may be arrogant, but he tipped his hand when he got mad. He couldn't stop talking about his relationship with RTG. So we know that's his highest priority. He doesn't want other lawyers involved. He wants to be the white knight who saves the day, so he keeps his coveted position as trusted advisor."

"Why is the white guy always the good guy?" Rett asked.

"What?

"White knight, douchebag."

"Ok, ok, sorry. He wants to be the African-American knight. How's that? But we know the relationship is huge for him. And that they don't want the perception that we're dictating who runs the company. All that's great info for us. If we can package a settlement demand that helps them with those points, they might jump at it."

Rett stood above me with her arms folded and grinned. "You're playing hoops, aren't you?"

"I am!"

"Damn, Ben, you're good. I knew it. You just hide it so well. So what do we do?"

"Let's figure out a counter offer. And let's run it by Liza. We need to get her buy in. No more vague instructions from her now."

61

We called Liza and put her on the speakerphone and brought her up to speed.

"You really asked for 2 million dollars?"

"We did," I said.

"But they don't take that seriously, right? Do you think they'll replace Nick and Jerry?"

"Whoa!" Rett said. "You shouldn't expect that, Liza. That's a crazy request on our part. Really just to test their pressure points and give us bargaining room on realistic issues."

"Yeah," Liza said, "but why do they get to keep their jobs when I'm out of work? Why would RTG want rapists running the company?"

Rett walked over to me and punched me in the arm. Then she took my arm and pulled me to her and whispered, "That's what you get for asking for the moon."

"Hey, Liza," I said. "Maybe let's not get hung up on any specific part of our settlement offer. We asked for a lot of things that are not realistic. But we figured we'd never know what they might be willing to do if we didn't ask. It's part of negotiating. But now we're at the tough part." I looked at my watch.

"It's after 1 o'clock. We don't have much time left," I said. "I think it's more productive to focus on what they're offering. They're at $200,000. I'm guessing we might get a little more out of them, but not much. Four years of pay would be $240,000. Do you think you could live with that?"

"So what would that amount to? You get a third, so that's 80 grand for you and 160 for me, right?

And after taxes, I'd get what, like $100,000? So really, I'm only getting like a year and a half."

"Do you want us to think about taking less than our third?" I asked.

Rett jumped and grabbed my t-shirt and shook me back and forth. "Are you crazy?" she whispered.

"No, no, no," Liza said. "You guys are great and you deserve every penny you can get."

I winked at Rett.

"I guess what I'm thinking," Liza said, "is that $240,000 sounds like a fortune, but at the end of the day, it won't even last me until I'm 40."

"Don't forget," Rett said, "that if you were working and earning 60 grand a year, you'd be paying taxes on that, too, and probably taking home something like $40,000. So if you net $100,000, that's really two and a half years' pay. Also, because of the assault, you won't have to pay taxes on all of your portion."

"Ok," Liza said, "let's say that gets me to age 42. What do I do then? What else can we do?"

"Well," I said, "the rest of what they're offering is still what they started with. You can't say anything bad about them. They get to make a public statement that they only settled this to avoid the nuisance of litigation. And you have to keep the settlement confidential."

"Why do they get to say that my claims had no merit, and I don't get to say anything? This is bullshit."

"If we could improve on that, would you be ok with it?"

"It just doesn't seem right. They drugged and raped me! If it's confidential, what's to stop them from doing it to someone else? They've probably been doing this to women for years. Do you know how many women left RTG? I don't think I could live with myself if I knew that someone else got raped because I settled just to be done with this."

"Ok," I said. "We get it. I don't know if there's anything we can do about that, but let us work on it. Would you be willing to live with it if we got you something closer to $300,000?"

There was a long pause. Rett looked at me and threw up her arms.

"Liza?" I asked.

"It's not right," she said quietly.

"How much is enough?" Rett asked, not bothering to hide her annoyance.

I put my hands up to calm her down.

"Liza, if I'm reading you right," I said, "I think you could live with $300,000 if we satisfied some of your other concerns?"

"Yeah, I guess so. I don't know."

"We really need to know," I said. "We can't negotiate without knowing what you'd be willing to take."

"Fine," Liza said. "Get me 300,000 and fix the rest. Just don't make me worry that I put other women at risk. Ok?"

"Ok," I said. "Got it. Don't go anywhere. We'll be in touch."

We hung up. Rett was pacing. "Damn, I wish she were more appreciative. I can't believe we got $200,000 out of them. That's crazy. How the hell are we going to get this done?"

"I don't know. But isn't this great? We demanded more than we ever dreamed they'd pay, and they're willing to fork over the money. Pretty cool, isn't it?"

"Yeah, but we're not close to a deal. What can we get to satisfy Liza?" Rett asked.

"What about this? Shaw said we can't require them to fire Stanton and Greyson. But what if we get close? You know, demand things that they can live with that encourages the Board to fire them? Then they'll do whatever they do, but it will be obvious that Liza was telling the truth."

"How do we get close?"

"I don't know. What if we require a donation, some big donation to a women's group?"

"I like that!" Rett said. "How about the Rape Crisis Center?"

"Oh, that's perfect!"

"Do you think the Board would feel compelled to fire them?" Rett asked.

"I doubt it. But I don't see how we can force that."

"Can we ratchet it up more?" Rett asked.

"With what?"

I looked at my watch. It was 1:45. Shit, we were late!

"We have to call Shaw," I said.

Just then the phone rang. It was Shaw.

Rett pointed at herself. She hit the speakerphone button.

"Loretta Anderson!" she barked.

We looked at each other and grinned.

"This is Alexander Sebastian Shaw. I thought you were going to call me at 1:30?"

"Sorry," Rett said. "But we don't have much to report. Our client isn't interested in your offer."

"Do you have a counterproposal?"

"Listen, Alex," I said. "We've got an issue here. Liza wants a trial because she's adamant that Stanton and Greyson have to be out. She doesn't want it on her conscience that some other woman gets raped because she didn't fight. And who knows how many others they've done this to. You've kicked the hornet's nest with Liza. She won't walk away quietly. On top of that, she won't accept that she's unemployed and dealing with this trauma while Stanton and Greyson go merrily to work every day collecting their massive paychecks."

"I'm telling you, there is no chance, no chance in hell, that this company will consider removing them as part of a settlement. It just won't happen."

"What if we tried something else?" I said. "We don't know if Liza would live with this. But what if RTG made a significant contribution to the Rape Crisis Center here in Cleveland?"

There was a long pause. "I don't like the message that sends," Shaw said, "and neither will RTG."

Rett jumped in. "Can't you turn this into a publicity win? You could make a public statement that although RTG won't talk about this case or its resolution, you take these issues very seriously and want to make clear how important the proper treatment of women is."

There was another long pause. Finally, Shaw said, "I can discuss that with RTG. There might be some hope there."

Rett looked at me and winked.

"We would also want training at RTG," she said.

"Pardon me?"

"As part of this, we would want training for everyone at company headquarters on sexual harassment and sex discrimination in the workplace."

"The company does training at regular intervals," Shaw said.

I jumped in. "Well, then that shouldn't be much of an issue, right? But it would give Liza comfort that the company is taking steps."

"I'll take it to my client."

"Alex," I said, "part of this also has to be that there's no public statement demeaning this lawsuit. If Liza can't talk about it, then neither can the defendants. None of this crap that you're settling just to be done with this nuisance."

"So you want both sides to say this was resolved to their satisfaction and nothing more?"

I looked at Rett. She gave me a thumbs up.

"We could live with that," I said.

"Ok," Shaw said. "I'll call you back."

"2:15?" I asked.

"Make it 3:15." He hung up.

Rett and I gave each other high fives. We might get it done! Rett gave me a big hug. As she did, Joss opened our office door. I looked back over my shoulder at her.

"Sorry, I should have knocked," Joss said.

She left, and pulled the door shut behind her.

62

"I'll be right back," I said to Rett.

I hurried out of the office. "Where are you going?" Rett called.

I didn't wait to respond. Joss was headed down the hall towards the staircase. "Joss, wait. Please. Just a second."

Joss stopped and turned. I walked towards her. Suddenly a door opened, and Lynn walked out of a shrink's office. I stopped.

Lynn looked at me. "There you are," she said. She stepped up and threw her arms around me. "I don't know if we should be doing this. I can't help myself. I've been trying to reach you."

Joss turned and walked down the steps. I stepped away from Lynn. "Joss," I called. "Please." She kept going.

I turned and looked at Lynn. "Listen, Lynn."

Lynn looked towards the steps and back at me. "Don't worry, Ben. I get it. I'll make this right."

Lynn hurried down the steps after Joss, who was on her way across the street to The Fairmount. I followed behind them. Lynn hustled up to Joss and put her hand on her shoulder. They stopped in the crosswalk and Lynn said something to Joss. Lynn looked at me and held her hand up, telling me to wait. I stood on the sidewalk and watched them. After a minute they turned and started walking toward The Fairmount. Lynn looked back at me and winked.

A couple hundred yards down the street, I saw the headlights on a white SUV in a parking space flash on. I couldn't see the guy behind the wheel, but he floored it trying to get out of his space, and smacked into the corner of the car in front of him. He threw it in reverse, cutting the wheel, and slammed into the car behind him.

Suddenly, he raced out of his spot, clearing the car in front. He swung wildly onto Cedar Road, swerving into the opposite lane, coming towards us. I looked at Joss and Liza, and suddenly I knew.

I sprinted towards them as fast as I could. The SUV roared up the hill towards Joss and Lynn. They saw the car coming and froze. The car accelerated towards them. Joss grabbed Lynn's arm and started to pull her, but there wasn't time. I increased my stride and put my shoulder down and hit Lynn in the waist at full speed, driving her into Joss. I kept my legs churning and dove, parallel to the ground, shoving them between two parked cars. I pulled my legs in before I hit the ground, and the SUV clipped my foot as it roared by, spinning me around as I crashed to the road. I lurched back as the car sped past, the rear wheel inches from my head. It screeched to a stop, and the driver threw it in reverse. The car came back at me. I tried to scramble to my feet, but my right foot ached and I stumbled.

Suddenly I felt Joss grab my arm. Somehow she yanked me out of the car's path, between the parked cars. The SUV slammed to a stop. A second later it roared up Cedar Road. We waited between the cars until we could see it was gone.

63

Joss and Lynn kneeled beside me. "Oh my god, Ben," Lynn said. "Are you ok?"

"I think so." My ankle throbbed, but luckily the car just nicked me while I was in the air.

Joss got on her knees and hugged me.

I sat up. "Do you know who that was?"

"No," Joss said. "The plates were covered. That was insane."

"Lynn?" I asked. "Was that your husband?"

"I don't know. It wasn't his car. But I don't know."

I stood. My ankle hurt like hell, but I think it was ok.

"C'mon," I said. "Let's get back to my office."

"We should get you to a doctor," Lynn said.

"No. There's no time now. Let's go back to my office."

"I should leave you two," Lynn said.

"No!" I said. "Lynn, you need to come with us."

We made our way back across the street, Lynn and Joss on either side of me, each holding onto an arm. I didn't think I needed the help, but I wasn't going to complain.

We got up to my office and stood in the hall.

"Listen, Lynn," I said. "You have got to leave your husband. That had to be him. Who else would do that?"

Lynn looked at me and didn't say anything.

"Goddamnit, Lynn. How many times is he going to beat you before you do something? Someone just tried to kill you. It's enough."

Joss looked back and forth at us. Lynn stared at me. She looked lost. She was always in control with me, and she had none here.

Joss moved next to Lynn and put her hand on Lynn's back. Lynn jumped, and turned and looked at Joss. Joss took Lynn's hand in hers and held it. She stepped up to Lynn and put her arms around Lynn. Lynn stiffened, but Joss held steady.

"I've been there," Joss whispered.

Lynn looked at Joss, and then rested her head on Joss's shoulder.

After a minute, they stepped away. Lynn smiled, that frown grin, and wiped a tear away. She took a deep breath and sighed.

"C'mon," I said. "Let's go in and sit for a minute."

We went into my office. Rett jumped up. "Where the hell have you been, Ben?" She looked at Joss and Lynn. "What's going on? We don't have time for this."

I shot Rett a look and put my hand on Lynn's back. "It's ok," I said. "Lynn, this is my partner, Loretta Anderson."

Lynn stepped up to Rett and shook her hand. "Hi," she said, "I'm Brooklynn Lawson Stanton."

I stared at Lynn. What?

"You're Brooklynn?" I asked.

"I've been trying to reach you since I read about the case," she said.

"Holy shit," Rett said.

"I wasn't avoiding your calls, Lynn," I said. "I don't have your number. And it doesn't show up on our caller ID."

"I know," she said. "I didn't want you calling me at the wrong time."

I sat on the couch.

"You're Nick Stanton's wife?" Rett asked. "Why are you here?"

I glanced at Joss. "It's a long story," I said. "I've known Lynn for a little while, but I had no idea she was married to Nick."

"Are we allowed to be talking?" Lynn asked.

I looked at Rett. "We are," Rett said. "But we probably shouldn't talk about the case. I don't want any claim of impropriety."

"We haven't talked about the case," I said. "I know this is really bad timing, but Rett and I are in the middle of some tough work issues. We should probably get at it."

"Ok," Lynn said.

"Wait," I said. "Where are you going to go? You can't go back to that guy. Please."

"I guess I can stay in a hotel."

"Don't use a credit card. Don't let him know where you are."

"You can stay with me," Joss said.

Lynn looked at Joss uncomfortably. Joss smiled at her.

"Are you sure?" Lynn asked.

"Come on, it'll be fine. I've got plenty of room."

Joss put her arm through Lynn's and they started to walk out.

"Wait!" I said.

They turned and faced me. I got up and hobbled over to my desk.

"Here, Lynn," I said. "You should take this." I handed her a copy of Stanton's deposition transcript. "I think you'll be happy."

Lynn looked at me and raised her eyebrows. She walked over and hugged me. "Thank you," she whispered.

Lynn turned back and looked at Joss. Joss smiled at her.

"Come on," Joss said, "let's go get settled. There's lots to talk about."

64

"What the hell is going on?" Rett asked. "How do you know Stanton's wife?"

"It's a long story. But there's no time for that now. We have to talk to Liza before it's too late."

We called Liza and gave her an update on the negotiations. She still sounded unhappy. I was starting to get frustrated.

"Liza," I said, "listen. We're getting to the end here." It was nearly 3:00. "We have to file our brief in 90 minutes. That means we have about an hour to get a deal done or walk away from this. You have to tell us if you're willing to accept this."

"Did you get the $300,000?"

"No. We really didn't talk about that piece of it," I said.

"I want the money and I want Nick and Jerry out."

"We're trying to see what we can do about Nick and Jerry," Rett said. "But they're never going promise us that they'll fire those guys. You know that if we win at trial, the jury can't fire them, right? The only thing the jury can do is award you money. And this is a settlement with all three defendants, even though RTG will pay whatever amount we settle on. Nick and Jerry will never agree as part of a settlement that they should be fired. But listen: you worked there for 20 years. If there's a public announcement that the case is settled, that you're satisfied with the settlement, and they make a public contribution to the Rape Crisis Center, and then they give all headquarters employees training on sexual harassment, what do you think will happen? Isn't that essentially telling the world that you're right, that Nick and Jerry did exactly what you said?"

There was a long pause. "It's never happened before," she said. "You know, you're probably right. It would be humiliating for Nick, who cares more than anything what people are saying about him. I think everyone would know exactly what happened."

"Soooooo, what do you think?" Rett asked.

"If you think I should take it, then it's fine, if it's what you want."

"I'm sorry, Liza," I said. "That's just not good enough. We can't settle this without you telling us it's what you want."

"Do you think I should take it?"

I looked at Rett. She said, "Liza, I spent almost two years working on the company side of these things. I read all of the settlements my firm did over the last 15 years. I can tell you that I've never seen a company agree to what we're talking about so early in the litigation. And at $200,000, they're offering you three and a half years pay. So if you're asking us if this is a good settlement, as far as employment cases go, it's phenomenal."

"This is more than an employment case," Liza said quietly.

"We know it is," I said.

Liza said something. We could barely hear her. "I'm sorry, Liza," I said. "We couldn't hear you."

"Fine," she mumbled.

I looked at Rett. She rolled her eyes at me.

"Are you sure, Liza?" I asked.

"I said fine!" she yelled.

She hung up on us.

65

Shaw called at 3:30. We put him on the speakerphone.

"Ok," he said. "Here's what the Board is willing to do: they'll agree that both sides will say publicly that this was resolved to their satisfaction. They'll agree to a $25,000 donation to the Cleveland Rape Crisis Center. They'll agree to do training at headquarters. I need a certification from you that the sex tape and all copies have been destroyed. They'll agree to pay Liza $200,000. Obviously, it has to be confidential, with a comprehensive non-disparagement clause. Any violation by Liza means liquidated damages of five times the $200,000. Do we have a deal?"

"Hang on," I said. I put the phone on mute.

"What are liquidated damages?" I asked Rett.

"That means if Liza breaches the confidentiality agreement, or if she disparages them, she agrees that they've been harmed in the amount of five times $200,000, and she has to pay them that. They don't have to prove they've been harmed in court – she automatically owes them a million bucks if she talks."

"So if she tells a friend what happened to her, and there's no harm to RTG, she still has to pay?"

"Yup."

"That's bullshit."

I took the phone off mute. "Ok, Alex. Here's the deal. No liquidated damages. Liza will agree to confidentiality, and both sides have to agree not to disparage the other, but if you think she talked to someone, you have to prove that you've been harmed, and how much. We won't agree to liquids."

"The Board needs a guillotine hanging over Liza's head so she has an incentive to keep quiet," Shaw said. "Otherwise, what's to stop her from bragging about this to all her friends?"

"No chance, Alex," I said. "Liza's got enough to struggle with. She's not going to have your guillotine on top of everything else. If she breaches confidentiality, you have to prove how it's harmed you."

Shaw sighed. "If we agree to that, do we have a deal?"

"No," Rett said. "We need $100,000 to the Rape Crisis Center."

"That's outrageous!"

"Oh, cut the crap, Alex" Rett said. "It's tax deductible. That's not even a fly on RTG's ass. Make it $100,000 so it will make a difference for the Center."

"If we do, then do we have a deal?"

'The training at headquarters has to be by an outside company that both sides agree to," Rett said. "We'll need written confirmation from the company that the training occurred and that every employee at headquarters has taken it."

"That's fine," Shaw said. "Are we done?"

"No," I said. "There's an issue with the money for Liza."

"The Board said $200,000."

"Right. But we haven't accepted that," I said. "We'll call you back in five minutes." I hung up.

"What do you think?" Rett said. "Tell him it's got to be $300,000?"

"I don't know. Have you noticed that he stopped talking about Stanton and Greyson? It's all about the Board now."

"So?"

"Well what does that mean? That sounds like he's making sure the Board is happy with him. Maybe the Board is distancing itself from Stanton and Greyson."

Rett looked at her watch. "Fuck, Ben, it's nearly four already. We've got to get this done. What do you think? They're putting a lot of money on the table. This is a really good deal. And Liza's falling apart just trying to talk to us about this. She'll never survive a trial. We should just take it and get out."

"Liza said $300,000. We can't settle without that."

"You're taking a huge risk here," Rett said. "It's $200,000 for Liza and $100,000 for the Rape Crisis Center. That's the same pain for RTG."

"Yeah, I guess. We have to call."

I called Shaw back.

"Alexander Sebastian Shaw!" he barked.

"Hi, Alex," I said.

"Do we have a deal?"

"The money's a problem."

"The money? Are you kidding me?"

"No. $200,000 won't cut it."

"That's more than three years. Now your client is just being greedy."

"Greedy?" Rett said. "Are you fucking kidding me? What is $200,000 to your clients? I looked at your 10-K filing. Stanton made 14 million last year. Greyson made 3 million. Stanton makes more in a week than you'd be paying Liza."

"Yeah," Shaw said, "but she's a secretary."

Now that made me mad. "You're offering Liza less than a week of Nick's pay," I said. "Less than a week, for what they did to her? And that's supposed to last her a lifetime?"

"Well," Shaw said, "your client's not a CEO.

And mine is. Two hundred thousand is really good money for a secretary. Now she'll have time to seduce all the executives she wants."

Man, now I was really pissed.

"They raped her, Alex. How much would be enough if she were your daughter? She doesn't deserve these scars. How dare you judge her. Our settlement demand stands."

"What demand?"

"We told you. Two million for Liza."

"What are you talking about?" Shaw yelled. "We've been discussing $200,000!"

"You have," I said. "But our last demand was two million and we've never budged from it."

It was 4 o'clock. Time was running out.

"We've got to file our brief and our ethics motion," I said. "Do we have a deal?"

"We certainly do not. We do not. I have to talk to the Board. We're out of time here. Why don't we get an extension of your filing deadline so we can see if we can get this done?"

Rett jumped in. "We can only get an extension from the Judge, and we both know he's probably on the golf course."

"Come on, Ms. Anderson," Shaw snarled. "I'm sure you can get anything you want from the Judge."

Rett grinned and wiggled her hips at me. Neither one of us responded to Shaw.

"Come on!" Shaw said. "I can give you written assurance that we won't oppose a late filing."

"No, thank you," Rett said.

There was silence for a moment. "I can't believe you're going to file an ethics motion," Shaw said.

"We've told you that from the beginning, Alex," I said. "If we don't have a deal, we're filing."

"I can't give you an answer now," Shaw said.

"Two million is insane. Every time we have an employee issue, they'll come asking for two million. There's no way we can do that."

"We've agreed to confidentiality," I said. "So that's it. At two million, with the other things we discussed, we have a deal. But we're out of time here. We'll give you until 4:15. You have 15 minutes. If we don't hear from you by then, we're filing."

I hung up.

66

Rett grabbed my shirt and shook me. "What are you doing? Oh my god! Two million dollars? What if this all falls apart? Liza said $300,000! She'll be furious!"

"I know. I know."

"Are you crazy?"

"I don't know. You said it yourself. They don't care about the money. They'll pay that to the lawyers if we go to trial. And that fucker really pissed me off. I can't believe the way he talked about Liza. Screw him. That's the kind of attitude that enables men to abuse women."

"Yeah," Rett said, "and who is he to pass judgment on how a woman copes with something like this. Right, Ben?"

"Right!" I said.

Rett folded her arms and stared at me. "Ben?"

"What?"

"What kind of arrogant asshole assumes he knows how a woman should cope with something like this?" Rett stared at me and waited.

Oh, shit. Had I been no better than Shaw? What could be more humbling? I closed my eyes and nodded.

Rett looked at her watch. "Shit," she said. "Shit. This is crazy. It's 4:10. We have five minutes. What if he says, 'no'?"

"Then we tell Liza what happened and we file our brief. Damn, the ethics motion will have to wait."

"I can get that done first thing tomorrow. What if he doesn't call? It's 4:11 now. Should we call him?"

"No. We're doing what we said. If we don't hear from him by 4:15, we're filing.

"Goddamnit," Rett said. "It's 4:13. I've got to get this filed."

"I guess I should ask," I said, "how do you plan to file the brief with the court?"

Rett rolled her eyes at me. "How can someone so smart be so dumb? We can do it electronically, dipshit. Otherwise we'd be racing downtown to the court to file it by hand. But with all the log-ons and screens, it'll take me a good ten minutes."

"Well, we have to file. If we miss the deadline, the case gets thrown out and we've committed malpractice."

"Shit! It's 4:14! Why isn't he calling?"

Rett was pacing back and forth. I sat in my chair and put my feet up on the window ledge. I wondered where Joss was.

"Fuck! Ben! It's 4:15. I can't believe he hasn't called. Yes I can! Why would he call? Why in the world would they pay two million dollars? We could win at trial and not get anything close to that. Fuck!"

"You have to file, Rett. He's not calling."

"Goddamn it! We walked away from $300,000. Do you know what a third of $300,000 is?"

"I think it's about, oh, I don't know. How much is it?"

"Stop being a smart ass, you fucker. We could use that money. I'm too damn old to borrow from my parents. Goddamn you, Ben. I should fucking strangle you. I wish I didn't like you so damn much."

Rett sat at the desk and started pounding on her computer.

"Ok. I'm logged on. I'm attaching our fucking brief. Goddamn, Ben."

"What time is it?"

"It's 4:25. I have to submit it."

Just then the phone rang. It was Shaw.

"Yes," I said.

"Have you filed yet?"

"We're just about to press the send button."

"We'll pay you one million, that's it."

"No," I said.

"You're a fucking bastard," Shaw said.

"Do we have a deal? Two million and the other terms?"

Shaw waited. "Yes, we have a deal, goddamn you."

Rett jumped in. "We need you to send an email to the Judge right now, with a copy to us, saying that we don't need to file a response to your Motion because the parties have reached a settlement."

"That's fine, I'll get to it," Shaw said.

"No, Alex," I said. "Right now, while we're on the phone. If it's not sent in the next 90 seconds, we're filing our brief."

Shaw didn't respond, but I could hear him typing. A minute later I heard a 'bing' from Rett's computer. She looked up and gave me a thumbs up.

"Can you have a draft of the settlement agreement to me by tomorrow?" Rett asked.

"You'll have it Monday, not a day sooner."

"That's fine," she said. "We'll send you an email confirming the terms of the settlement. Have a nice weekend."

We hung up.

67

Rett and I looked at each other from behind our desks. Then we started jumping up and down. Really. We had no idea how to process this.

"Holy fuck!" Rett yelled. "I can't believe it!" She sat on the couch. Then she jumped up and shoved me with both hands in the chest. I just stood there grinning like an idiot.

"I can't believe it!" she said. "Did you see that veneer of sophistication evaporate?" She laughed and clapped her hands. "We have to call Liza. Fuck, we have to send Shaw an email confirming the deal."

"I can do that," I said. "I'm not completely insane like someone else in this room."

I sat down and typed an email confirming the terms of the deal. "Here, make sure I didn't miss anything."

Rett stood next to me and read it, her hand resting on my shoulder. Her heel was tapping about 1,000 times a minute. She looked up at me. "Timing!"

"What?"

"Timing! We have to say when the payments will be made."

"What's typical?"

"Thirty days. And put in there that they'll make one payment to Liza and one to us for our fees. That way we get our money directly from RTG when Liza does, and don't complicate the tax issues. And tell him that if we don't hear back from him immediately, we understand that he confirms this description of the agreement."

I typed for a few minutes and looked up.

"Good?"

"Let 'er rip."

Rett looked at me. She shook her head. "Holy fuck, Ben. We did it. Can you believe this?"

"I can't. We need to tell Liza."

Rett pulled the phone over and started to call.

"Wait," I said. "Let's go over there. We should tell her in person."

Rett raced down stairs, and I hobbled after her. We hopped in Rett's car like a couple of high school kids. Rett kept looking at me and pounding the steering wheel with her hand while she drove. I couldn't help but laugh, watching how excited she was.

We got to Liza's and knocked on the door. She was in her baggy sweats, looking like she hadn't slept for days. She opened the door and looked at us. Then she turned around and walked into her living room.

We followed her in. She stood next to the fireplace, leaning against the wall.

"Bad news, I assume?"

Rett looked at me and grinned. I nodded to Rett.

"It's really good news, Liza," Rett said. "Amazing news. We have a deal. I can't believe this. But they're going to pay the Rape Crisis Center $100,000. They're going to make an announcement that the abuse of women is unacceptable and they want to support groups that work to protect women. They're going to give mandatory training to all employees at headquarters on the sexual harassment laws. They won't say anything bad about you. You can tell everyone that the case was settled, and you're satisfied with the result. And Liza?"

"Yeah?"

"They're going to pay you two million dollars."

Liza stared at Rett. She looked at me and back at Rett. "What?"

"I know. I can't believe it. Ben was incredible. But they're going to pay you two million dollars. I've never seen anything like it."

Liza walked to the couch and sat down. She just sat there, watching the fire.

I looked at Rett and turned to Liza.

"Are you ok?"

"What about Nick and Jerry? What happens to them?"

"We don't know. That's not part of the settlement. But our sense is that the company is distancing itself from them."

"So they get to keep their jobs?"

"That's something we raised, but they refused to discuss it with us," I said.

"Don't forget," Rett said, "that if we had a trial and won the case, the jury couldn't remove Nick and Jerry from their jobs. The only thing a jury can do is give you money. So that kind of thing really isn't part of settlement discussions. We got you things a jury could never do, like the money for the Rape Crisis Center, the training, and the agreement about what they'll say about you. But it's not realistic that they would negotiate with us about what happens with Nick and Jerry."

Liza sat there with the stone face. Rett looked at me and threw up her hands.

"What are you thinking, Liza?" I asked.

She sat there watching the fire. After a while, she said, "What about a job?"

"What do you mean?"

"I don't get my job back, right?"

I sat down next to Liza. "Would you really want it?"

411

"No, I guess not."

"Liza," I said, "they're giving you two million dollars. We get a third, but that still leaves you with over $1.3 million. That's more than 20 years of pay. You don't have to work."

She looked up at me, and the tears came pouring down her face. "What am I going to do? Sit here every day staring at this fucking fireplace?"

"Listen, Liza," I said. "I can't conceive of how painful this is for you." I slid closer to her and said, "You have to take a deep breath and find a way to manage it. You've got your whole life ahead of you. We've talked about this lawsuit only being able to do so much. It got you financial security and vindication from a public standpoint. That's worth a lot. And now we can put the legal nonsense aside and get at the really hard work of getting your life back. This isn't a miracle cure. But for what a lawsuit can do, it's everything we could have dreamed of."

Liza looked at me and nodded.

"Two million?" Liza asked.

"Two million dollars," Rett said.

"Wow. Nick must be furious. That's great."

"It is great," Rett said. "Unlike anything I've ever heard of."

"I'm sorry if I'm being a shit," Liza said. "Thank you. Both of you. I really appreciate what you've done."

"We're going to get a drink," I said. "Do you want to come with us?"

Liza sighed. "No. You guys go."

"Ok," I said. I stood up. "Are you ok, Liza?"

"Yeah. This was a tough day, worrying about what was going to happen. I'm glad we're not having a trial."

"Liza, you should be proud of yourself," I said.

"You stood up to them and told them that they can't get away with this. And you won. That took incredible strength. You should be really proud."

Liza stood and walked to the fireplace. She stared at the floor and wiped a tear away. Without looking up, she said, "Thanks."

68

Rett and I went to Nighttown to celebrate. When we got there, David and Joss were sitting at a booth in the back. David waved us over.

"Do you mind if we join you?" I asked Joss.

"That's fine. How's your ankle?"

"I'm fine," I said as we slid in. "Where's Lynn?"

"She's at my condo," Joss said. "I thought it would do her some good to have time to herself."

Rett did a drumroll on the table with her hands. "We got a settlement done! I'm so pumped!"

"Really?" David asked. "Is it a good deal?"

Rett looked at me and winked. "We are bound by confidentiality and can't discuss it. Liza can discuss it with you in therapy. She'll be bound by confidentiality too, but there will be an exception for her doctors."

David and Joss looked back and forth at us. "Without talking at all about the settlement," Rett said, "we are very, very happy at this moment."

"How is Liza?" Joss asked.

"You know," I said, "she was really subdued. I guess I was a fool thinking that she'd be overjoyed."

"She should be overjoyed," Rett interrupted. "Overjoyed like no plaintiff has ever been before."

"We just came from her house," I said. "She said she wanted us to get a deal done. And we did. A better deal than any of us could have dreamed of. But it seemed like it upset her. She was focused on Nick, and still being out of work, and how she was going to fill her time."

The waitress brought a round of beers.

"You have to understand," David said. "This lawsuit was a source of anxiety for Liza. But it served many purposes, one of which was keeping her occupied. Even though it's logical that she should be happy with a good result, now she's left with the harsh reality of having been brutally raped and abandoned by someone she thought loved her."

We sat there looking at our beers.

"But let's not avoid the obvious," Joss said. "If you got her a great result, then you did as much for her as you could. And if the settlement allows her to start confronting her demons, then you've done her a fantastic service. Come on, let's toast."

Joss raised her glass and smiled at me. My heart melted. There she was.

I put my glass down and slid out of the booth.

"Can we go, Joss? I need to talk to you."

"What the fuck!" Rett said. "We need to celebrate. This was a life changing day for us."

"We'll celebrate later," I said. "Please, Joss? I have to talk to you."

Joss looked at David. "Sure," she said. She slid out of the booth.

I pulled my wallet out and started to pull out some bills.

"I got it, Ben, you dipshit," Rett said. "I can afford it now."

69

Joss and I walked outside. "Is your car here?" I asked.

"Sure."

"Let's go. I know the spot. I'll drive."

We drove without talking to the lake in Shaker Heights that I had run to the other night. We parked and walked through the woods. It was warm and the sun was setting across the water. I led Joss toward the lake to the giant square boulder. We climbed on top and sat, shoulder-to-shoulder, watching the sun sink on the other side of the pond.

"Joss," I said. "Can we just start over?"

"Nope."

"No?"

"You have to understand how much baggage I have, Ben. I'm pretty good at managing it. But getting close to someone scares the hell out of me. I haven't done it since freshman year of college. And last time I got close to someone, it didn't work out so well for me."

"I'm not him."

"I know."

"I would never, never hurt you, Joss."

"I know that, consciously. You're the kindest person I've ever met."

I spun and faced her. I couldn't stop smiling.

"But you have to understand how much that scares me," she said.

I leaned forward and kissed her on the lips. Softly. Slowly.

Joss held her lips to mine and breathed deeply.

"Every time I yearn for you or feel close to you," she whispered, "I panic."

I leaned my forehead against hers.

"You have to understand clowns like Westy," she whispered. "They're safe for me. I feel nothing, but at least it's human contact. It's better than being alone every minute of every day."

"A distraction, like Liza and her lawsuit?"

Joss sighed. "Exactly."

"Joss, I have to ask. You're such an intuitive, impressive, insightful person. And I'm… I'm not. Are you only here because it's safe with me? I don't want to be your next distraction. Your next Westy."

Joss stood and pulled me up. "You don't see it, Ben. You're so much more. You've been scampering alone so long you're afraid to see it. I love knowing how good you are. But it's more than that. You make me feel alive. You make me laugh. You make me feel free to be goofy and dance in the halls. I work and hang with guys like Westy because it gets me through the present. But when I think about you, I get excited about the future. I can't tell you what a gift, what a frightening, wonderful gift that is."

She pulled me to her and kissed me passionately.

"Wanna spend the present in my apartment?" I asked.

She tugged on my ear with her teeth. "We're going to spend the present right here on this rock," she whispered. She took my hand and pulled me down on top of her.

"This is the best present ever," I said.

No doubt about it. It was the greatest day of my life.

Epilogue

I can't believe how Liza's case changed things. Two months after the settlement, RTG announced that Nick and Jerry would be stepping down at the end of the year as part of a "general business restructuring." The public announcement of our settlement, accompanied by RTG's "donation" to the Rape Crisis Center, and the change in management at RTG, sent a message to the public that Liza had been telling the truth all along. Even though she couldn't talk about the settlement, when people asked, Liza responded that she was satisfied with the resolution, and oh, by the way, Nick and Jerry were no longer working at RTG. People got the idea. It was hard to believe those two bastards would ever find work again.

I hadn't heard from Lynn, but Joss told me that she and Nick were getting a divorce. At the right time, I'd get in touch with her. Who knows, maybe she'd help with our firm's marketing.

And somehow, word leaked out in the legal community that Rett and I had gotten Liza a monstrous settlement. We had an angry call from Shaw one day, accusing Liza of breaching the confidentiality agreement. We asked him if he had any proof, and of course he had none. Liza told us that everyone at RTG was talking about it, and we have no doubt that RTG employees are the ones who spread the word. Rett and I shared that with Shaw, and he swore at us and hung up. Funny how that polished demeanor dissolved when things didn't go his way.

It's been amazing what the case did for Rett and

me. We got over $600,000 from the settlement. I never dreamed of that kind of cash. But when word of the settlement got out, we started getting calls from people who wanted to hire us. Just flooded with calls. Twenty a day from women who were abused, from employees who were mistreated at work. Sex, age, race discrimination claims. Sexual harassment. Discrimination against people with medical conditions. It's hard to believe what goes on out there. It's pretty clear, though, as long as people have to interact with people, we will never want for work.

Our firm is blossoming. We rented the office next to ours and convinced the landlord to let us knock out the wall in between. So now we have this huge open space. The nerf hoop is still up over the couch, and Rett and I play HORSE every day.

We got so busy that we needed to hire an office manager. And it dawned on us that we knew the perfect person. We called Liza, and she was giddy about coming to work with us. She runs the show now. She screens the calls coming in, pays the bills, keeps us organized, and has more common sense about running a business than Rett and I have, that's for sure. She's fantastic at getting to know our clients, being empathetic about their situation, making them comfortable, getting them talking. She's an invaluable part of the firm, and I like to think that's been therapeutic for her. She wanders down the hall and meets with David a couple times a week, and seems to be getting healthier.

And Rett is the perfect partner. She's so passionate about everything, always doing battle with the world. We laugh and joke and debate every day, pushing each other to better places. What a joy it is to work with a true friend, someone who always has my back, no matter what.

And then there's Joss. Beautiful, sexy, soulful Joss. We started spending all our free time together. Man, we have cavernous insecurities, no doubt. But we're tending to each other. Last week my phone rang on Saturday at seven in the morning. It was Joss, and she told me to come down to the front of the building. I wandered out of bed and looked out the front door, and there she was, standing next to a rented U-Haul, high kicking in the street in her shorts and t-shirt with a huge smile on her face. I went outside and she climbed the steps and put her arms around my waist.

"Want a roommate, Benny?" she asked, brushing my lips with her tongue.

"Sure. Who'd you have in mind?"

She mussed my hair and we started carrying her bags. That's how far we've come. She was certain she wanted to live with me, and certain I would want her to. And she was right.

Every night we climb into bed and wrap ourselves around each other, safe and content at home. What could possibly be better?

Sanctioned

ACKNOWLEDGMENTS

First, I want to thank all of you who had the patience and stamina to read drafts of this novel and offer me candid criticism. You were immensely helpful to me, as well as kind in managing my fragile ego. I am eternally grateful for your help.

I would also like to express my immense gratitude to my many clients over the years who suffered the agony of discrimination, and particularly those who were the victims of sexual harassment and abuse. I am in awe of the strength you have had, and the character you have demonstrated, in dealing with this trauma and fighting to take back your lives. I am so lucky that you were willing to share yourselves with me, and that I was able to witness the courage you displayed in opposing this abominable behavior.

I am deeply obliged to the incomparable Geoffrey Baker, who created and provided the picture for the cover of this book. For those of you who wish to enrich your lives, his artwork can be found at geoffreybakerphotography.com.

Finally, I would like to thank my wife, Carolyn, and our children, for their love and support and humor as this old guy plods forward in his stubborn and stumbling way. You have made this journey an absolute joy, even with all that snickering you think I cannot hear.